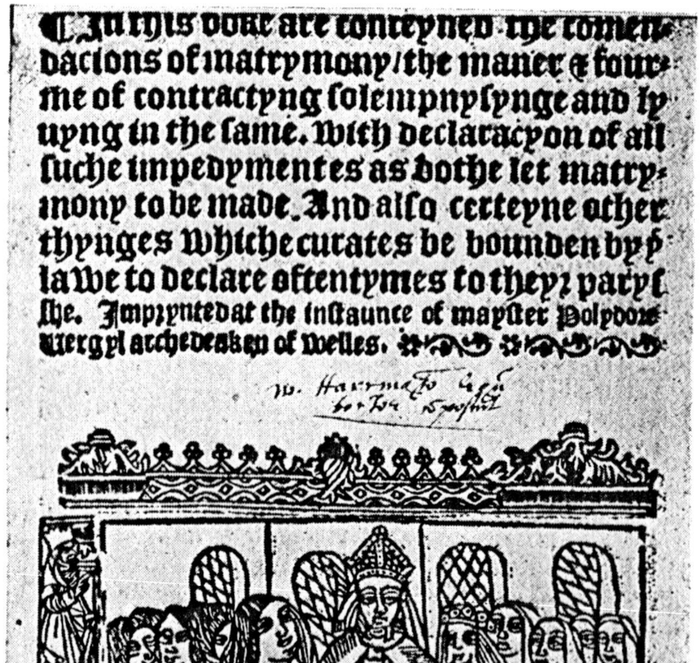

In this boke are conteyned the comen-
dacions of matrymony/the maner & four-
me of contractyng solempnysynge and ly-
uyng in the same. With declaracyon of all
suche impedymentes as dothe let matry-
mony to be made. And also certeyne other
thynges whiche curates be bounden by ye
lawe to declare oftentymes to theyr parys-
she. Imprynted at the instaunce of mayster Polydore
Vergyl archedeaken of Welles.

TITLE PAGE OF HARRINGTON'S BOOK

(Cut shows marriage scene)

ENGLISH DOMESTIC RELATIONS

1487—1653

A STUDY OF MATRIMONY AND FAMILY LIFE
IN THEORY AND PRACTICE AS REVEALED
BY THE LITERATURE, LAW, AND
HISTORY OF THE PERIOD

BY
CHILTON LATHAM POWELL, PH.D.
INSTRUCTOR IN THE JOHNS HOPKINS UNIVERSITY

THE LAWBOOK EXCHANGE, LTD.
Union, New Jersey
2001

ISBN 1-58477-096-1

Printed in the United States of America
on acid-free paper

The Lawbook Exchange, Ltd.
965 Jefferson Avenue
Union, New Jersey 07083-8605

Please see catalogue at rear of this volume
or our website www.lawbookexchange.com
for a selection of our other fine facsimile reprints
of classic works of legal history.

Library of Congress Cataloging-in-Publication Data

Powell, Chilton Latham, 1885-
English domestic relations 1487-1653: a study of matrimony and family life in theory and practice as revealed by the literature, law, and history of the period / by Chilton Latham Powell.
p. cm.
Originally published: New York : Columbia University Press, 1917.
Includes bibliographical references and index.
ISBN 1-58477-096-1 (cloth : alk. paper)
1. Marriage--Great Britain--History. 2. Domestic relations--Great Britain--History. 3. Divorce--Great Britain--History. I. Title.

HQ613.P8 2000
306.81'0941--dc21 00-023850

ENGLISH DOMESTIC RELATIONS

1487—1653

A STUDY OF MATRIMONY AND FAMILY LIFE IN THEORY AND PRACTICE AS REVEALED BY THE LITERATURE, LAW, AND HISTORY OF THE PERIOD

BY
CHILTON LATHAM POWELL, PH.D.
INSTRUCTOR IN THE JOHNS HOPKINS UNIVERSITY

New York
COLUMBIA UNIVERSITY PRESS
1917

Printed from type, March, 1917

This Monograph has been approved by the Department of English and Comparative Literature in Columbia University as a contribution to knowledge worthy of publication.

A. H. Thorndike,
Executive Officer

PREFACE

The present work was undertaken in the belief that considerable knowledge of any particular subject could be gained by examining not only the literature centering around it but also whatever other expression of fact or opinion might exist in connection with it during the period under consideration. The subject of my investigation here is that of domestic relations in England, including both the contract of marriage (its making and breaking) and the subsequent life of the family. The period involved extends from the first appearance of the subject in English writing up to its first great crisis, a height of clear thinking and vigorous expression on which Milton and Cromwell stand alone. Although it has been necessary to thus limit the work in regard to time and place, an effort has been maintained to make the field of investigation within these limits as all-inclusive as possible.

I cannot fairly claim to be entering *terra incognita* in this study. Legal writers have already covered the field as thoroughly as available material from legal sources has allowed them to go; historians have also done something, though not a great deal, in tracing the development of the different marriage ceremonies during the period; and students of literature have made a few blind thrusts here and there whenever they found their heroes, like Milton, stepping aside from the fields of the imagination to discuss a "business of such concernment to the life of man." No one, however, has used all possible sources of information —

history, law, literature, and actual practice — to concentrate research from different angles upon all the interests involved; and since the information hitherto discovered, except in the legal field, is scant to the point of being negligible, it is only by using all available sources and combining the results thus gained that the actual conditions of the period may be set forth and the contemporary literature on the subject properly understood.

As is suggested above, the field of literature (using the term broadly to include all kinds of writing) has been almost entirely neglected in connection with the present subject. For this reason, we may expect to find it, as an expression of current thought and practice, the most profitable source of information, particularly such works as may be eliminated from the stricter limits of literature on the ground of being utilitarian rather than artistic. On the legal and ecclesiastical status of matrimony, the conditions and opinions of the day are to be found principally in tracts, controversial and otherwise the Thomason collection being especially valuable, in confessions and defenses of faith, and occasionally, as a side issue, in books on domestic life. It is only when a writer turns aside from controverted subjects and aims to present his conception of ideal family life that we meet with books of any length or anything like a series of works that we may class together as a type or genre. The demonstration of such a series, developing from the beginning of the English Reformation up to the days of the Commonwealth and running parallel to legal and ecclesiastical agitation in the same field, is perhaps the most important contribution of the present study to the history of literature; but from a wider point of view, its contributions to the history of law and practice in church and state as well as its assemblage of legal and historical material not elsewhere so available, may be thought to be of equal moment. Attention should also be called to the first two appendices, which on account of their growth under investigation had to be removed from the main body of the book. The first presents the only existing account of the English writings on the divorce suit of Henry VIII, correcting many bibliographical errors previously made and discussing several important books hitherto practically unknown (*e.g.* those of John Fisher); and the second attempts to overthrow altogether the present conception of Milton's early married life and the supposed cause of his tracts on divorce.

Although this book was undertaken upon my own initiative and has been worked out according to my own ideas, I am indebted to others for incidental assistance. To Professor Charles William Wallace, of the University of Nebraska, I wish to express my gratitude for his ever ready kindness in helping me with bibliographical work at the British Museum. To Professors Ashley H. Thorndike, Jefferson B. Fletcher, George Philip Krapp, and Munroe Smith, of Columbia University, and to Rev. Dr. J. G. Dangar, Prebendary of Exeter Cathedral, I am also duly grateful for valuable suggestions on certain details. Professor Smith's final approval of my investigation may be taken as a guarantee of its accuracy in points of law. Finally, I take this opportunity of expressing my appreciation of the privileges kindly extended to me by the following institutions, where my studies were carried on — the British Museum, the Bodleian Library, Oxford, the libraries of Christ College and St. John's College, Cambridge, the University of Edinburgh Library, the Peabody Institute, Baltimore, and the Bar Library of Baltimore.

BALTIMORE, MD.
June, 1916.

C. L. P.

CONTENTS

APPENDICES

BIBLIOGRAPHIES

ENGLISH DOMESTIC RELATIONS

1487–1653

CHAPTER I

INTRODUCTION

I. The Laws of Marriage

The legal aspects of marriage, in regard to both the original contract and the resultant relations of husband and wife, have been pretty thoroughly treated in books of law,[1] but it is necessary to have the principal facts involved

[1] A brief but sufficient statement of the development of the legal history of marriage, including the principal points of Roman canon law, may be found in an article by Munroe Smith in the *Universal Cyclopedia* under the heading of *Marriage*. The best statement of the canon law of marriage is in Esmein, *Le Mariage en droit canonique*. For the Roman canon law of marriage and divorce, see Coudert, *Marriage and Divorce Laws in Europe;* for the relations of Roman canon law to English law, see Maitland, *Roman Canon Law in the Church of England;* for English ecclesiastical law, as modified by the Reformation and subsequent practice of ecclesiastical courts, see Phillimore, *Ecclesiastical Law of the Church of England* (Pt. III, ch. VII). An excellent book for the lay reader on the development of marriage and related subjects, from a broader and less legal point of view than the above works, is Howard, *History of Matrimonial Institutions*, which contains copious notes and the best existing bibliographies on the general subject. The only early legal work unknown to Howard which I have found, is Ridley, *A Viewe of Civile and Ecclesiasticall Law* (published in 1607); but in addition to this, practically all the books discussed in my second, third, and fourth chapters below are here examined for the first time in connection with the subject of marriage. Other useful works are mentioned in the notes to the present chapter.

immediately before us. Although in the early stages of the development of the Aryan races, marriage was regarded as a religious affair, and although one of the earliest forms of Roman marriage was of a religious nature, the only element required by the later Roman law to establish the validity of a marriage was the consent of the contracting parties. The Christian church, from its first organization, made a consistent and increasing effort to gain control of matrimonial affairs; but although by the beginning of the thirteenth century it had almost complete power over both marriage and divorce, it still recognized a privately contracted marriage, made by mutual vows only, as valid, and was unable to stop altogether the practice of private divorce. The constitution of marriage as a sacrament by the Council of Florence in 1439 — a conception that had been slowly maturing for centuries — was the obvious device to explain and perpetuate the doctrine of ecclesiastical jurisdiction; but not until the Council of Trent in 1563 did the church declare officially that marriage not contracted in the presence of a priest and witnesses should be void. This decree was, of course, too late to affect England, which had thrown off Papal supremacy in 1534; thus the English Reformation had to deal with the entire question of marriage and divorce in the vaguely defined status it enjoyed in the early sixteenth century. Previous to the Reformation, however, the case of England was identical with that of other Roman Catholic countries, its affairs ecclesiastical being regulated entirely by canon law, which in regard to matrimonial causes had drawn its whole theory of consent from Roman civil law.[1]

[1] The church, however, was seldom permitted to decide questions of property, inheritance, etc., involved in cases of marriage or divorce; it acted only in regard to the validity of the contract and the right of dissolving it.

The period which we are investigating in this book lies altogether within the days of church supremacy, and the conception of marriage with which we must start is that of the mediaeval Church of Rome. To understand the various elements here involved, it is necessary to look more closely into the regulations and ceremonies of marriage as it was then practiced. The fifteenth century is the time of our investigation for the moment, although very little change took place between the twelfth and the seventeenth.

The first step in the contract of marriage was called spousals, which, roughly speaking, correspond to the betrothal of preceding times and to the engagement of today.[1] Spousals differed widely in kind but were similar in effect. There were two distinct types, *de futuro* and *de praesenti.* Spousals *de futuro* were merely promises made by or for two persons to marry some time in the future, *deo volente,* and might be broken for any just and reasonable cause by either party. Such spousals might be made by parents for young children, just as vows are made for them at baptism, but these promises might be repudiated for any reason whatever by either of the young people upon coming to marriageable age. Spousals *de praesenti* were a far more serious matter. They were vows made similarly to the *de futuro* but in the present tense, and were in effect, though not in name, marriage itself.[2] They could be broken only by death and by entrance into holy orders. In case of cohabitation after either form of spousals, and without any marriage ceremony, the offenders laid themselves open to

[1] For a full discussion of this subject from a legal point of view, see Swinburne, *A Treatise of Spousals;* for a treatment from a more general viewpoint, see Jeaffreson, *Brides and Bridals.*

[2] Thus the Duchess in *The Duchess of Malfi* says:

"I have heard lawyers say, a contract in a chamber
Per verba praesenti is absolute marriage."

punishment by the church, but their union was recognized as a valid marriage by both church and state. It was thus possible to contract an irregular but perfectly legal marriage without the sanction or the intervention of either civil or ecclesiastical authority. Spousals of either type might be pure or conditional, sworn or unsworn, public or private, but these details were of no actual importance, although publicity was strongly urged in all cases. Private spousals could be accomplished by any of the lovers' formulas of today for becoming engaged, and in public spousals there was also a certain amount of latitude allowed. In the most orthodox form of the latter, a priest was present, and a regular ceremony consisting of vows similar to those of a present-day wedding was gone through with.[1] From the great diversity of practice here possible and the secrecy with which private spousals might be made, it is evident that, as the church was the only authority in disputes concerning spousals and marriages and as this authority was usually administered by local courts or priests, a great latitude of interpretation and practice was possible, especially as the ecclesiastics were extremely open to bribery

[1] Readers of literature of this period (up to 1650) are likely to fall into two errors in regard to spousals, — first, that of not recognizing a private spousal and its importance when it occurs, and second, that of mistaking a public spousal for a marriage. Of public spousals we have good examples in *Twelfth Night*, V, 1, and in *The Taming of the Shrew*, III, 2 (see below, p. 19). After spousals, the engaged couple might call each other "husband" and "wife," although they were not really so. Thus Olivia calls Cesario (mistaking him for Sebastian) husband, and likewise Petruchio calls Katherine wife and Baptista father. In Shakespeare, the exchange of rings is a fairly good guide to a modern audience that a spousal is taking place, *e.g.* *Merchant of Venice*, III, 2. An excellent example of a private spousal *de futuro* occurs in Heywood's *English Traveller*, II, 1.

of one kind or another. Despite this fact, so much importance was attached to these contracts that a secret unsworn spousal could invalidate a later regular and church-blessed marriage and render the children of it illegitimate.[1]

The legal age for marriage, which might follow spousals immediately or after an interval of any length, was fourteen for males and twelve for females.[2] But the church performed

[1] The point here was that persons who had made a contract were married by that act "in the eyes of God," and were controlled by the text, "What God hath joined together, let no man put asunder." The proper application of this text in various instances was obviously difficult. Milton, remarking upon it and its effects, says that it is "as obscure as any clause fetched out of Genesis, and hath increased a yet undecided controversy of clandestine marriages." *Prose Works*, II, 17. We find several instances of precontract in old plays. Beatrice in *The Changeling*, in order to escape from her contract with Alonzo, contrives to have him murdered. In *The Roaring Girl*, Mrs. Gallipot, in order to gull money out of her husband for her paramour, Laxton, tells him that she was once contracted to Laxton. He thereupon bribes Laxton not to bring suit, and furthermore says to his wife,

> "If thou shouldst wrestle with him at the law,
> Th'art sure to fall, no odd flight, no prevention."

In *The Miseries of Enforced Marriage*, a private contract occurs between Scarborow and Clare, after which he says to her father,

> "Your daughter's made my wife, and I your son."

When his uncle later tries to contract him to another, he objects on the ground that it would make him an adulterer, "my babes being bastards, and a whore my wife." When this marriage is finally forced upon him, Clare, hearing of it, says,

> "Whoe'er shall marry me
> I'm but his whore, live in adultery."

[2] It was presumed that twelve and fourteen were the ages of puberty for girls and boys respectively. The validity of a marriage rested on whether or not both were capable of sexual union rather than on their actual ages. For examples of child marriages, divorces, etc., see Furnivall's reprint of the Chester records under the title of *Child-Marriages*,

marriages upon infants in arms, their parents consenting, and recognized the age of seven as that when parental consent was no longer absolutely necessary. Such marriages, however, were voidable by either party upon coming of age (fourteen and twelve respectively) unless cohabitation had taken place. As indicated above, a valid but clandestine marriage might be made merely by sexual intercourse preceded by promises to marry; but all such unions were stigmatized by public and ecclesiastical opinion. In order to increase the publicity of marriage and thus diminish the number of those clandestinely made, the practice of publishing banns grew up and became pretty general by the middle of the fourteenth century. Furthermore, only certain times of the year were proper for marriage,[1] although in case this rule was not observed, the contract was none the less valid.

The final recognized step in the consummation of matrimony was the performance of the marriage right of *carnalis copula* or bodily union. Legislation concerning the effect

Divorces, etc., and also the references in Howard, *Hist. Mat. Inst.*, I, 357–8. Children have been married, divorced, and widowed before reaching puberty.

Heroines of tender years are not uncommon in Elizabethan drama. Juliet, it will be remembered, was only thirteen. Manthea in *Englishmen for my Money* at the age of twelve cries,

> "Good God, how abject is this single life.
> I'll not abide it."

[1] The prohibited times varied somewhat in different localities but always occurred at the three chief sacred seasons of the year. They embraced Advent and shortly after, a part of Lent, and from Rogation Sunday to Trinity. For further details, see Jeaffreson, I, 285 ff. Since the Reformation, no season has been prohibited, but the former ones continued to be observed for some time. In the fifteenth century, a marriage had to take place before twelve o'clock, just as it must be before three in England today. However, all these obstructions could be set aside by the purchase of a special license.

of the performance or omission of this act was scant, but the opinions of the church fathers, which in the absence of canons on the subject had the force of law, were both numerous and conflicting. From our discussion of spousals, it will be seen how great was the importance laid upon this act, as it might in itself convert either form of spousals into actual marriage or might legalize the marriage of children under age. It is impossible here to go into the effect of its total omission; it will be enough for our purpose to say that in such a case an applicant for divorce might find a court which would thereby make a point in his favor, and again he might not.[1] At any rate, a marriage was regarded as much more firmly cemented if copulation had taken place.

From the foregoing discussion, it will readily be seen that the question of divorce, or rather of annulment, which turned on the original validity and subsequent nature of a marriage, was one of the most vexing problems that the church ever brought upon itself. We are not here concerned with civil legislation, for although it may have differed in a few details where rights of property and so forth were involved, it left the actual granting of divorces entirely in the hands of the church.[2] Such cases were usually decided in local ecclesi-

[1] Henry VIII, in seeking a divorce from his wife Catherine, tried to establish the fact that her previous marriage with Arthur had been consummated by bodily knowledge; but although the judges seem to have been convinced that such was the case, it is far from clear whether this decision had any real effect in the suit.

[2] Milton, with his usual acumen, says on this point: "The Popes of Rome, perceiving the great revenue and high authority it would give them even over Princes, to have the judging and deciding of such a main consequence in the life of man as was divorce; wrought so upon the superstition of those ages as to divest them of that right." *Prose Works*, II, 53. Almost the same language had been previously used in the act by which Henry VIII tried to reform the abuses of the church in divorce matters. See p. 62, below.

astical courts, but might be carried to Rome on appeal. In the Roman Catholic Church, there never has been any such thing as divorce in the modern sense of the word. Here the term was used as a general one to include two types of separation, neither of which corresponds to the divorce of today. The first of these was *divortium a mensa et thoro*, which was simply a separation and did not allow either party to remarry.[1] The causes for this were various, but those usually plead were adultery, heresy or apostasy, and cruelty. The second type was *divortium a vinculo matrimonii*, which took the form of a declaration that the marriage had been illegally contracted and was therefore null and void *ab initio*, that any children born during it were bastards, and that either party might marry again without further ado.[2] The state of abuse into which matrimony had fallen is well illustrated by the fact that there were more grounds for the annulment of marriage than for separation *a mensa et thoro*.

This brings us to another large and vaguely settled question, as to what conditions prohibited a marriage, or if it were already made, what causes, previously existing, were sufficient to nullify it. Here we must distinguish, for there

[1] Nevertheless, second marriages after such a separation were practiced to a certain extent, either by legal manipulation or by pleading St. Paul's words, "It is better to marry than to burn," and obtaining an indulgence. For a discussion of this practice in England, see below, p. 87, n 1. The separation *a mensa et thoro* is, of course, the only type of divorce granted by the Catholic Church today, except the complete annulment of marriage.

[2] Up to 1337, children were not bastardized if their parents had married in ignorance of an existing impediment. After that date, both civil and church law held them to be illegitimate if a divorce was obtained; otherwise they were legitimate, although legal grounds for divorce actually existed. For further discussion of these points, see Pollock and Maitland, *History of English Law*, II, 373 ff.

were a number of impediments which obstructed marriage but which if unobserved were not weighty enough to have any further effect except that of subjecting the offenders to the discipline of the church. These were set forth in verse form as follows:

> "*Ecclesiae vetitum, tempus, sponsalia, votum*
> *Impediunt fieri, permittunt facta teneri.*" [1]

The impediments which forbade marriage and annulled it completely if already contracted were, "poetically comprised":

> "*Error, conditio, votum, cognitio, crimen,*
> *Cultus disparitas, vis, ordo, ligamen, honestas,*
> *Si sis affinis, si forte coire nequibis,* —
> *Haec socianda vetant connubia, facta retractant.*" [2]

[1] This verse is taken from Renton and Phillimore, *Comparative Law of Marriage and Divorce*, p. 24. Its source is not given, and I have not seen it elsewhere. The impediments are: veto by the church, improper time, precontract (i.e. *de futuro*), and informal vows.

[2] This verse is given by Hemmingius, *Libellus de Coniugio, Repudio, & Divortio*, p. 137, by the author of *A Curtaine Lecture*, p. 141, who attributes it to Cardinal Cajetanus, and by Godolphin, *Repertorium Canonicum*, p. 493, who attributes it to Thomas Aquinas. Renton and Phillimore, *Comparative Law of Marriage and Divorce*, p. 19, cite a similar verse, except that the third line is increased to two, in which *aetas* (minority) and *si clandestinas et impos* (if clandestine and unconsummated) are added. The source of the verse is not given. Coudert, *Marriage and Divorce Laws in Europe*, p. 7, gives still another and longer verse, not mentioning the source, which adds the further impediments of *amentia* (insanity) and *raptio* (abduction).

Erasmus, *Matrimonii Christiani Institutio*, f. e6 ff., discusses the impediments at great length, but does not distinguish between the absolute and the prohibitive. He mentions eighteen altogether: *interdictum ecclesiae sive generale, tempus anni, conditio* (i.e. *honesta, turpis, indifferens, impossibilis, et hinc mille casuum varietatis*), *error, votum castitatus, ordo, cognitio, adoptio et arrogatio* (*adoptantur filii familias, arrogant qui sui juris sunt*), *cognatio spiritualis, affinitas, publica honestas, consuetudo sive constitutio, crimen, dispar cultus* (*hoc est diversa religio*),

As interpreted by the church, these impediments were respectively: mistaken identity, certain conditions of one party unknown to the other, solemn religious vows, relationship within the forbidden degrees,[1] criminality,[2] difference of religious faith, fear (caused by threats etc.), membership in holy orders, prior marriage or contract *de praesenti* (with any one still living), lack of public decency, affinity,[3] and impotency.[4] It may be seen from the number and diversity of these causes that a marriage might be annulled for

metus, praecedens obligatio, inhabilitas corporum ad usum matrimonii, ubi dissidium est animorum et inamabilis cantio est. Commenting upon these impediments and their effects, he says, "*Quorum alia sunt eius generis, ut non dirimant contractum, sed obsistant contrahendo, & contemptorem impedimenti crimini faciant obnoxium, non depellant ab uxore: alia dirimunt ad tempus: alia & contrahendo obsistunt, & contractum distrahunt. Quaedam dirimunt matrimonium ratum, non dirimunt consummatum. . . . Rursus alia dirimunt coniunctum domesticum aut societatem thori, alia restituunt marem & foeminam in integrum. . . . Iam circa unumquodque impedimentorum mille quaestionum examina pugnaeque innumerabiles opinionum humanarum.*" *Op. cit.*, f. e7.

Wm. Harrington, the first to set forth the impediments in English, in 1528, agrees as well as can be expected with those given here. See below, p. 72, n. 2.

[1] *Cognatio* or relationship was of three kinds: (1) blood relationship within four degrees (before 1215 within seven degrees); (2) spiritual relationship (abolished in 1563), which existed between all persons taking part in the baptism or confirmation of a child; (3) relationship by adoption, forbidding marriage between adopter (or his wife) with the adopted and between the adopted and the children of the adopter.

[2] By criminality was meant one of two things: (1) the murder of a person who obstructed a contemplated marriage, and (2) adultery with promise of marriage at the death of obstructing person.

[3] Affinity existed between each party and the relatives of the other both in the case of a married couple and in that of a couple who had had illicit relations.

[4] For further explanation of the impediments, with qualifications, exceptions, etc., see Godolphin, p. 492 ff., Renton and Phillimore, p. 19 ff., and Coudert, p. 7 ff.

almost any reason that the church wished to sanction in any particular case, a condition of affairs that was widely taken advantage of. "No exercise of its power yielded more money, or caused more scandal. So tangled was the casuistry respecting marriage, at the beginning of the sixteenth century, that it might be said that, for a sufficient consideration, a canonical flaw might be found in almost any marriage." [1]

The impediments which were surest of recognition and which were oftenest plead, were precontract, that is spousals *de praesenti*, and consanguinity or affinity between the contracting parties. Voluminous and widespread was the writing on the latter case, especially after Henry VIII's divorce, opinion differing chiefly as to how many degrees of relationship should be forbidden, and in Henry's suit as to whether the Pope had exceeded his authority in granting the original dispensation by which the King was enabled to marry Catherine.[2]

The Reformation in Germany, in regard to matrimonial affairs, was like the voice of John the Baptist crying in the wilderness, but unfortunately its message was hampered to no small extent by the fact that the leaders of thought there still tried to reconcile the authority of the Scriptures with the reason of every-day demands.[3] Consequently the chief actual result was to set ideas to work which ultimately brought some kind of order out of chaos, but which for a century after Luther's time could accomplish very little in

[1] Thwing, *The Family*, p. 83.

[2] For an account of the English writing on the subject of the royal divorce, see below, Appendix A.

[3] Almost all the leaders of the German Reformation contributed something to the discussion of marriage and divorce, some of them writing books on this subject alone. For further account, see Milton *Prose Works*, II, 231 ff., Woolsey, *Divorce and Divorce Legislation*, p. 126 ff.

themselves. The most important step taken was to deny the sacramental character of marriage, which Luther did in his *De Captivitate Babylonica* in 1520.[1] He also wished to do away with the distinction between spousals *de futuro* and *de praesenti* and to make all such contracts either simple betrothals, like the present-day engagement, or else marriages *per se;* but this proposition was not accepted. With the greatest evil in marriage and divorce legislation, — the multiplicity of impediments and the consequent ease with which a divorce *a vinculo matrimonii* might be obtained — the Reformers did nothing at all, although they seem to have realized the need of some action in regard to these conditions. In the field of divorce itself, perhaps the greatest immediate results were attained. Separation, or divorce *a mensa et thoro*, was abolished altogether, and in place of it was established a divorce resembling the modern type, by which the children remained legitimate but the innocent party might remarry without further suit in either spiritual or civil court.[2] For such divorce the ordinances of Wittenberg in 1534 and 1553 give two recognized causes, adultery and desertion.[3] Finally, all questions and suits in regard

[1] In this he was followed by Calvin in his *Institutiones*, 1536, and in the discipline of the Geneva church, which became the model for the church discipline of Holland and Scotland and influenced the *Thirty-nine Articles* of the Church of England.

[2] This was the origin of divorce as it is practiced today in Protestant countries. The only difference between a modern divorce and one under the German Reformation, is that nowadays either party may remarry.

[3] Divorce for adultery was based on the words of Christ (*Matt.* V, 32, and XIX, 9); that for desertion was based on those of St. Paul (I *Cor.* VII, 5). But the latter was taken in a more general sense than the literal meaning of the word, and included other causes, such as the refusal of the marriage right. The Wittenberg ordinances expressed the most conservative opinion. That of Zurich in 1525 stated that adultery, desertion, etc., were not only causes for divorce but represented

to marriage and divorce were placed partly in the hands of the parish clergy and partly in those of secular judges. Owing to the confusion of opinion arising from this arrangement, the result was hardly an improvement over the old system of jurisdiction except in principle; and this fact, together with the failure of the Reformers to attack the evils of impediments and nullification, in the end produced conditions which were actually much the same as those preceding, except for the possibility of remarriage after a divorce for adultery or desertion.

What has been said of the Roman Catholic Church in general prior to Luther's time, applies also to England before Henry VIII precipitated the whole Reformation question by his divorce from Catherine. Some one has made a remark to the effect that Henry first saw the light of the Reformation in the shining eyes of Anne Boleyn; and although this is no doubt true, the conditions he brought into the forum of public opinion were real faults in civil and ecclesiastical jurisdiction; and however insincere may have been his own concern in the general question, his personal attitude and the publicity of his case instigated thought and argument, which by provoking a wide controversy, finally resulted in great benefit to the realm.

II. Practice and Customs of Marriage

As a matter of actual practice, aside from ecclesiastical or civil concern, we may say that marriages were of three kinds, — those of children, those clandestinely performed by persons either under or over the age of puberty, and

also the standard of abuse which it was designed to remedy, "and to the judge it is left to decide what other causes shall be put by their side." Woolsey, p. 132. For further discussion, see Woolsey, *ibid.*, and Howard, II, 60 ff.

those openly and formally made with the blessing of the church and the celebration of friends. As we are interested in the practices and customs herein involved, as well as the legal aspects of the contract, we must examine briefly each of these three methods of marriage.

Infants, that is "those Younglings and Babes which as yet cannot speak" could not effect any kind of contract, but their parents could "make marriages" for them regardless of their age. These so-called marriages, however, had only the force of promises *de futuro* and were of no legal standing. The youngest couple reported in the Chester records is that of John Somerford, age three, and Jane Brerton, age two. The testimony, descriptive of the wedding, given later at John's suit for divorce (when fifteen years old), was as follows:

> "Johannes Somerforth . . . dicit, that he was present bie, when John Somerforth and Jane Brerton were maried together in the parish church at Brerton about xij yeres ago. . . . He saies that he carried the said John in his armes, beinge at the tyme of the said Mariage about iij yeres of age, and spake somme of the wordes of Matrimonye, that the said John, bie reason of his younge age, cold not speake hym selfe, holdinge him in his armes all the while the wordes of Matrimonie were in speakinge/ And one James Holford caried the said Jane in his armes, beinge at the said tyme about ij° yeres of age, and spake all, or the most parte of, the wordes of matrimony for her; and so held her still in his armes." [1]

The reasons for such child marriages were several. First, the parents were fulfilling the responsibility of settling their children in marriage, or at least taking steps thereto, which was one of the recognized duties of parenthood. Secondly, a peaceful treaty or alliance was often formed by families or countries hostile to one another by means of such a union. Thirdly, in case of the death of a father,

[1] Furnivall, *Child-Marriages, etc.*, p. 25.

by the laws of feudalism, the crown or its grantee had the right of the persons and estates of the children and might sell them to its own advantage; this the parents obviated by marrying their children as soon as possible. Fourthly, if the child was seven years old, the parents might benefit by the marriage settlements. It cannot be determined how common these child marriages were, but references to them are sufficiently numerous to make it clear that the practice was by no means out of the ordinary, especially among noblemen. Becon, writing about 1562 of the causes of the low esteem in which marriage was held, says: "First as touching men of nobilitie, wee see dayly by experyence that they for the moste parte marrye theyr chyldren at theyr pleasure whan they are verye yonge, euen to suche as wyll geue them most mony for them, as men usė to sel theyr horses, oxen, sheepe, or any other cattel. Who that wyl geue most mony, shalbe sonest sped."[1] Although it was a deplorable state of affairs that children should have been married for financial considerations only, the duty of parents to provide for their children in marriage is so clearly expressed in the domestic conduct books of the time that it is only fair to suppose that the impulse to settle them as soon as possible proceeded in most cases from worthy motives.

[1] Becon, *Worckes*, Pt. I, f. cccclxiiii. It may be objected that the children could break these contracts upon coming of age; but it must be remembered that "of age" in those days meant twelve and fourteen instead of eighteen and twenty-one, and it is hardly to be thought that such children would be able to act for their own best interests even if they realized what their rights or their interests were. If the marriage was made at the parents' instigation after the children were of age, whether the latter knew what they were doing or not, it was accomplished once and for all. Milton calls this practice a "savage inhumanity," and says that "the law which gives not all freedom of divorce to any creature endued with reason so assassinated, is next to cruelty." *Prose Works*, I, 373.

Clandestine marriages were those performed by children over seven years of age, either publicly or secretly, without parental consent, or those performed secretly by youths of fourteen and girls of twelve. In either case, the church condemned the practice but recognized the marriage as valid; but, as stated above, in the case of children under the age of puberty, the marriage had to be ratified later by both. An interesting wedding is cited in the Chester records as having been clandestinely performed by a priest between a boy of eleven and a girl, "a bigge damsell & mariageable," as follows:

> "Jacobus Hartley . . . Dicit, that he hard say that the said James and Anne articulate, were Maried in the parish Church of Colne, upon the xijth even in the Christmas shalbe v yeres, comme the Twelfth even next, about x of the Clocke in the night, — the said James at that tyme beinge about xj or vnder xij yeres of age,— without the consent of any of his frendes, bie one Sir Roger Blakey, then Curate of Colne . . . he saies, that the same night, this deponent was in the house of Christopher Hartley of Wwller, vncle to the said James libellate, and sawe when the said James [Ballard] was brought into the said house about Midnight bie ij^{o} fellowes, which (as this Deponent supposethe) had bene at the said Mariage. And in the morowe after, the same James [Ballard] declarid vnto his Vnckle, that the said Anne had intised hym with two Apples, to go with her to Colne, and to marry her. . . . And further he saieth, that the said Curate was ponished by the Archbushop of York his grace, for marieng at inconvenient tymes and vnlawfull persons." [1]

Between persons of age, clandestine marriages were made simply by exchanging such words as "I take thee for my wife" and "I take thee for my husband." Such a contract was in name a mere spousal *de praesenti*, but in effect it was a marriage, and if it was followed by cohabitation, it became automatically recognized as such. Swinburne,

[1] Furnivall, p. 45.

writing about 1600, says on this point, "Albeit there be no Witnesses of the Contract, yet the parties having verily (though secretly) Contracted Matrimony, they are very Man and Wife before God; neither can either of them with safe Conscience Marry elsewhere, so long as the other party liveth." [1] The contracted parties were man and wife before the law as well as before God, although the lack of witnesses made the proof of the marriage difficult. The form of such spousals might be anything from a simple promise to the complete ceremonial for public spousals as far as could be managed under the circumstances. At least the bride and groom might exchange a handclasp and a kiss, both of which had from ancient times been associated with the marriage contract. Great significance was also attached to the gift of a ring, usually given by the man to the woman or by each to the other, and one was always provided, if it could possibly be afforded, even in the most secret marriages.

As has already been said, both the child marriage and the union by means of spousals only were somewhat irregular though not unusual. The former had to be ratified at the children's coming of age, and the latter was always regarded with disfavor and was the cause of much legislative dispute. In the regular course of events leading to marriage, both spousals, either *de futuro* or *de praesenti*, and the solemnization by the church of the contract so made, were conducted openly and with a certain amount of set formality. A marriage might include both forms of spousals as well as the church celebration, but this would naturally occur seldom, as the latter embraced all the necessary vows and the ecclesiastical benediction in one service. On the other hand, no contract at all was required before the wedding ceremony, for the same reason. However, the contract

[1] Swinburne, *Treatise of Spousals*, p. 87.

itself, whether made in secret, in a private gathering of friends, or in the church service, was the essential feature of matrimony, the ceremony of the church being quite secondary in importance. On this point the publisher of Swinburne's book says, "In all Marriages Solemnized after the most strict manner, the Contract of Parties is the principal Ingredient and most essential Part, all other Matters being only as it were Foreign and Extrinsical to its Nature." [1]

In regard to the forms of spousals *de futuro* and *de praesenti,* they were so nearly alike, in whatever sentences they were expressed, that we may say that if the words spoken gave the impression that the parties at that moment took one another in the contract of matrimony, the spousals were *de praesenti;* if the words implied a promise against the future, a *de futuro* spousal was established.[2] Indeed, the simple intention to marry, though accompanied by the wrong formula, was sufficient to effect the contract. Swinburne says here, "Albeit the words of the Contract, neither of their own natural signification, neither yet by common use and acceptation conclude Matrimony; Yet whereas the Parties do thereby intend to Contract Matrimony, they are inseparable man and wife, not only before God, but also before Man; in case their meaning may lawfully appear." [3] Furthermore, for the protection of innocent girls against evil men, "when the words of the Contract are indifferent or equally flexible to the signification of Spousals *de futuro,* or Matrimony; In this Case the Law

[1] Swinburne, f. A3.

[2] Howard, I, 340 ff, brings considerable evidence to bear that the distinction between *de futuro* and *de praesenti* spousals was not understood or recognized by the humble people, but was in fact mere ecclesiastical hair-splitting. This was also Luther's view. Swinburne acknowledges the difficulty but upholds the distinction at length. *Ibid.,* secs. III, X, XII.

[3] Swinburne, p. 87.

presumeth Matrimony to be contracted, except in certain cases."[1] Spousals might be qualified to some extent by the stipulation of certain conditions. This subject is treated at length by Swinburne,[2] but is not of sufficient importance to be considered here.

The public spousal was performed either at the bride's house or at the church porch, but in either case the priest was recognized as the official witness. Here the vows were exchanged for either a future or a present union, but the couple was not pronounced to be man and wife, nor were they supposed to cohabit until the contract was solemnized by the church ceremony for marriage. Next to the vows, the exchange of gifts, principally from the man to the woman, was the most important feature of spousals. The ring of betrothal was worn on the right hand. A public spousal in full form is described by the priest in *Twelfth Night* between Olivia and Sebastian:

> "A contract of eternal bond of love,
> Confirm'd by mutual joinder of your hands,
> Attested by the holy close of lips,
> Strengthen'd by interchangement of your rings;
> And all this ceremony and compact
> Sealed in my function, by my testimony."[3]

[1] Swinburne, p. 88. Throughout his treatise, Swinburne uses the terms matrimony and spousals *de praesenti* as synonyms.

[2] *Ibid.*, sec. XII.

[3] Shakespeare, *op. cit.*, V, 1. In *All's Well*, II, 3, a contract is performed by the King between Helena and Bertram. The ceremony is appointed to be held that night, and the "solemn feast" later. A spousal similar to the *Twelfth Night* one takes place in Reade's *The Cloister and the Hearth*, although it is not described in detail. It is interesting to note that although this union was not solemnized by the church, the birth of a child was no stigma to the bride, except for the fact that her "bethrothal paper" was missing.

Here we find all the principal details, the handfasting, the kiss, the exchange of rings, and the benediction of the priest. But, so far as we know, there were no other witnesses. An espousal or a marriage was supposed to be witnessed by two persons, but it seems likely that the presence of a priest served just as well.

The time between the performance of spousals and the celebration of marriage varied. Since the publishing of banns was usually done on the three successive Sundays after the spousals, a space of about three weeks was the proper minimum; on the other hand, it might extend to years, as is often the case with engagements of today. The banns publicly asked in church as well as posted in public places of the town, were devised to make sure that no impediments existed which might later invalidate the marriage. In case any of such nature were discovered, the contract was annulled *ipso facto* without any formality at all, and was of no force in obstructing a later marriage. In Cromwell's time, the betrothed couple were given the choice of being "asked" on three Sundays in church or "cried" by the town bellman on three successive market days, and it seems that the latter method was the more popular.

The modern marriage ceremony originated in times too remote for us to investigate. The general form and phraseology of it go back to the twelfth century and became perpetuated in England for all succeeding time, with but slight changes, by the first English *Prayer Book*,[1] published by

[1] Many things in our modern ceremony are significant of old practices. One may notice that the vows made at the chancel steps are future in tense, corresponding to the ancient spousals *de futuro*. The bride's father accompanies her through these, as he did formerly, and then drops out altogether, since originally this was where he presented his daughter's dower to the groom and gave the bride herself into the hands of the priest. The vows now made at the altar rail are present in tense, corresponding to the spousals *de praesenti*. The earliest Prot-

order of Edward VI in 1549. The service of the Church of England today is practically the same as this.[1] The orthodox ceremony of the period we are studying used a form which was simply a repetition of spousals *de futuro* and spousals *de praesenti*, followed by the minister's pronouncing the couple to be "man and wife" and the prayers of the congregation for the success of the union. The publisher of Swinburne's book explains this clearly in his preface. "In our Publick Office of Marriage," he says, "Spousals and Matrimony[2] are united, and performed in one continued Act; When the Minister demands, *Wilt thou have this Woman to thy wedded Wife, &c.* And the Man answers, *I will,* and so the Woman *vice versa,* there's a Specimen of *Spousals de futuro.* When the Man repeats the words, *J. N. take thee N. to my wedded Wife, &c.,* and so the Woman *vice versa,* there's the form of *Spousals de praesenti,* which in Substance are perfect Matrimony. . . . When the Minister adds his Benediction, and pronounces them to be Man and Wife, then 'tis a perfect Marriage to all constructions and purposes in Law." [3]

estant marriage ceremony seems to have been drawn up by Bugenhagen in 1523. (See his *De Conjunctio episcopum.*) Since the Reformation, the minister has performed the legal marriage in pronouncing the couple "man and wife." The purely religious part of the ceremony, which followed, has been much curtailed in Protestant churches, but among Catholics the mass is still used to complete the marriage. In the American branch of the Church of England, the introductory part of the service has been shortened by the omission of much of the explanation of the uses and abuses of matrimony, which to our taste is offensive and ill-timed.

[1] The practices of the other churches and the origin of their ceremonies are discussed in the next chapter.

[2] The writer follows Swinburne's usage of these terms, applying them to spousals *de futuro* and *de praesenti* respectively.

[3] Swinburne, f. A3 *b**. It must be remembered that this book was written after the Reformation and treats of the Church of England only.

* The letter *b* indicates the back side or *verso* of the folio mentioned.

The marriage itself, through the part just described, was performed in the church porch;[1] the company then proceeded within the church, the bridal couple entering the chancel itself; and the blessing of God was spoken over them, as they kneeled beneath the "care-cloth," which was held by four ecclesiastics.[2] Jeaffreson picturesquely describes a wedding ceremony in full form as follows:[3]

"To the church-porch . . . the espoused woman of pre-Reformation times, with loosened locks falling to the waist, came on her wedding day, preceded by minstrels and vase-bearer, conducted by bride-knights or pages, attended by maidens, surrounded by her kindred, and followed at a distance by her father. There she met her espoused groom and became his wife, in the presence of God, the priest and the people. If she had previously gone through no ceremony of public betrothal, the earlier part of the proceedings at the porch corrected the omission. In answer to the priest's inquiry, she declared her wish to obey, serve, love, honor, and keep, alike in sickness and in health, the man who had just before in the hearing of the congregation expressed his desire to be her loving, worshipful, and considerate husband. The marriage followed immediately on the utterance of her wish for it.

"She stood at the groom's left hand. . . . Firmly pressing with his grasp the unreluctant hand . . . the groom said, 'I, * *, take the * *, to my wedded wyf, to have and to holde, fro this day forwarde, for bettere for wers, for richere for porere; in sykeness and in hele; tyll dethe us departe: if holy chyrche it wol ordeyne;

[1] Thus the Wife of Bath, "Housbondes at chirche-dore she hadde fyve." Marriage was performed in the body of the church for the first time in the reign of Edward VI, but this practice did not become universal until about a century later.

[2] If either bride or groom had been previously married, the care-cloth was not extended over them.

[3] Jeaffreson places his description before the Reformation probably because several variations of usage came in shortly after it. His account, however, does very well for the orthodox practice in post-Reformation days.

and therto I plight the my trouthe.' The hands of the spouses having been momentarily separated, the fairer and gentler of the two caught the other's large hand with a nervous grasp, and said, 'I, * *, take thee, * *, to my wedded husbonde, to have and to holde, fro this day forwarde, for better for wors; for richer for porere; in syknesse and in hele; to be bonere and buxom, in bedde and at borde, tyll dethe us departhe, if holy chyrche it woll ordeyne; and therto I plight the my trouth.'

"Next came the use of the ring. . . . Together with the ring the groom put gold and silver on the officiating priest's book; and after the symbol had been duly consecrated before the assembly, . . . he took it up with the thumb and two next fingers of his right hand, and placed it with peculiar ceremoniousness on the particular finger of the bride which it was destined to adorn.[1] 'With this rynge I the wed, and this gold and silver I the give, and with my body I the worship, and with all my worldely chatels I the endow,' he uttered following the priest's voice. . . . The ceremony of placing the ring on the bride's ring-finger was followed by the priestly utterance of a benediction[2] . . . which was followed by the recital of verses of the 68th Psalm, and the delivery of other blessings, that terminated the proceedings at the church-door."[3]

The real ceremony of the wedding was now complete, but prayers, additional benediction, and mass or sermon were yet to follow within the church.[4] These, however, were not

[1] The third finger of the left hand. In case the maiden already wore a bethrothal ring, it became the marriage ring also and was shifted from the right hand to the left.

[2] At this point, in post-Reformation times, the minister declared the couple to be "man and wife."

[3] Jeaffreson, I, 88 ff. Further details of the trappings of marriage — costumes, music, the ring, the feast, etc. — are set forth in this interesting book. These are particularly valuable in throwing light on the stage-business of contemporary drama, as in the case of the wedding of Petruchio and Katherine and the former's abuse of the conventional ceremonials.

[4] After the Reformation, the mass was given up as part of the marriage ceremony when the church dropped its use altogether. The

essential to a marriage. Before leaving the church, the bridal party partook of wine, bread, and sweetmeats, blessed by the priest, who also gave the groom a benedictional kiss, which the latter conveyed to the bride.

The ceremony over, the whole company adjourned to the house of the groom, where a feast was provided. Indeed, the groom's friends usually started feasting before they attended the church ceremony, a custom that unfortunately has not yet altogether died out. This practice and the evils resulting from it, are commented upon by Bullinger in his *The Christen state of Matrimonye*, as follows:

> "But the deuell hath crept in her also / & though he can not make the ordinaunce of goying to the church to be vtterly omitted & despised / yet is he thus mightie / & cā bring it to pas / that the ordinuance is nothing regarded but blemished with all maner of lightnesse: In so much that early in the morning the wedding people begynne to exceade in superflous eating & drinkyng / wherof they spytte vntill the halfe sermon be done. And whan they come to the preaching / they are halfe dronke / some alltogether / therfore regard they nether the preaching ner prayer / but stonde ther onely because of the custome. Such folkes also do come vnto the church with all maner of pompe and pryde / & gorgiousnesse of rayment and Jewels. They come with a greate noyse of basens and drommes / wher with they trouble the whole church / & hindre them in matters pertayninge to god." [1]

The propriety of celebrating marriages with feasting and

sermon was not a part of the ceremony in England until it was introduced by the Reformers. After about 1650, it was postponed until the first Sunday after the wedding.

[1] Bullinger, *op. cit.*, f. L. Bullinger was not an Englishman, but the fact that Coverdale, who translated his work, retained this passage, is evidence that the description represents English practices accurately enough. That Coverdale was not above taking liberties with his text is shown by the variations in the different editions of the book in question.

merrymaking seems to have been under debate, but if conducted with moderation, both were approved by clergy and laity alike, as proper and fitting, even upon Scriptural authority. William Perkins, a Puritan of the less radical type, writes in 1590:

"Heere question is moued, whether mariage is to be solemnized with mirth and feasting. Answ. I. It is lawfull and warrantable to vse feasting and mirth at mariages, because these be things indifferent, and wee haue examples thereof in the Scriptures. . . . Christ himselfe did approue the resort of people to the mariage at Cana in Galilee, both by his presence, and by that honorable gift of sixe water-pots of best wine, Ioh. 2. 2. 7. 8. II. It is not only lawfull, but conuenient and fit to be done, if there be abilitie; according to the commendable custome of the place & countrie wherein men do dwell; so as in the vse thereof, these cautions bee obserued. First, that in mirth and merry-making, there be care had that nothing be done which is dishonest, prophane, or of ill report. Philip. 4. 8. Whatsoeuer things are honest — pure — of good report, thinke on these things. Secondly, that ioy in them be mixed and moderated with feare of God, without which Laughter and reioycing is meere madnesse, Eccles. 2. 2. Thirdly, That it be performed in a moderate and sober vse of the creatures, without riot & excesse. Thus we reade at the great feast of Ahashuerosh, it was appointed by the King himself, that they should drink orderly, & none might compel another to drinke more then he thought conuenient. Ester I. 8." [1]

William Gouge, a later Puritan, goes still further, declaring that such a feast partakes of the nature of a civil ceremony and is "very requisite."

"Though vpon the forenamed consecrating of mariage it bee in regard to the substance thereof fully consummate, yet for the greater solemnity of so honourable a thing, it is very requisite that further there be added a ciuill celebration of it: vnder which I comprise all

[1] Perkins, *Christian Oeconomie*, p. 96.

those lawfull customes that are vsed for the setting forth of the outward solemnitie thereof, as meeting of friends, accompanying the Bridgroome and Bride both to and from the Church, putting on best apparell, feasting, with other tokens of reioycing: for which we haue expresse warrant out of Gods word." [1]

Among the Independents, who opposed all ecclesiastical performance of marriage, the rejoicing and feasting of friends was regarded almost as an essential part of the wedding, in order to make it public and to take the place of the church ceremony. Under the caption "How must they be duelie ioined in mariage," Robert Brown, one of the leaders of the sect, lays down these principles:

"Their bethrothing & espousing must be further made known vnto witnesses. Their friendes must be glad and reioyce together, in some ioyefull and seemelie manner." [2]

The elaborateness of these festal celebrations depended, of course, upon the position and wealth of the bridal couple. In full form, they lasted two or three days, and included banqueting, dancing, song, games (particularly of a kissing nature), outdoor sports, sometimes masques or interludes, and finally a levee held by the bride and groom to their nearest friends in the bed chamber, the receiving couple being enthroned in the bed.[3] It may readily be imagined that at a time of such general abandon, abuses and excesses might easily take place. This was indeed the case, and the evil practices are often commented on by the writers on marriage. Bullinger's description, in his *Cristen state,* of such an afternoon and evening is too good to miss.

[1] Gouge, *Domestical Duties,* p. 120.

[2] Brown, *Life and manners of true Christians,* cap. 172.

[3] In *The Changeling,* the inmates of a mad-house are hired to amuse a wedding company on the third day of the feast. In *The Wonder of Women,* a pageant takes place in the bridal chamber.

"After the bancket and feast / there begynneth a vayne / madd/ and vnmanerly fashiō. For the bryde must be brought in to an open dauncyng place. Then there is such a renninge / leapinge/ and flynging amonge them / then there is such a lyftinge vp and discoueringe of damesels clothes and of other wemens apparell/ that a man might thinke / all these dauncers had cast all shame behinde thē / and were become starke madde and out of theyr wyttes / and that they were sworne to the deuels daunce. Then must the poore bryd kepe foote with all dauncers / & refuse none/ how scabbed / foule / dronkē / rude and shamels so euer he be. Then must she oft tymes heare and se much wickednesse / & many an vncomely word. And that noyse and rōbling endureth euen tyll supper.

"As for supper / loke how much shamels & drōken the euenyng is more then the murnyng / so much the more vyce / excesse/ and mysnourtoure is vsed at the supper. After supper must they begynne to pype and daunce agayne of the new. And though the yonge parsones / beynge weery of the bablyng noyse and inconuenience / come ones towarde theyr rest / yet can they haue no quietnesse. For a man shall fynd unmanerly & restlesse people/ that will first go to theyr chābre dore / and there syng vycious and naughtie balates that the deuell maye haue his tryūphe now to the vttermost."[1]

With the coming of Puritan and Independent ideas after the Reformation, both ceremony and custom underwent certain changes. Those described above, however, may be taken as representative of the so-called Church of England after it broke away from the Pope. For the severing of the Anglican Church from the Church of Rome, so far as marriage and divorce were concerned, had no effect upon general conditions whatsoever.

[1] Bullinger, f. L *b*. A similar description of wedding revelry occurs in the old morality play *The Disobedient Child* (Dodsley, *Old Plays*, ed. Hazlitt, II, 300). Another, but with fewer details, is given by Chaucer, Merchant's Tale, ll. 465 ff.

CHAPTER II

CONTROVERSIES REGARDING MARRIAGE

I. HISTORICAL SITUATION

THE first years of the Reformation in England were picturesquely and aptly described by Thomas Fuller in a sermon in 1643. "King Henry the eight," he says, "brake the Popes necke, but bruised not the least finger of Popery; rejecting his Supremacy, but retaining his superstition in the six Articles. The Reformation under Edward the sixth, was like the Reformer, little better then a child. . . . As Nurses to woe their Children to part from knives do suffer them to play with Rattles; so the State then permitted the People (infants in Piety) to please themselves with some frivilous points of Popery, on condition they would forsake the dangerous opinions thereof. As for Queene Elizabeth, her Character is given in that plaine, but true expression, that shee swept the Church of England and left all the dust behind the door." [1] The Puritan doctrines referred to here, which began to make themselves felt in Elizabeth's reign, were advanced in their early conception in both England and Germany long before this name was attached to the sect in 1564. Indeed, the beginning of this agitation may be traced back without break to Wiclif; but although the present movement was the result of principles similar to those of the Lollards, as a historical development it is so clearly the immediate outcome of the Reformation that the earlier influences may be quite disregarded here.

[1] Fuller, *A Sermon of Reformation*, p. 7. The passage given is quoted by Fuller from some work which he does not name. He repudiates the characterization of Elizabeth's reign, but history rather supports it.

As early as 1550, the effect of the German Reformation and the still more sweeping reform ideas, many of which were not as yet in actual operation anywhere, began to have some influence in England. Many of the future leaders of English thought, such as Hooper, Coverdale, Rogers, and Ridley, "the first race of Puritans," were at this time returning from their exile on the continent, and by sermons and teaching began to spread the doctrine of the purification of the English Church from Popish practices and Popish form of government. Although in the succeeding years under the oppression of Elizabeth, this purification was still aimed at certain ceremonial details, — the minister's robe, the ring of marriage, etc. — and some historians have represented the Puritan movement as originating from the desire to get rid of these, the fact is that prelatical episcopacy in its fundamental conception was attacked, by some at least, from the very first. Hooper, in his *Declaration of the Ten Commandments*, published in 1550, spends three chapters in expounding the nature of ecclesiastical law and the necessity of avoiding the decrees and interpretations of Popish bishops.[1] And Bucer, in his *Draft of a more primitive Church system*,[2] in 1557, goes so far as to advocate provincial synods as well as a council of bishops and presbyters.

The Puritan form of church government in its complete conception was first drawn up in England by a committee of sixty divines, of which Cartwright and Travers were

[1] Hooper, *Early Writings*, p. 270 ff.

[2] Contained in his *De Regno Christi*. Such a form of church government was instituted by Calvin in Geneva in 1541, having been submitted to the civil authorities in 1536. Church government by synods of clergy and laity had been established by Zwingli at Zurich as early as 1528. Bucer's ideas were, of course, taken from continental practice, which influenced Hooper and the other English Reformers also.

members, in 1576. Here we find provisions for three types of governing bodies, — classes, comitial assemblies, and provincial synods — following the form of Calvin's church government at Geneva. These, under different names, continued to be advocated as the disciplinary powers of the Reformed church. These principles of ecclesiastical government had been previously set forth in 1574 in a Latin book by Travers, *Ecclesiasticae Disciplinae, et Anglicanae Ecclesiae . . . explicatio*, which was translated by Cartwright in the same year under the title of *A full and plaine declaration of Ecclesiasticall discipline, etc.* A second Latin book by Travers, in 1584, since known as the *Book of Discipline*, was also translated in that year by Cartwright, but its publication was suppressed.[1] Robert Brown, later the founder of the Brownist sect, issued a book in 1582, *The life and manners of true Christians*, which for the first time set forth in English the Puritan interpretation of Scriptural instruction for life and church government. But with the establishment of the Court of High Commissions in 1571 and the increasing power of Archbishop Whitgift, the advance of the Puritan cause was brought almost to an

[1] This is the book which was found among Cartwright's papers after his death and published in 1664 under the title of *A Directory of Church-government*. Neal (*History of Puritans*, I, 358) confounds these two translations from Travers. Heylyn (*History of Presbyterians*, p. 291) speaks of a *Form* by Cartwright as being popular in 1582. This was the translation of the first book. The confusion of the two works, which existed from Neal's time until 1872, is set right by the editor of the reprint of the 1664 edition of Cartwright's *Directory*. Both books, however, contain the same principles. The Elizabethan names for the *Directory* were *The Book of Discipline*, *The Form of Discipline*, etc. The editor of the reprint says that this was "no doubt the same book as that referred to in the proceedings of Parliament in 1584, under the title of *A Book of the Form of Common Prayer, Administration of the Sacraments, etc.*" I think he is mistaken here, as a book of this name and date is extant which bears no resemblance to Cartwright's.

end, although its adherents held their ground and spread their gospel by personal teaching and suffering. It was at this time that the Puritans were martyrs as non-conformists to ritualistic details rather than as advocates of a reform of church government, as it was easier to convict a man of ceremonial omissions than of doctrinal opinions. For this reason, it is natural that most of the public expression of the time in sermons, petitions, tracts, etc., is concerned with superficialities rather than fundamentals, the famous Marprelate tracts being a case in point; but the treatises mentioned above show clearly that the real trouble was more than surface deep.

In the reign of James I, there was no change in the condition of affairs except for the slackening of persecution. In the *Humble Petition to King James* and at the Hampton Court Conference, only minor points were discussed, and the only things obtained by the Puritans were the King's scorn and enmity. The limitation of the power of the ecclesiastical courts, which Neal says were an "insufferable grievance" on account of the "bottomless deeps of canon law," and the widening of the jurisdiction of the civil magistrate on much the same lines as were afterwards established in Charles' time, were advocated by William Bradshaw in his *English Puritanisme*, published in 1605. The same views were for the first time expressed in Parliament in 1607, in a speech which is important both in showing the coming attitude of the period and in throwing light upon previous history. The following is extracted from it:

"And whereas by the laws of God and the land, ecclesiastical persons should use only the spiritual sword, by exhortation, admonition, and excommunication, which are the keys of the church, to exclude impenitent sinners, and leave the temporal sword to the civil magistrate, which was always so used in England, till the second year of the reign of king Henry IV. at which time the Popish prelates got the temporal sword into their hands; which statute was since by several acts of Parliament made void; yet by virtue of that temporal authority once for a short space by them used, some ecclesiastical persons do use both swords, and with those two swords the oath *ex officio*, which began first in England by the statute of the second of king Henry IV. being contrary to the laws of England, and, as I verily think, contrary to the laws of God." [1]

But nothing came either of Bradshaw's book or of this speech. Another attempt was made in the same direction by a petition in 1610, but the King was still obdurate.

The Puritan movement was once more changed from an aggressive to a defensive cause under the high hand of Archbishop Laud in the reign of Charles I. So bitter and so sweeping was this prelate in his attack against the followers of the antipapal movement that the various sects of non-conformists which had split off from time to time from the established church almost lost their individuality in the defense of their common doctrines, especially as there was no occasion to quarrel over the details of Protestantism until Popery, now in the ascendent, was cast from the realm. In this period we find but few publications on the Puritan side, as Laud suppressed them as thoroughly as he could. A few, however, appeared anonymously, but their supposed authors were severely dealt with, Prynne, Burton, and Bastwick being imprisoned, tortured, pilloried, and fined. Under Elizabeth and Whitgift, the High Commission Court had been oppressive enough; but Laud, by obtaining from Charles a decree removing ecclesiastical courts from state control, became himself the absolute master of every church and every minister in the country. This, of course, could not have been the case had he not had the support of all the bishops, — with the exception of a few who had become non-conformists — for they, realizing that their positions

[1] Neal, *History of the Puritans*, II, 68 ff.

were to be maintained only by the continuance of the existing form of church government, upheld the Archbishop and opposed the growing attitude of independence in the House of Commons. In 1640, Laud's power reached its zenith, as expressed in the canons of that year. Canon 6, "that all archbishops, bishops, priests, and deacons take oath upholding the present doctrine and discipline of the church," was aimed directly at all those opposed to orthodoxy, with the intention of driving every non-conformist from his church or subjecting him to such punishment as Laud's courts saw fit.

But such autocracy could not be maintained indefinitely. Already ministers and congregations were fleeing the country to Holland, Geneva, and America in order to escape persecution and to worship as they pleased. In 1640, the House of Commons asserted itself, repudiated the canons just passed, and resolved "that the clergy of England . . . have no power to make any constitutions, canons, or acts, whatsoever, in matters of doctrine, discipline or otherwise, to bind the laity of the land, without consent of Parliament." [1] Laud was sentenced to the Tower in 1641, and Parliament set about to strip the church and the bishops of the power obtained under his administration. By this time, the Puritans and their fellow non-conformists represented not only the general opinion but also the real power of the entire kingdom; hereafter their labors were to be directed merely towards forcing their desired reforms from the House of Lords and the King.

The bishops in the House of Lords stubbornly blocked every effort of the Commons for reform; but the Commons, supported by the populace of London and the greater part of the laity of the upper house, were becoming too powerful to be resisted. In 1641, the Star Chamber and the Court

[1] Neal, II, 319.

of High Commissions were abolished; and in 1642, a bill was railroaded through both houses taking all temporal jurisdiction from the bishops. Thus the first obstacle to complete church reform was overcome. The King, who by this time was pretty well intimidated by Parliament, was approached in the same year with a summary in nineteen propositions of the reforms desired, the most important of which for us was "that your Majesty will be pleased to consent, that such a Reformation be made of the Church-Government and Liturgy as both Houses of Parliament shall Advise; wherein they intend to have Consultations with Divines." [1] These propositions were not granted in any satisfactory way, and the deadlock between the King and the country, which embraced other matters than ecclesiastical, finally resulted in civil war.

It is not possible here to go sufficiently into the history of this period to show the various efforts and the failures thereof on the part of Parliament to obtain a real reform of ecclesiastical affairs. It will be enough for our purpose to set forth the propositions for church government submitted to the King at Uxbridge in 1645. These, though not accepted by him, are important in that they express the general principles of all the non-conforming parties, of which the English Puritans and the Scotch Presbyterians were the leaders, and also because they became in the next year the basis of the church doctrine and government under the Commonwealth. The new doctrine was set forth in a *Directory for Public Worship*, which was to supersede the *Book of Common Prayer* of Edward VI. It was drawn up by the official assembly appointed in 1643.[2] It contained, beside an introduction explaining its origin, the proper

[1] Rushworth, *Historical Collections*, Pt. 3, I, 723.

[2] The *Directory* was not made law until January 3, 1645. It may be found in Scobell, *Acts and Ordinances of Parliament*, I, 76 ff.

forms and usages connected with the functions of the church under the following headings: (1) Assembling the Congregation, (2) Public Reading of the Holy Scriptures, (3) Public Prayer before the Sermon, (4) Preaching the Word, (5) Prayer after the Sermon, (6) The Sacrament of Baptism, (7) The Sacrament of the Lord's Supper, (8) The Sanctification of the Lord's Day, (9) The Solemnization of Matrimony, (10) Visitation of the Sick, (11) Burial of the Dead, (12) Public Solemn Fasting, (13) Observance of Days of Public Thanksgiving, (14) Singing of Psalms, and (15) an Appendix on the Days and Places of Public Worship. The government of the church was to be in the hands of congregational, classical, and synodical assemblies, in practically the same manner as that of Calvin's church at Geneva, which had been advocated by Cartwright in England in the previous century.[1]

This form of church government became established nationally, by way of trial, under the Commonwealth in 1646. The order of bishop was abolished, London was divided into twelve classical elderships, each containing twelve parishes, and persons were appointed by Parliament to settle the counties of England and Wales into provinces, as had already been done in Scotland by the Presbyterian Church. The eldership of each parish was obliged to meet every week, the classical assemblies once a month, provincial assemblies twice a year, and national assemblies as often as summoned by Parliament. The exact limitations of the jurisdiction of the church under this régime

[1] See his *Directory* and *Discipline*. Some similar form of church government was established as early as 1576 by Cartwright in the islands of Guernsey and Jersey, which had obtained royal permission to manage their own ecclesiastical affairs. But I have been unable to find any further information on the subject, except that this arrangement came to an end in the latter part of James I's reign.

cannot be determined. The sole disciplinary function seems to have been to deprive individuals of the Holy Communion in cases of sufficient offense. The ordinances "that cognizance and examination of any capital Offence, shall be by the Magistrate thereunto appointed," and that "the Presbytery . . . shall not have cognizance of anything wherein any matter of Payment, Contract, or Demand is concerned, or of any matter of Conveyance, Title, Interest, or Property,"[1] which had been established in 1645, give us the general status of the case but leave us in the dark as to the particular interests of our investigation, namely marriage and divorce. The abolishing of the temporal power of the bishops in 1642, and the utter overthrow of their office in 1646, together with the final establishment of the new form of government in 1648, when the power of the assemblies was limited to settling points of faith and to excommunication for disorders,[2] would seem to make it clear that questions of marriage and divorce were, at least officially, taken entirely out of the jurisdiction of the church. On the other hand, no law was passed touching upon either subject, and no new method of judicature has been discovered as operating at the time.

This situation was brought to an end by Cromwell's marriage act in 1653, in which it was provided that marriage should be performed by the local justices of the peace, and that all controversies or exceptions concerning contracts and marriages should also be referred to them or to such other persons as Parliament might appoint.

[1] Rushworth, Pt. 4, I, 212.

[2] Scobell, I, 165 ff. The whole form of church government, as then established, may be found here.

II. The Puritan Platform in regard to Marriage

The above brief outline of the general Puritan movement will be sufficient to enable us to place the various reforms in regard to marriage in their proper historical setting. In looking more closely into the legislation and practice centering about this subject, it is necessary to consider not only the history of the Puritans, but also that of the other non-conformist bodies, in England, Scotland, the Continent, and America. Historians seem to have neglected this very important period in the development of the present-day conception of marriage, and have contented themselves with saying that civil marriage originated in Holland and spread from there to England and America.

The mistake here arises from a failure to distinguish between a legal marriage, which might be merely spousals *de praesenti*, and the "solemnization of matrimony" by the church, which was no more than an ecclesiastical blessing upon an already established union. The church, from the beginning of the Christian era on, had attempted to put the emphasis upon the solemnization, although it always recognized a privately contracted marriage as valid. Luther's teachings, on the other hand, while retaining the church service as a beneficial custom,[1] threw the emphasis upon the previous contract, where in the light of actual law it belonged. It was doubtless the result of Luther's teachings, passed on by Calvin, that two of the Netherland provinces, Holland and West Friesland, established civil marriage in 1580 upon gaining independence from Spain.[2]

[1] Luther drafted a model ceremony for use where desired, which was followed with variations in the chief church ordinances.

[2] "There the law was 'that those of any religion, after lawful and open publication, coming before the magistrates in the town-house,

But this ceremony did not replace that of the church, as has been usually thought; it was merely a legal recognition and sanction of the marriage contract, which up to this time had been performed in private, with or without witnesses, as spousals *de praesenti*. That the ecclesiastical solemnization continued to be practised in Holland, as an additional ceremony, is shown by the presence of the usual church service in the old Dutch liturgies [1] and is testified to by the Brownists' *Confessions of Faith*.[2] Furthermore, among the forms and ceremonies established by the National Synod of Dort in 1618-19 for all the reformed churches of the Netherlands, *The Celebration of Marriage before the Church* is printed for general use.[3] It is thus clear that in Holland the so-called civil marriage was no great innovation at all, but was merely the old private marriage, by means of spousals *de praesenti*, conducted according to legal form.

That this explanation of the case, which is important both for itself and for its later bearing upon England and America, is the correct one, is further shown by the church service itself, in which the man and the woman are regarded and referred to as already married but "desire here openly to have your marriage-bond confirmed in the name of God

or stadt-house, were to be by them orderly married, one to another.'" Bacon, *Genesis of New England Churches*, p. 340. See also Bradford, *History of Plymouth Plantation*, I, 217.

[1] See Bibles, liturgies, etc., published at Delft, 1582, and Leyden, 1589, under title, *Biblia, dat is De gantsche Heylighe Schrift, etc.*, and also the comments on the English Reformed church in Holland, pp. 43–44 below.

[2] This book is contained in *An Apologie or Defense of . . . Brovvnists*, 1604. Baillie, in his *Dissvasive from the Errours of the time*, p. 42, quotes this passage from it: "The Dutch Church at Amsterdam celebrates mariage in the Church, as if it were a part of the Ecclesiastick Administration, while it is in the nature of it meerly civill."

[3] See *A Catechisme of the Christian Religion, etc.*, trans. from the Dutch, p. 81.

before his church." [1] An interesting comment, which again supports my view, is made upon this ceremony in the account of the Synod of Dort, published by order of the Synod of Walloon Churches, held in 1667: "*Comme il se trouve que jusques à present on use par tout de deverses manieres touchant les Mariages, & toutefois est convenable d'entretenir Uniformité en cest endroit, les Eglises continuëront l'Usage qu'elles on eu jusques à maintenant, conforme à la Parole de Dieu & aux predecentes Ordonnances Ecclesiastiques, jusques à ce que par le Magistrat Superieur (lequel on requerra promptement pour cest effect) eu soit establie, avec l'advis des Ministres, une Ordonnance generale, à laquelle ce Reglement Ecclesiastique se rapporte quand à ce point.*" [2] In such form, civil and ecclesiastical, marriage continued to be celebrated in Holland throughout our period.

In England, even in the established church, conditions were similar to those in Holland, except that the presence of civil authority was not required, and in public opinion, though not in either ecclesiastical or civil law, greater emphasis was laid upon the church ceremony. William Harrington, whose views were orthodox even to the point of including marriage among the sacraments, makes these points clear. Writing in 1528, he says:

"It is to be knowen that man and woman dothe entre this holy ordre and sacramente of matrymony by expresse and free consente

[1] *Catechisme of the Christian Religion*, p. 83. In putting the vows to the bridal couple, the minister is directed to say "to the married persons":

"N. doe you acknowledge here before God, and his Holy Church, that you have taken, and doe take to your lawfull wife N. here present," etc.

Note the tenses. Furthermore, there is no pronouncing of the couple to be "man and wife," as this would have occurred, if at all, at the civil ceremony.

[2] *La Confession de Foy des Eglises Reformées du Païs-Bas, etc.*, p. 78.

of bothe partyes / that is to say: when bothe the man and the woman dothe consente bothe in one tyme to be husbonde and wyfe / and that consente doo shewe eyther to other by expresse wordes of the tyme presente, as by these wordes or other lyke / I take the to my wyfe / or I frome this tyme forwarde wyll haue the to my wyfe. . . . But and they vse wordes of the tyme to come . . . then it is noo matrymony. . . .

"Moreouer this consent which doth make matrymony ought to be expressed & shewed in open and in honest places afore & in the p̄sence of honest and laufull wytnesses called specyally therfore, ii at ye leest / for & it be otherwyse yt is to say / yf ye man & woman or theyr proctours do make matrymony secretly by them selfe without any recorde or but with one wytnesse yt is called matrymony clādestinat whiche for many causes is forboden by the lawe . . . notwithstondyng that matrymony is valeable and holdeth afore god. . . .

"And when matrymony is thus laufully made / yet the man maye not possesse the woman as his wyfe / nor the woman the man as her husbonde . . . afore suche tyme as that matrymony be approued and solempnysed by oure mother holy chyrche / and yf they do in dede they synne deedly." [1]

Thus in England, as well as elsewhere, marriage by means of spousals *de praesenti* was recognized by both church and state, but the church had managed to become accredited as the proper authority for the solemnization of it. Nevertheless, as this authority was self-assumed and as the sacramental character of marriage was repudiated in the *Thirty-nine Articles* of 1552, it had only the validity of tradition.

That the civil authority should take charge of affairs matrimonial, does not seem to have been advocated in the first meeting of Puritan divines, in 1576. As yet the Reformers were too much occupied with planning the mere

[1] Harrington, *Cōmendacions of matrymony,* f. Aiii ff. For a fuller quotation from Harrington, see Appendix C, below.

form of church government to give attention to the division of power between church and state, although they went as far as to determine that the classical assemblies should decide "doubts and difficulties touching the contract of marriage." Cartwright's *Directory* also omitted any mention of civil jurisdiction. His directions as to marriage itself are interesting as the first Puritan expression in England on the subject.

"Let espousing goe before marriage. Let the words of espousing be of the present time, and without condition, and before sufficient witnesses on both sides. It is to be wished that the Minister or an Elder be present at the espousals, who having called upon God may admonish both parties of their duties. . . .

"The Espousals being done in due order, let them not be dissolved, though both parties should consent. Let the marriage be solemnized within two moneths after. Before the marriage let the promise be published three severall Sabbath daies; but first, let the parties espoused, with their parents or govenours desire the publishing thereof of the Minister and two Elders at the least, that they may be demanded of those things that are needfull, and let them require to see the instrument of the covenant of Marriage, or at least sufficient testimony of the Espousals." [1]

It is important to notice here the emphasis laid upon spousals and the insistence that they be *de praesenti* and before witnesses. In this we see the influence of Luther's teachings in England even before they became established by law in Holland.

From the appointment of Whitgift as Archbishop of Canterbury in 1583 to the fall of Laud in 1641, the Puritans were persecuted to such an extent and the publication of so-called seditious pamphlets was so rigorously suppressed that it is difficult to find much expression of opinion on the subjects of church government and marriage. Neverthe-

[1] Cartwright, *Directory*, f. B3.

less, on the latter topic I have found enough writing to be able to present a definite account of its theory and practice. William Perkins, in his *Christian Oeconomie,* 1590, gives the fullest discourse, of which the following are the most important passages:

"Mariage is that, whereby the coniunction formerly begunne in the contract, is solemnely manifested, and brought to perfection. Mariage is consummate by three sorts of actions; one of the parents of the Bride and Bridegroome, the other of the Minister in publicke, the third of the persons coupled together. . . .

"The second Action . . . is the blessing and sanctification thereof, which is a solemne worke, whereby the Minister pronouncing the parties contracted to be man and wife before the whole congregation, commendeth them and their estate vnto God by solemn prayer. . . .

"Now that this action is to be approued and vsed in the Church, appeares by these reasons. I. Mariage as it is a publicke action, so it is after a sort a spirituall and diuine ordinance, whereby it differeth from the contract: For the contract being meerely ciuill, as it standeth by consent of man, so by the same consent, it may bee broken and dissolued, but with mariage it is otherwise. II. Marriage is the Seminarie of the Church and Common-wealth. III. It was the practise of ye Primitive Church." [1]

As in the case of Cartwright's *Directory,* it should be noted that the church ceremony is not regarded here as the actual marriage — that had already taken place in the spousals *de praesenti* — yet it is strongly recommended that the church should bless and solemnize the union. This attitude is more definitely expressed in a statement made

[1] Perkins, *op. cit.*, pp. 83, 94, 94, respectively. The Biblical authority cited by Perkins for making marriage an ecclesiastical affair is: (1) God said to Adam and Eve, "Increase and multiply" (*Gen.* II, 22); and (2) St. Paul said, "Let all things be done decently and in order" (I *Cor.* XIV, 40).

by John Paget [1] in a collection of letters entitled *An Arrow against the Separation of the Brownists*, published at Amsterdam in 1618. "For marriages," says this writer, "we do not hold it as a thing of necessity that they should be celebrated by Ministers in the church; we judge them lawful marriages that are made by the Magistrates, without Ministers; but yet we hold it lawful, more convenient and comfortable, that they be accomplished in the church by Ministers, both for showing the duties of the persons married, and for obtaining a special blessing by the prayers of the congregation." [2] The writers who attack more directly the civil marriage of the Brownists take the same attitude. Thomas Edwards in his *Antapologia: or, A Full Answer to the Apologeticall Narration*,[3] asks, "Whether also, one of these Apologists, was not so farre gone in the principles of the new Church-way, as that he would not be married by Ministers, but deferred marriage till he came into Holland, where presently after his comming he was married, (not in the way of the Reformed churches there,) but by the Magistrates according to the way of the Brownists, as it is laid down in Robinsons *Apologie*." [4] Another Puritan writer, Ephriam Paget, in his *Heresiography*, a book on the various nonconformist sects, describes the Brownists as being "as malevolent to the Dutch and French churches as to us," and among the reasons given for this antipathy is the fact that they celebrate marriage in the church. "Is not this a foule fault?" asks Paget ironically, "Is it not better to

[1] This Paget is not included by Brook in his *Lives of the Puritans*, but there can be no doubt that he represents Puritan beliefs.

[2] Hanbury, *Historical Memorials*, I, 334.

[3] The *Apologeticall Narration* was written by several Brownists in defense of their doctrines.

[4] Edwards, *op. cit.*, p. 22. For account of Robinson's *Apologie*, see below, p. 53, n. 1.

be married in the Congregation with prayers and Gods blessing pronounced upon them by the minister, then to be contracted privately, and entered into a book as men do horses in Smithfield?" [1]

Summing up these opinions, we have clear and abundant evidence that the Puritans, while not condemning marriage by magistrates as unlawful, considered it "lawful, more convenient and comfortable" that it should be solemnized by the church.

III. The Position and Practice of the Independents

From the passages cited above, it will readily be seen that the Brownists or Independents went much further in their emancipation from ecclesiastical jurisdiction in marital affairs than did the other reformed churches.[2] This innovation was originated by Brown himself, who probably developed it from the teachings of Luther — perhaps through Cartwright's *Directory* — and from the practice of Holland.[3] It was first expressed by him in his book, *The life and manners of true Christians*, published at Middelburg in 1582, the principles of which he and his assistant Richard Harding preached upon their return to England

[1] Paget, *op. cit.*, p. 50.

[2] Historians and legal writers have failed entirely to realize this fact, namely, that the Brownists differed radically from the other reformed churches in their ideas of marriage. The point is, however, of extreme importance: from a historical standpoint, it explains the origin of the civil marriage of New England, and from a literary one, it throws considerable light upon Milton's conception of marriage. These points are both demonstrated below.

[3] Brown had been a disciple of Cartwright and "built his schism upon Cartwright's principles" (Heylyn, p. 295). It is evident that Brown goes much further in his "schism" than did Cartwright.

in 1584. In speaking of marriage, Brown makes no mention of the church at all. The important things connected with marriage he declares to be espousals and cohabitation. The chief points to be observed are set forth as follows:

> "Mariage is a lawfull ioyning and fellowship of the husbande and wife, as of two in one fleshe, by partaking the vse of eche others loue, bodie, and giftes, in one communion of dueties: and especiallie in generation and bringing vp children. . . .
>
> "The couenant of Mariage is an agreement or partaking of conditions, to hold the communion thereof, so long as death or lawfull separation and divorcemēt doth not breake it.
>
> "There is also a couenant before mariage as by bethrothing, espousing and agreement of friends and kindred.
>
> "Bethrothing is a couenant betweene the parties to be married, whereby they giue their troth that they will and shall marrie together, except some laweful vnmeetnes and disliking eche of the other do hinder it in the meane time.
>
> "Espousing is the couenant betweene them, whereby they are pronounced before witnesses, to giue them selues, and to be giuen eche to other to become husband and wife." [1]

This account, however, does not express definitely that marriage is a civil affair only and that the church has nothing to do with it, although such were clearly Brown's views. But in 1587 we find these doctrines not only expressed but publicly proclaimed before the Court of High Commission by John Greenwood, a member of the Brownist sect. This was the first voice raised in England against marriage as

[1] Brown, *op. cit.*, secs. 169 and 171. This important book is occasionally mentioned by historians but seems to have escaped examination, although Hanbury quotes a few definitions from it. (*Hist. Mem.*, I, 19 ff.) In the passage above, Brown uses the term *marriage* to mean not the ceremony but the state, the term *betrothing* to mean spousals *de futuro*, and the term *espousing* to mean spousals *de praesenti*.

practised by the established church.[1] The following questions and answers took place at Greenwood's trial:

"Q. What say you of marriage? Did you not marry one Boman and his wife in the Fleet?

"G. No. Neither is marriage any part of the minister's office.

"Q. Who used prayer?

"G. I think, that I used prayer, at that time.

"Q. Who joined their hands together?

"G. I know no such thing. They publicly acknowledged their consent before the assembly.

. . . .

"Winch. They make such marriages under a hedge. It hath been an order long received to marry by a minister.

"G. There were many faithful witnesses of their mutual consent. And if it were not lawful, we have many ancient fathers, who, by your judgement, did amiss." [2]

The evidence of Brown and Greenwood, somewhat incomplete in itself, is fully substantiated by Robert Barrow in his book *A Brief Discovery of the False Churches*, published in 1590,[3] three years before he was executed along with

[1] I do not take into account here the many objections which had been raised by the Puritans against ceremonial details in the orthodox marriage service. For notice of these, see Hooker, *Ecclesiastical Polity* (ed. Rhys), II, 391 ff., and notes there.

[2] Brook, II, 35. It should be noted here that even the Bishop of Winchester acknowledges the validity of privately contracted marriages, although accomplished in the way he describes in the slang of the day. (Cf. Jaques' speech to Touchstone, "And will you, being a man of your breeding, be married under a bush, like a beggar? Get you to church, and have a good priest, that can tell you what marriage is." *As You Like It*, III, 3.)

[3] This book also has been entirely neglected by students of marital affairs, although quotations from it occur in Hanbury (I, 39 ff.). I have been able to find only the reprint of 1707, the editor of which, says Hanbury, "destroyed all the raciness of the original."

Greenwood on the charge of writing seditious pamphlets. As this book gives the fullest expression I have found of the Independents' principles in regard to marriage, I am led to quote from it at some length. Referring to "this so famous Church of England," Barrow says:

"Not to speak of their Orders or Injunctions which are Four times in the Year to be solemnly read, nor to repeat their Penance, with the bitter Curses and Comminations, their Lentfast; they have yet the Holy Ceremony of Marriage, solemnly kept in the Church (for the most part) upon the Lord's-day: And an especial Composed Communion for the same. This Action is to be performed by the Priest, &c. who instructing the Parties to be joined in Wedlock what to say, and when to pray, &c. teacheth the Man to wed his Wife with a Ring, in the Name of the Father, of the Son, and of the Holy Ghost. . . .

"But in the mean time, I would fain know of the most Learned among them all, either Foreigners or Natives, where they find in the Old or New Testament, That Marriage is an Ecclesiastical Action, belonging to the Worship of God in his Church, to be done by the Minister as part of his Office and Function, and that in the Church, with such a Set of Collects, Exhortations, Psalms, Anthems, and Blessings composed for that Purpose. . . . I have always found it the Parents Office to provide Marriages for their Children, whilst they remain under their Charge and Government: And that the Parties themselves affianced and betrothed each other in the Fear of God and the presence of such Witnesses as were thought fit to be present, and that in their Parents or other private Houses, without being obliged to go to Church for an Ordinance and Action of the Second Table, and see not why they might not as well bring any other Civil Business as this into the Church, for few believe themselves to be rightly Married except it be done by a Priest, after the prescribed manner, and that also in the due Seasons. . . . though all these Ceremonies are not observed in all the Reformed Churches." [1]

[1] Barrow, *op. cit.*, p. 190 ff.

The religious platform of the Brownists was officially drawn up in a *Confession of Faith* by the exiles in Holland in 1596 and published in 1598,[1] addressed "To the reuerend and learned mē, Students of the holy Scripture, in the Christian Vniversities of Leyden in Holland, of Sanctandrewes in Scotland, of Heidelberg, Geneva, and other like famous scholes of learning in the Low countries, Scotland, Germany, and France." This book gives their general beliefs and their platform of church government, but is not detailed enough to be of assistance in the present study. But in their *Third Petition to King James*, their principles in regard to marriage are clearly expressed:

"The Ministers aforesaid lawfully called by the Church where they are to administer ought to continue their functions according to Gods ordinance, and carefully to feed the flock of Christ committed vnto them: Being not inioyned or suffred to beare civil offices withall, neither burthened with the execution of civil affaires, as the celebratiō of Mariage, burying the dead, &c. which thinges belong as well to those without as within the Church." [2]

That the Independents continued this practice in England is shown by a passage from Rogers' *Matrimoniall Honovr* in 1642. In discussing marriage by ministers, he says: "In the Scriptures, we see it was civilly carried, and dispatcht by the Elders at the gate: and now in some of the reformed

[1] These dates are given in the prefaces contained in *An Apologie or Defense of . . . Brovvnists*, pp. 15 and 5 respectively. Baillie (*Dissvasive*, f. *4 *b*) gives the date 1602 for the publication of the *Confession of Faith*. This *Confession* is also contained in the *Apologie*.

[2] *Third Petition* (contained in the *Apologie*), p. 54. Further evidence showing the opinion and practice of both the Independents and the Puritans may be found in *Certain Letters* (from exiles in Holland), 1602 (Hanbury, I, 144); *A Confession of Certain Christians in England*, 1616 (Hanbury, I, 300); Francis Johnson, *A Christian Plea*, 1617 (Hanbury, I, 319). See also the quotations from J. Paget, Edwards, and E. Paget, pp. 43–44, above, and those from Baillie and Robinson, pp. 52–53, below.

Churches, we see its performed in like sort, officers being appointed to take their names, to booke them in a Record and so with a short ceremony to dismiss them." [1] Finally, in 1653, Cromwell established civil marriage by law.

IV. Continental, Scottish, and American Churches

We have already seen that in Holland the state declared marriage a civil affair and insisted that the contract be made before a civil magistrate; we have also seen that the church continued to celebrate it by a solemnization of the vows previously made before the state. Calvin does not seem to have expressed himself in print on the question of the contract of matrimony; but from the fact that the Holland and Scottish churches, which emphasized the civil celebration, took their discipline directly from the church of Geneva, it is clear that the church there also followed Luther's principle of making the spousals the all-important element. This fact is borne out by the form of ceremony of the English church of Geneva, which was approved by Calvin himself. Instead of combining the forms for spousals *de futuro* and *de praesenti* with prayers and ceremonies by the minister, as is the case in the marriage service of the English *Prayer Book* of Edward VI, the Geneva reform liturgy, after preliminary exhortation and public inquiry as to impediments, simply requires the man to declare himself according to the following oath put by the minister:

"You, N. shall protest here before God, and his holy Congregation, that you have taken, and are now content to have N. here

[1] Rogers, *op. cit.*, p. 110. Any description of the civil ceremony approved by the Independents is lacking, but it would seem that it consisted merely of a few words spoken by the magistrate immediately after the public performance of spousals *de praesenti*. The ceremony, however, was clearly a civil procedure and not merely a form of public spousals.

present to your lawfull wife, promising to keep her, to love and intreat her in all things according to the duty of a faithfull husband, forsaking all other during her life, and briefly, to live in a holy conversation with her, keeping faith and truth in all points, according as the word of God and his holy Gospel doth command." [1]

The points to be noted here are: first, there is no marrying or proclaiming of "man and wife" by the minister; second, there is nothing to the effect that "God hath joined together"; and third, the words on the part of the contracting couple are merely an acknowledgment that they have, before this time, taken one another as man and wife. These points contrast strongly with the orthodox ceremony of the Edward VI *Prayer Book* and later liturgies. Thus marriage at Geneva, like the one overseen by Greenwood in the Fleet prison, was merely a contract before witnesses, which the church might bless with its solemnization and prayers if the parties so desired.

In Scotland to this day marriage may be made without any official intervention, by means of spousals *de praesenti* either with or without witnesses. This is both interesting and important, as it shows that although the Scotch Presbyterian Church had a marriage ceremony in its liturgy, it nevertheless considered the actual marriage contract a private affair. In other words, the Romish influence in Scotland has never at any time been strong enough to make

[1] *The Forme of Prayers and administration of the Sacraments*, p. 25. The woman, of course, makes a similar vow. Preceding the *Form of Marriage* in these liturgies, there is this note of direction: "After the banes or contract have been published three severall dayes in the congregation (to the intent that if any person have interest or title of either parties, they may have sufficient time to make their challenge) the parties assemble at the beginning of the Sermon, and the minister at time convenient saith as followeth." Then comes the exhortation etc. as described above. Compare this ceremony with that of the early Dutch church, pp. 38–39 and note, above.

secularly performed marriages in any sense clandestine. But the church did provide a ceremony for those who wished it and doubtless urged its use upon the people. Its form was taken over bodily in 1564, along with the rest of the service book, from the English church at Geneva, which has already been discussed.[1] The only other note that I find in regard to the Scottish ceremony is an item in the *Second Book of Discipline*,[2] 1581, to the effect that among the duties of a minister "it belongs to him likewise, after lawful Proceeding in the matter by the Eldership, to solemnize Marriage betwixt them as are to be joined therein, and to pronounce the Blessing of the Lord upon them."[3]

In considering the Puritans of New England, we must bear in mind that they were of the Independent sect and shared the extreme views already discussed. It is well known that marriage in New England was a civil affair from the first, but the origin of this practice has not heretofore been definitely determined.[4] From my demonstration of the practice of the Independents, together with the fact that it was the congregation of John Robinson, Brown's leading disciple, which first emigrated to this country, it is fairly obvious that the early American civil marriage was a direct result of the principles and practice of the Independent Church, encouraged perhaps by the state laws of Holland. But as the point is here made for the first time,

[1] This fact is stated on the title page of the Scottish book of liturgies, which may be found in *The Confessions of Faith of the Church of Scotland*. John Knox (*History of Reformation in Scotland*, p. 333) states that the Church of Scotland sent an official reply in 1566 to the confession of faith of the continental Reform churches to the effect that "they agreed in all points with those churches and differed in nothing from them" except in the keeping of certain festal days.

[2] Contained in *The Confessions*.

[3] *Op. cit.*, p. 459.

[4] Howard, II, 127 ff., devotes several pages to the different supposed causes of the New England civil marriage.

it will be well to quote some further evidence in support of it.

This evidence we find in contemporary pamphlets, by which we are able to set forth the whole course of events. Robert Baillie, writing in 1595 of the Independents, says: "For the marriage blessing, they applaud the Brownists Doctrin, they send it from the Church to the Town-house, making its solemnization the duty of the Magistrate; this is the constant practise of all in New England: the prime of the Independent Ministers now at London, have beene married by the Magistrate, and all that can be obtained of any of them, is to be content that a Minister in the name of the Magistrate and his Commissioner may solemnize that holy band."[1] A passage from Ephriam Paget serves to continue the story. Speaking of the spread of the Brownist doctrines, he says: "The first man of note that held their opinions (as Mr. Edwards writeth) was one Mr. Robinson, who leaving Norwich male-content, became a rigid Brownist: but afterwards by some conference with learned men, he was brought to some moderation, and writ a book recanting some of his opinions. This man dying,[2] many of his congregation went from Leyden unto New England, and planted at new Plymouth, whither they carried Mr. Robinsons opinions, which spread far there: and by letters also and other meanes were conveighed into old England: and to this purpose he citeth a letter by Master Cottens."[3] Finally, we have the expression of Robinson himself in his defense of the Brownists in 1619. "We cannot assent," he says,

[1] Baillie, *Dissvasive*, p. 115. See also Lechford, *Plaine-dealing: or, Newes from New England*, p. 39, which Baillie cites as his authority.

[2] The writer is mistaken here. The Mayflower sailed before Robinson's death.

[3] Paget, *Heresiography*, p. 69. The reference to "Mr. Edwards" is to Thomas Edwards, *Answer to the Apologeticall Narration*. "Master Cottens" is doubtless John Cotton.

"to the receaved opinion and practice answerable in the Reformed Churches, by which Pastours thereof do celebrate Marriage publiquely and by vertue of their office."[1]

The first marriage in New England was that of Edward Winslow and Susanna White in 1621, performed "according to the laudable custome of the Low-countries . . . as being a civill thing."[2] There is no reason to think that the church was not allowed to invoke a blessing upon this union, for even the Brownist Greenwood offered a prayer at the marriage in the Fleet; nevertheless the ceremony itself was a civil one. "Thus, in the first New England wedding, a precedent was given which has never yet been set aside, and which marked clearly the distinction between the jurisdiction of the civil power in 'causes matrimonial' and the legitimate jurisdiction of the church."[3] The same kind of ceremony is recorded by Governor Winthrop at a wedding solemnized at Boston in 1647. The minister of the bridegroom's church had been asked to preach, but the magistrates objected to this and gave as one of their reasons that they "were not willing to bring in the English custom of ministers performing the solemnity of marriage, which sermons at such times might induce, but if any ministers were present, and would bestow a word of exhortation, etc., it was permitted."[4] The practice recorded in these two

[1] Robinson, *Apologie*, p. 40. This book was first published in Latin in 1619 under the title *Apologia . . . quorundam Christianorum . . . dictorum Brownistorum.* It was translated in 1625 under the title *A iust and necessarie Apologie of certain Christians . . . called Brownists or Barrowists.* It must not be confused with the anonymous *Apologie or Defense of . . . Brovvnists*, 1604.

[2] This was Winslow's second marriage. He was first married in Holland "before the magistrats in the Town or Stat house." Bradford, *History of Plymouth Plantation*, I, 216 and n. 4.

[3] Bacon, *Genesis of New England Churches*, p. 341.

[4] Winthrop, *History of New England*, II, 382.

instances was first given legal authority in Massachusetts, in 1646, when a statute was passed providing "that no person whatsoever in this Jurisdiction shall joyne any persons together in Marriage, but the Magistrate, or such other as the General Court, or Court of Assistants shal Authorize."[1] Commenting upon the New England marriage ceremony, Howard says: "The conception of wedlock which existed there from the beginning was identical with that which later found expression in the writings of Milton and the legislation of Cromwell."[2]

V. The English Church of the Commonwealth

It is impossible to believe that these conditions in the churches of the continent, Scotland, and New England, together with the practice of the Independents in England itself, should not affect both English public opinion in general and the doctrines of the more conservative Reformed churches of England in regard to marriage. The separation between the latter and those outside the mother country was much less than may be thought. There was constant intercourse and exchange of views among all parties, both by actual meeting of representatives and by letters to and fro. Among the tracts of the Thomason collection, are letters from one church to another asking advice and discussing practices, pamphlets of all kinds on ecclesiastical questions of the day, petitions, protests, apologies, defenses, etc. Ministers and others even returned from the New England colonies and advocated the practices in vogue there. Edward Winslow, above mentioned, on a visit to England in 1634, openly defended the practice of civil marriage and was imprisoned in the Fleet for seventeen

[1] Whitmore, *Colonial Laws of Massachusetts*, p. 172.

[2] Howard, II, 127.

weeks as a consequence. Despite the censorship of the press, a good deal of controversial writing by the adherents of the various sects got into print, but on account of the number and importance of other questions, there is little that throws any light upon the trend of public opinion on our subject. The tracts already cited, together with Winslow's imprisonment, incline us to believe that the more conservative reformers clung tenaciously to the ecclesiastical ceremony, but at the same time they give evidence that this was done more for the sake of expediency than because marriage was thought to be essentially a religious affair.[1] John Donne probably expressed the general conservative point of view in saying, "As marriage is a civil contract, it must be done so in public, as that it may have the testimony of men; as marriage is a religious contract, it must be so done, as that it may have the benediction of the priest: in a marriage without testimony of men they cannot claim any benefit by the law; in a marriage without the benediction of the priest they cannot claim any benefit of the Church."[2] On the other hand, it is certain from such testimony as that of Rogers and Baillie that among the Independents marriage was actually performed by the magistrate.[3]

The result of all these influences upon the parliamentary assembly of divines was to effect a compromise by which it was "judged expedient that marriage be solemnized by a lawful minister," but evidently from the phraseology used, a marriage made either privately or by magistrate was still deemed valid. This decision, drawn up by the assembly in 1643, was made law by act of Parliament on Jan. 3, 1645,

[1] See especially the quotation from E. Paget, pp. 43–44, above.

[2] Donne, *Works*, IV, 33. See also the preface to the marriage service in the *Directory*, p. 56, below.

[3] See above, pp. 48, 52.

and published in the *Directory of Public Worship*. The ceremony itself was adapted from that of the Scotch Presbyterian church, which, as said above, came *verbatim* from the English Church at Geneva. A prefatory paragraph gives the authorized position of the Reformed churches on the subject:

"Although Marriage be no Sacrament, nor peculiar to the Church of God, but common to mankinde, and of publique interest in every Commonwealth, yet because such as marry are to marry in the Lord, and have especiall need of Instruction, Direction, and Exhortation, from the Word of God, at their entring into such a new condition; and of the blessing of God upon them therein, we judge it expedient, that marriage be solemnized by a lawfull Minister of the Word, that he may accordingly councel them and pray for a blessing upon them." [1]

The ceremony itself consists of a short exhortation and instruction, the exchange of vows between the man and the woman, the pronunciation of them as "man and wife" by the minister, and a concluding prayer. Altogether the form is much shorter and much simpler than that of the Edward VI *Prayer Book*, towards which the Reformers were united in their objection. The vows, similar for both man and woman, followed these words:

"I, N, doe take thee N. to be my married Wife, and doe, in the presence of God, and before this congregation, promise and covenant to be a loving and faithful Husband unto thee, untill God shall separate us by death." [2]

This ceremony acknowledges the office of the church to a greater extent than did the original one of Geneva, as approved by the Synod of Dort in 1618, the chief difference being the minister's pronouncing the couple "man and wife." But it must not be supposed that the ancient custom

[1] Scobell, I, 86.

[2] *Ibid.*, I, 87.

of marriage by spousals *de praesenti* was given up; on the contrary, the omission of the first part of the existing orthodox ceremony from the new form, is evidence that it continued to be used as the form for spousals. Furthermore, in legal circles, both civil and ecclesiastical, spousals *de praesenti* were still regarded as marriage and impeded any other union.

We may infer from this and from Cromwell's marriage act eight years later that the conflict of authority in the two methods of effecting matrimony still produced an unsatisfactory state of affairs; or, to put it differently, the particular conditions which previously had been a source of evils and entanglements in the ecclesiastical courts, remained unaltered. As a result, it was soon realized that marriage must be regarded as either entirely a civil or entirely an ecclesiastical affair, and that any combination of the two authorities was sure to be disastrous.

The question before the English nation evidently was: Should the contract, or spousals *de praesenti*, already acknowledged as marriage itself, be considered as the authorized ceremony; or should the church be given complete authority to perform marriage, and some attempt be made to invalidate the force and permanency of the private contract? [1] For some reason, there seems to be little or no expression of opinion on this subject from the time the assembly deemed it expedient that marriage be an ecclesiastical office to the passage of the civil marriage act; but we may be sure, from the previously expressed sentiments

[1] No one hitherto seems to have looked at the question in this way. The general impression among historians seems to be that Cromwell's act flew in the face of all existing conditions and instituted an entirely new marriage process. I think I have demonstrated that such was not the case, especially as the church ceremony continued to be used in addition to the civil after the latter was established in 1653.

of the Independents and from the readiness of Parliament to pass Cromwell's act, that the subject continued to be debated with increasing tendency towards the more radical attitude. At any rate, the decision was finally reached to follow the teachings of the German Reformers and the English Independents and the practice of Holland and New England, and to put all marital affairs into the hands of the state. That is, the power of the church was abolished, and spousals *de praesenti* performed before the civil magistrate and in the presence of two witnesses, became the actual and authorized form of marriage. This was accomplished by an act of Parliament in 1653, according to which the ceremony consisted simply of the vows as set forth in the *Directory*, slightly changed in wording, without prayer or exhortation. The act concludes:

"And it is further Enacted, That the Man and Woman having made sufficient proof of the Consent of their Parents or Guardians as aforesaid, and expressed their consent unto Marriage, in the maner and by the words aforesaid, before such Justice of the Peace in the presence of two or more credible Witnesses; The said Justice of the Peace may and shall declare the said Man and Woman to be from thenceforth Husband and Wife; and from and after such consent so expressed, and such declaration made, the same (as to the form of Marriage) shall be good and effectual in Law. And no other Marriage whatsoever within the Commonwealth of England after Sept. 29, 1653, shall be held or accompted a Marriage according to the Laws of England." [1]

My contention that this was not a revolutionary measure but merely a shifting of the emphasis from the ecclesiastical

[1] Scobell, II, 236; also to be found in the newspapers of the time. Howard, I, 424 ff., makes a great deal of the stipulation in this act that marriages must be properly recorded in special parish registers. He seems to overlook the fact that this same clause was contained in the *Directory* eight years earlier.

celebration to the private, is borne out by the lack of writing in opposition to the change [1] and by the continuation of the church ceremony as a blessing of God upon the contract civilly made, just as the Independents had consistently claimed it to be. Jeaffreson in his *Brides and Bridals* makes the statement that usually "the wedding was religiously solemnized in the church, after or before the performance of the purely civil affirmation in the magistrate's parlour . . . in accordance with the instructions of the *Directory for Public Worship*." [2] There can be no doubt, however, that the civil marriage was condemned by the more orthodox clergy, especially those who still supported episcopacy, and by the political and religious enemies of Cromwell, who saw in the act only another unreasonable measure by a tyranical usurper. The act, nevertheless, had the support of the Independents at least, of whom Milton was the most prominent and the most powerful.

[1] Of course, the censorship of the press might account for this to some extent. In looking through the Thomason tracts of the period, I find only one, aside from newspapers (which contain nothing of importance), that mentions the subject at all. This is a *Letter from a Gentleman in the Country*, which is chiefly a defense of the form used by the church and an expression of the writer's failure to see any need for the new act. Howard, I, 432, n. 1, accepts Friedberg's suggestion (*Eheschliessung*, 328, n. 2) that the controversial literature on the subject may have been great, but observes that, if so, little has been preserved. In the Sutro collection (San Francisco) of thousands of pamphlets of the time, he was able to find only one, omitting newspapers, on this topic. Friedberg, he says, had a similar experience in the Berlin library. The British Museum, according to my experience, yields but one more, and that not controversial. It seems time, therefore, to give up the idea that there was written controversy on the subject, especially as Thomason is known to have obtained practically all tracts of any importance during this period for the Museum library. Of course, satirists took occasion to poke fun, but such writing may be disregarded here. For references to it, see Howard, I, 432–3.

[2] Jeaffreson, II, 69. See also Howard, I, 419, n. 2.

In his treatise *The Likeliest Means to remove Hirelings out of the Church*, published in 1659, he reasserts the position originally laid down by the Brownists, summarizes the history of ecclesiastical marriage, and upholds firmly Cromwell's act:

"As for marriages, that ministers should meddle with them, as not sanctified or legitimate, without their celebration, I find no ground in scripture either of precept or example. Likeliest it is . . . that in imitation of heathen priests, who were wont at nuptuals to use many rites and ceremonies, and especially, judging it would be profitable, and the increase of their authority, not to be spectators only in business of such concernment to the life of man, they insinuated that marriage was not holy without their benediction, and for the better colour, made a sacrament; being of itself a civil ordinance, a household contract, a thing indifferent and free to the whole race of mankind, not as religious, but as men: best, indeed, undertaken to religious ends, and as the apostle saith, I Cor. vii, 'in the Lord.' Yet not therefore invalid or unholy without a minister and his pretended necessary hallowing, more than any other act, enterprise, or contract of civil life, which ought all to be done in the Lord and to his glory: all which, no less than marriage, were by the cunning of priests heretofore, as material to their profit, transacted at the altar. Our divines deny it to be a sacrament; yet retain the celebration, till prudently a late parliament recovered the civil liberty of marriage from their encroachment, and transferred the ratifying and registering thereof from the canonical shop to the proper cognizance of civil magistrates." [1]

[1] Milton, *Prose Works*, III, 370. Notice that it is the "ratifying and registering" on which Milton lays emphasis, following out the theory that marriage itself was a private affair, "a household contract."

CHAPTER III

THE ATTEMPTED REFORM OF DIVORCE

I. Legal Situation

When England under Henry VIII broke away from the Church of Rome, the canon laws of Catholicism in regard to divorce remained in operation; indeed, the English Protestant church never has drawn up a code of laws to supersede them. The first movement towards any actual reform of the Roman Catholic doctrines or church government was the appointment of a committee, in accordance with the act of 25 Henry VIII, ca. 19 (1534), to draw up a new platform for the ecclesiastical doctrine and discipline of England. In the meantime, however, it was provided that "suche canons constitucions ordynaunces and Synodals provynciall being allredy made, which be not contraryant nor repugnant to the lawes statutes and customes of this Realme nor to the damage or hurte of the Kynges prerogatyve Royall, shall mowe styll be used and executed." [1] The loose terms herein contained were never more fully defined; and the evil practices in divorce cases, which continued unabated pending the action of the committee, led to the King's wholesale attempt in 1540 to stop divorces and separations altogether, except in cases of marriage within the forbidden degrees. Previous to this date, Strype tells us, divorces, or rather annulments of marriage, "mightily prevailed. . . . For it was ordinary to annull marriage and divorce man and wife on some pretext of precontract." [2]

[1] *Statutes of the Realm*, III, 461.

[2] Strype, *Memorials of Cranmer*, I, 114.

The preamble to the famous act of 1540, known as 32 Hen. VIII, ca. 38, is very instructive in regard to the conditions of the time, and expresses practically the same opinions concerning ecclesiastical jurisdiction over marital affairs as were later proclaimed in Parliament in 1607 and by Milton in his pamphlet of 1659;[1] but it is too long to quote in full. It may be abbreviated as follows:

> "Whereas heretofore the usurped power of the Bishop of Rome hathe alwayes entangled and troubled the mere jurisdiction and legal power of this Realme of England and also unquietid muche the subjectis of the same . . . by making that unlaufull whiche by Goddis wourde is laufull bothe in mariages and other thinges; . . . mariages have been brought into suche uncertainty thereby that no mariage coulde be so surely knytt and bounden but it shulde lye in either of the parties power and arbitre . . . to prove a precontracte a kynnerede an alliance or a carnall knowledge to defeate the same. . . . Be it therefore enacted . . . [that] . . . suche mariages being contracte and solemnised in the face of the churche and consūmate with bodily knowledge . . . shalbe . . . taken to be lauful good juste and indissoluble, . . . notwithstanding any precontracte . . . not consūmate with bodily knowledge . . . [or] . . . any dispensation prescription lawe or other thinge . . . And that no reservation or prohibition, Goddis law except, shall trouble or impeche anny mariage without the Leviticall degrees."[2]

The church, however, maintained its former power on the ground that the phrase "God's law excepted" applied to all marriages made in the face of the recognized ecclesiastical impediments, and that any such contract was void *ab initio*. Thus the entire act was made of no effect in actual application. Of conditions following this attempt to curtail the power of the church, T. E. says: "This Statute, though it seemed to be made vpon good and great considera-

[1] See Strype, *Memorials of Cranmer*, I, 30, 57.

[2] *Statutes*, III, 792.

tions, (because precontracts too too slenderly proued, and sometime but onely surmized, helped the Romish oppression . . .) yet many did after the making of it, very dissolutely come from their first vowes, . . . slipperily leauing their former Contracts." [1] Meanwhile the committee of thirty-two, provided for in the act of 25 Hen. VIII, ca. 19, was at work. According to Milton, it was composed of "divines and lawyers, of whom Cranmer, the archbishop, Peter Martyr, and Walter Haddon (not without the assistance of sir John Cheeke . . .) were the chief." [2]

The *Reformatio Legum Ecclesiasticarum*, as the decisions of this committee were called, shows clearly the influence of Luther's teachings and of German practices. The former were followed implicitly in the abolition of separation *a mensa et thoro* and in the establishment of actual divorce with permission for the innocent party to remarry for the causes of desertion, adultery, and other ill usages, in practical accordance with the Zurich marriage ordinance of 1525.[3] Furthermore, husband and wife were put upon equal footing in divorce suits. In regard to the impediments and the annulment of marriage, the King's committee expressed itself much more definitely than did the German Reformers, who rather shirked the whole situation; but in their recommendations thereupon they harked back to the Romish canons, and except for one or two details, suggested no changes in the existing conditions. The *Reformatio Legum* is important only in showing the attitude of the public leaders of the day, for Henry died before he could force it through Parliament, and it was defeated under Edward

[1] T. E., *Lawes Resolvtions of Womens Rights*, Bk. II, sec. xxix.

[2] Milton, *Prose Works*, II, 237. Milton is mistaken in saying (*ibid.*) that the committee was appointed by Edward VI.

[3] See above, p. 12, n. 3.

VI by the House of Commons.[1] Thus the old Catholic régime with all its abuses continued. Strype says that at this time annulment and divorce were frequent. "Noblemen would very frequently put away their wives and marry others if they like another woman better or were like to obtain wealth by her. And they would sometimes pretend their wives to be false to their beds and so be divorced and marry again such as they pleased." [2]

From this time on to Cromwell's day, actual conditions remained unchanged. The decree of 32 Hen. VIII, ca. 38, was repealed and repassed alternately until the Star Chamber finally established it permanently in 1601, but it seems

[1] That the bill was defeated by the Commons without ever reaching the Lords, is illuminating in showing how little the Reformation had as yet actually touched English public opinion.

[2] Quoted by Kitchin, *A History of Divorce*, p. 177. Kitchin adds: "Thus the Earl of Pembroke divorced his first wife and married a daughter of Sir Philip Sidney." He is badly mixed here. Sidney had but one daughter, and she married the Earl of Rutland. Pembroke's first marriage, however, was annulled, after which he did marry again; his second wife died, and he then married Mary Sidney, the famous sister of the poet.

The case of Mary Queen of Scots and Bothwell is still more interesting. In the first place, Bothwell got Mary's husband out of the way by murdering him (thus making any later marriage with Mary illegal). Then he was divorced from his wife in a Protestant court on the ground that he was an adulterer. But since he was not the innocent party in the divorce, the Protestant minister, Mr. Craig, refused to marry him to the Queen; nor would a Catholic priest perform the marriage, since that church did not allow remarriage after such a divorce. To obviate this predicament, an annulment of his former marriage was obtained from a Catholic court, especially appointed by Mary, on the ground of alleged affinity, which could be maintained only by admitting or inventing a former illicit connection with one of his wife's relatives. After this, a bishop was found to perform the marriage with Mary. Later, Bothwell's divorced wife married the Earl of Sutherland.

See also the statement of Bunny, p. 83, below. The divorce and remarriage of Lady Essex (Frances Howard) is another case in point here.

to have had no effect whatever at any time, as the church was able to escape its provisions through the loophole of "God's law excepted."[1] Edward VI showed his approval of the views of the German Reformers by bringing Fagius and Bucer over to Cambridge as professors of Hebrew and Divinity respectively;[2] but his beliefs, whatever they were, took no more active form, except for the repealing of the above law of Henry VIII. These two elements, the Romish practices and the principles of the German Reformation, continued as the grounds of contention in matrimonial affairs throughout our period, and indeed, they continue to the present day. The followers of the Catholic Church as well as those Protestants who clung to prelatical episcopacy, upheld the Roman practices; whereas the Puritans and the various sects which split off from them, not only upheld the principles of the German Reformers, particularly in their platform of divorce (with remarriage for the innocent party) for adultery and desertion, but also opposed the whole Roman theory of ecclesiastical jurisdiction in marital affairs. The efforts of these dissenting sects, however, have never been of sufficient weight in England to overthrow the influence of Rome except momentarily, and to this day the old impediments, the narrowness of the grounds for divorce, and the discrimination against the woman, are upheld to a greater extent in England than in any other Protestant country.

[1] This exception was perfectly well recognized in legal circles. Coke says on the point: "There be also other divorces [beside those for consanguinity and affinity] which declare the marriage to be void, as divorce *causa frigitatis*, where the party hath *perpetuam impotentiam generationis*, &c, and *causa metus*, *sive duritiae*, also *causa impubertatis:* these marriages are said to be prohibited by God's law, otherwise the statute of 32H8 would extend to them." *Institutes*, Pt. II, p. 687.

[2] Milton is mistaken in saying (*Prose Works*, II, 72) that Fagius was professor of Divinity.

So far we have concerned ourselves only with legislation. Almost as important is the jurisdiction thereupon, especially as the principles of separation, divorce, and annulment, and the grounds for such suits, varied greatly among the different churches, as will be shown more fully later on.

There can be no doubt that the proper and usual way to conduct any divorce proceedings was by means of the church courts, of which there were five recognized grades: (1) Archdeacon's, held by an archdeacon or his representative; (2) Consistory, held by cathedral officers, the bishop's chancellor or commissionary acting as judge; (3) Court of Arches, at London and York only, which handled appeals from Consistory courts; (4) Court of Delegates, or commissioners appointed by the sovereign, which handled appeals from the Courts of Arches; (5) Court of High Commissions for "all manner of jurisdiction, privileges, and preëminences touching any spiritual or ecclesiastical jurisdiction within the realms of England and Ireland." Besides these, there were other local courts, "some of them mere shops for the sale of 'dispensations, licenses, faculties, and other remnants of the papal extortions.'"[1] It was to these "mere shops" that people of meager circumstances went for divorce. Indeed, from the repeated references to "the minister," it seems as if questions were often decided and divorces granted by the parish priest alone.[2] Certainly among the Puritans, if their cases were submitted to legal jurisdiction of any kind, divorces for adultery or desertion, after 1603, must have been granted by a single minister or some sort of local magistrate or informal assembly, since the established church did not grant divorces on these grounds. Enough has been said elsewhere to show the corruption of the ecclesiastical courts in periods previous to the one under consideration here and the advantage

[1] Bacon, p. 77.

[2] E. g., see quotation from Perkins, p. 80, n. 4, below.

taken of these conditions by those who could afford it financially. That this state of affairs had not improved is abundantly shown by contemporary practices and comment. John Cotton, who spoke from experience, says, "The ecclesiastical courts are like the courts of the high-priests and pharisees, which Solomon, by a spirit of prophesy, styleth, *dens of lions*, and *mountains of leopards.* Those who have had to do with them have found them to be markets of the sins of the people, the cages of uncleanness, the forgers of extortion, the tabernacles of bribery, and contrary to the end of civil government."[1]

The jurisdiction of the ecclesiastical courts in divorce affairs, as has been shown, was of early origin, but with the coming of the Reformation and the conception of marriage as a civil affair and not a sacrament, we find a new conception of divorce arising also. This is that marriage is dissolved *ipso facto,* without any jurisdiction whatever, by the mere existence of causes recognized as proper grounds for its dissolution. The case here, as investigated up to date, is stated by Howard as follows:

"The researches of Stölzel have clearly established that in the beginning the reformers returned to the principle of self-divorce prevailing among the ancient Romans and Hebrews, and accepted by some of the early church councils. . . . When an adequate cause exists, a marriage is thereby dissolved in favor of the innocent person without any magisterial authority whatsoever. If in certain cases, in order to establish the existence of the grounds of dissolution, any action is needful, it is regarded as extra-judicial; and when gradually such informal proceedings have grown into an orderly process dealing directly with the question of divorce, this process concludes with a decree; not that the marriage *is* thereby dissolved, but that it *has* already been dissolved in consequence of the grounds now established. . . . Luther and other Protestant

[1] Brook, III, 155.

leaders accepted the theory just explained that a marriage is 'broken' or dissolved when a proper cause intervenes; and if without exception they insisted that the married persons should not separate themselves, but appeal to public authority, they had in mind, as Luther plainly shows, the establishment of the fact of wedlock already broken in order, where it was desired, to grant the permission of marrying again." [1]

Although this conception of the possibility and practice of private divorce, followed by civil sanction, after something the same manner as the Hebrew practice, seems to be generally admitted as having existed to some extent in Germany, no one has as yet traced its course in England. Whether the similar condition, which actually did exist in England, took its source from the German Reformation, or whether private divorce had continued unbrokenly in some measure from early times down, which seems unlikely, is hardly worth debating here. At any rate, we find exactly the same attitude existing in England as that just described of Germany. Hooper, after speaking of the causes of divorce, says, "The persons may by the authority of God's word and the ministry of the magistrates [2] be separated." [3] Whately in the beginning of the next century says, "Now if it shall fall out, that either of the married persons shall frowardly and peruersely withdraw themselves from this matrimoniall societie (which fault is termed desertion), the person thus

[1] Howard, II, 69. There is a reference to this practice of self-divorce in Bullinger's *Christen state of Matrimonye*, f. lxxvii, which by urging a regular proceeding upon the persons concerned, supports Howard's remarks. "Though they be persuaded to haue lawfull occasions of divorcemēt/ yet they may not be iudges in their awne causes/ nor take ought here in hād by their awne authoryte/ but let their matter come before their ordinate Judge."

[2] The word *magistrates* always refers to civil rather than ecclesiastical officers.

[3] Hooper, *Early Writings*, p. 379.

offending, hath so farre violated the couenant of marriage, that . . . the bond of matrimony is dissolued, and the other party so truly and totally loosed from it, that (after an orderly proceeding with the Church and Magistrate in that behalf) it shall be no sinne for him or her to make a new contract with another person." [1]

The decree granted by the civil or ecclesiastical court to permit the second marriage, had the effect, unintentional or not, of granting the previous divorce; so that to this extent any such private divorce differed from the old Hebrew practice. There is, nevertheless, evidence that the ancient practice of private divorce existed during our whole period, especially among the Independents.[2] Becon, in his *Homily against Whoredom*, has this passage: "Of this vice cometh a great part of the divorces, which now-a-days be so commonly accustomed and used by men's private authority, to the . . . breach of the . . . bond of matrimony." [3] In 1552, the use of such private divorce was deemed to be of sufficient prevalence to warrant its being mentioned and condemned in the *Reformatio Legum*. John Knox reports a private divorce with remarriage in Scotland in 1560, which though opposed by the magistrates was upheld by

[1] Whately, *Bride-bush*, p. 25. See also the doctrine of the Puritans as drawn by their assembly, p. 88, below.

[2] This practice among the Independents has been hinted at before, but never has any real evidence been brought to bear on the subject by either historian or legal writer. Inderwick comes the nearest of any to making a definite statement, in saying, "The Jewish law, to which they much adhered, provided for and regulated divorces." (*The Interregnum*, p. 46.) It is well known that the Jews in England continued their old practice of private divorce. Their laxity in this respect, says Inderwick, "was found in 1655 to be one of the strongest arguments against their proposed admission to the rights of citizenship." (*Ibid.*)

[3] Becon, *op. cit.* (pub. in *Catechism, etc.* by Parker So.), p. 647. This homily was included in the official book of homilies published by authority in 1547.

public opinion.[1] At the other end of our period, John Paget, writing to Ainsworth, a leader of some of the Independent churches, objects to the practice of that sect "that you also allow Divorces among yourselves, without authority of the magistrates." [2] At about the same time, Burroughes, in his lectures on Hosea, refers to the custom as then current: "It is true when a man putts away his wife for whoredom and giveth her a bill of divorce, he will never take her again." [3] Milton not only recognizes the practice but even makes the defense of it one of the principal points in his *Doctrine and Discipline of Divorce*.[4] Finally, Baillie, in 1645, commenting upon the Brownists, says, "As their mariage is private, so likewise must their Divorces, without cognizance either of Magistrate or Minister"; and of the Independents, he says, "Concerning Divorces, some of them goe farre beyond any of the Brownists: not to speak of Mr. Milton, . . . for I doe not know certainely whether this man professeth Independency (albeit all the Heretics here, whereof ever I heard, avow themselves Independents)." [5] Scattered as this evidence may seem, it is quite sufficient to establish the fact that divorce by private authority, without recourse to either magistrate or ecclesiastic, was practised throughout the whole of the period we are studying.

II. The Puritan-Anglican Controversy on Divorce

The controversy between the Puritans and the Church of England in regard to divorce, from the time of the Reformation to Cromwell's civil marriage act, ran somewhat

[1] Knox, *History of Reformation in Scotland*, p. 241.
[2] Hanbury, I, 333.
[3] Burroughes, *Exposition of Hosea*, p. 228.
[4] See below, pp. 96–97.
[5] Baillie, *Dissvasive*, p. 116; also in Hanbury, III, 146.

the same course as did that over the celebration of marriage, with which it is more or less connected. The controversy over the divorce of Henry VIII, which began in 1527, was the chief factor in precipitating the whole question; but as divorce matters had already been the subject of much discussion and some legislation among the Reformers in Germany, the King's affair can not be regarded as the entire cause of the dispute in England. Nevertheless, it brought to a head an illness of the church and state which otherwise might have increased and spread for some years to come. Yet the attention directed to the question at this time was, after all, but momentary, and after the immediate issue had been settled to the King's advantage, — if to no one else's — and he himself had made a desultory attempt to better conditions by means of the act of 1540, excitement died down and the first chapter of the controversy was over.

How far this chapter was a cause of the second and in many ways more important one, it is difficult to say. After the King's death, writing on the subject became directed more to the general field of divorce matters and less to the specific case of Henry and Catherine. One finds occasional references in the later books to the royal affair, but they are too few to argue from.[1] The most we can say, perhaps, is that the King's case, by bringing the subject into public discussion, stimulated thought and controversy upon it, which in the wider issue uncovered, soon lost sight of the particular instance. In this development we find no books on divorce alone until the question of remarriage arose, along towards 1600.[2] What expression there was, is to be found in books on domestic life, in tracts on the doctrine and government of the church, and in the Parliamentary debates on the subject of the reform of the ecclesiastical courts. The domestic books cannot be said to be written in the spirit of controversy; they are rather merely the expression of

[1] E. g., see below, p. 114, n. 1.

[2] See below, p. 81 ff.

individual standards and opinions, without much consideration of what any one else thought on the subject. On the whole, all the writers of these books advocate much the same principles, with one important exception. This is the stand made by the Puritans for divorce after the manner of the German Reformers, with permission for the offended person to remarry, instead of the separation *a mensa et thoro*, which continued to be maintained by the Church of England.

The views of the Church of England differed in no way in regard to divorce affairs from those of the Church of Rome; for, as Fuller said, the secession of the former from the jurisdiction of the latter "touched not the least finger of Popery." These views had already been set forth, for the first time in English, before Henry VIII's marital troubles existed outside of what he was pleased to call his conscience; and as they remained the accepted principles of the Church of England, it is perhaps worth while to state them briefly once again as put forth in this book, the *Cō-mendacions of matrymony*, by William Harrington, in 1528.[1] For divorce, he says, there is but one cause: if before *carnalis copula* one of the married persons goes over to a heretical religion and will not return. Separation is admitted if one of the couple is adulterous. The impediments to marriage are given in full by Harrington, and here we find the same confusion that we noted above between those which impede marriage but do not annul it and those which render it absolutely null and void *ab initio*, some of the causes being included in both lists.[2]

[1] It must be remembered that the interpretation of these principles was in the hands of the ecclesiastical courts, and on account of the corruption therein, the application of them was by no means consistent.

[2] See above, p. 8 ff. and notes. Harrington's book is the only one in English, either original or translation, that gives a list of impediments in anything like complete form. Although the most important book of

In Protestant writings, we find less discussion of the annulment of marriage through impediments and more attention to the granting of divorce for adultery, desertion, and other causes. Bullinger, in his book *The Christen state of Matri-*

all that I have seen, so far as definite information is concerned (giving more than all others put together), it seems to have been completely overlooked by all previous investigators, both legal and otherwise. The impediments, as here given, are worth quoting. They may be summarized:

I. Impediments preventing marriage, but not annulling it if already made:

1. Forbidden seasons of the year.
2. Inhibition or prohibition by the church.
3. Precontract.
4. Vow of chastity, previously made by either party.
5. Incest (*i.e.* adultery with any of betrothed's relations within four degrees).
6. Murder (committed in order to marry a certain person impedes such marriage).
7. Ravishment of another's wife.
8. Christening one's own child (impedes any second marriage).
9. The murder of a priest.
10. A solemn penance previously undergone.
11. The woman's being a nun.

II. Impediments preventing marriage and annulling it if made:

1. Wrong person (*i.e.* through mistaken identity, trickery, etc.)
2. An existing marriage on the part of either.
3. Solemn vow of chastity previously made.
4. Cognition:
    - *a.* Carnal (*i.e.* consanguinity or affinity within four degrees).
    - *b.* Contract or carnal knowledge (preventing marriage with any one within four degrees of the other party involved).
    - *c.* Spiritual (existing between persons joined by common participation in the baptism or confirmation of a child and also between the children of the same).
5. Adultery (preventing subsequent marriage with party involved).
6. Murder (as in above list).

monye, confines his remarks on the impediments to a treatment of the degrees of consanguinity and affinity, and discusses divorce in an entirely different part of the work. Here the Reformation ideas are advocated in liberal form, divorce being allowed for whoredom, adultery, murder, and poisonings. The author further remarks, "They therfore that in no case wyll helpe the oppressed persone / ner in anye wyse permytte diuorce to be made / do euen as the Pharisies / whych by reason of [following] the commaūdment of the Sabboth after the lettre / suffred men to be destroyed and to peryshe." [1]

Bishop Hooper, the first real Puritan to express himself on the subject, in his *Declaration of the Ten Commandments,* 1550, follows the German ideas in allowing divorce for adultery, and goes a step further than his English contemporaries in putting the man and the woman on the same footing in all matrimonial matters.[2] In the latter attitude he was supported by the committee which drew up the *Reformatio Legum* and later by some of the more important Puritan writers, Perkins, Whately, and Milton for example. But at the time, there was no agreement on this topic, and Hooper's opinions had evidently met with strong opposition

7. Difference of religion (no marriage to be made with Jew, Turk, Saracen, or such other).
8. The man's being a priest.
9. Impotency } But if either of these develop after the marriage,
10. Madness } "there is no remedy."

Interesting points to be noted about these lists are: (1) Impediments 4, 5, and 6 of the first list occur again as 3, 4*b*, and 6 of the second. (2) Precontract, which according to all other authorities annulled marriage (unless *de futuro* only), does not occur in the second list. Harrington is certainly wrong here. (3) If 4, 5, and 6 of list two had been strictly observed during the following century, many of the plots of the drama of the time would have been knocked on the head at the outset.

[1] Bullinger, *op. cit.,* f. lxxvii *b.*

[2] Hooper, *Early Writings,* cap. X.

from his associates, since he takes particular pains to refute their arguments and justify his own position. His treatise, bring a part of his discussion of the seventh commandment, does not touch upon other causes for divorce, although it seems to suggest that such exist, and makes no mention of the impediments. Becon, writing in about 1562, says that Christians may put away their wives for no fault either of body or mind "adultery only excepted." [1] He does not discuss the impediments at all, but attacks the English Church at length for not allowing remarriage after separation. After quoting many of the church fathers on this point, he reviews carefully the opinions of the writers shortly before him, considering in some detail those of Erasmus, Luther, Bucer, Melancthon, Bullinger, Peter Martyr ("that precious pearl and maruelous marguerite"), Musculus, Calvin, Sacarius, and Brentinus, all of whom agree in allowing the innocent party to remarry. Puritan expression after this allows divorce (with remarriage of the innocent party) consistently for adultery, usually for desertion, and sometimes for the other causes originated by Luther. Henry Smith, in 1591, is perhaps the least lenient of them all, declaring bluntly, "The disease of marriage is adultery, and the medicine heerof is Diuorcement." He continues: "If they might be seperated for discord, some would make a cōmodotie of strife; but nowe they are not best to be contentius, for this Law will holde their noses together, til wearines make them leaue strugling, like two spaniels which are coupled in a chain, at last they learne to goe together, because they may not goe a sunder." [2]

Meanwhile the established church was holding fast to its

[1] Becon, *Boke of Matrimony*, *Worckes*, Pt. I, f. DCxxviii.

[2] Smith, *A Preparative to Mariage*, pp. 90–91. Smith is known to have inclined strongly towards orthodoxy, but he was opposed to attempting to force it upon others.

old principles and practices under the favor of Elizabeth and the protection of the High Commission Court. Divorce with permission to remarry was still refused, although in actual practice little attention was paid to this prohibition once a separation was obtained.[1] The church courts, nominally under the power of the statute law but in reality subservient only to the High Commission Court, which was controlled by Whitgift, continued to annul marriage on the ground of impediments, real or fictitious, and to grant separations *a mensa et thoro*, which were quickly put into practice by the plaintiffs as actual divorces. In this condition of affairs, it became apparent to the Puritans that as long as the church courts existed in their present status, there could be no reform in the administration not only of divorce matters but of tythes, wills, and marriage contracts as well, all of which were being discussed equally with divorce. Thus it was that from this time on, the opposition of the Puritans was directed more towards the fundamental evil of ecclesiastical jurisdiction than towards any one of the interests that suffered therefrom.

We have already seen that as early as the middle of the century prelatical episcopacy had been attacked by Hooper and Bucer, and that the Puritan ideas for church government were given final and definite form by the assembly of divines in 1576.[2] Here we find the first platform for divorce proceedings, in the provision that the local classes should decide "doubts and difficulties touching the contract of marriage." This seems to be the only definite statement — and it is far enough from being satisfactory — as to the intended jurisdiction in matrimonial affairs.

In 1582, Robert Brown reopened the agitation in his book *The life and manners of true Christians*, by upholding the civil magistrates over the prelates; and by means of his writing and preaching started the Independents' move-

[1] See below, pp. 83, 87, n. 1.

[2] See above, p. 29 ff.

ment against all ecclesiastical jurisdiction in matrimonial as well as other affairs.[1] Of the church under the control of the bishops, he says:

"O, churche without eyes. For thy light is shutt vp at the Bishops *Beneplacitū*. Art thou the church of Christe, when thy starres be not in his hande, but the fystes of thy Bishoppes doo pull them downe from thee? Yet is this church of Englande the pillar and ground of trueth. For the Bishops overryde it. They are the trueth and it is the ground. It is the Beast and they are the Ryders. It stoupeth as an Asse for them to get vp. The whippe of their spirituall Courtes, and the Spurres of their lawes, and the Bridle of their power, do make it carie them." [2]

In the third section of the book, Brown describes the proper government by church and state. "Church gouenors are persons receyuing their authoritie & office of God, for the guiding of his people the church, receyued and called thereto, by due consent and agreement of the Church." Continuing, he says, "Ciuill Magistrates are persons authorised of God, and receyued by the consent or choyse of the people, whether officers or subiectes, or by birth & succession also, to make and execute lawes by publick agreement, to rule the common wealth in all outwarde iustice, & to maintaine the right, welfare, & honour thereof, with outwarde power, bodily punishmens, and ciuill forcing of men." The bishops,

[1] In the preface of Brown's book, there is an extended and confused discussion of pastors, bishops, and magistrates, under the title *Of Reformation without tarying for anie*. In this, bishops and magistrates are classed together, as if both were opposed to reforms, but this is merely the result of Brown's impatience at the failure of Parliament, fettered by the multiplicity of ecclesiastical affairs, to move as rapidly as he desired. The treatise is an excellent example of the confusion in popular minds of the authority of the parish priests, the civil magistrates, and the bishops' courts.

[2] Brown, *An Order for Studying the Scriptures* (contained in *The life and manners*), f. G3 *b*.

whom he calls heathen, he says, "shift and thrust themselves into Church gouernment as Antichristes . . . [and] . . . into ciuil gouernment as Tyrantes." [1]

Whether Cartwright took his ideas on the judgment of matrimonial causes from Brown or held similar ones previously, we cannot say; but in his *Reply to the Answer*, in c. 1573,[2] he puts Brown's general principles concerning the power of the temporal magistrates as to marriage and divorce legislation into definite expression. He says:

> "Another thing is that in these courts (which they call spiritual) they take the knowledge of matters which are mere civil, thereby not only perverting the order which God hath appointed in severing the civil causes from the ecclesiastical, but justling also with the civil magistrate, and thrusting him from the jurisdiction which appertaineth unto him, as the causes of the contracts of marriage, of divorces, of wills and testaments, with divers other such like things. For, although it appertain to the church and govenors thereof to shew out of the word of God which is a lawful contract or just cause of divorce, and so forth, yet the judicial determination and definitive sentences of all these do appertain unto the civil magistrate." [3]

Whitgift replied to this that there was no distinction between the civil and the ecclesiastical jurisdiction since both were executed by the Queen and emanated from her supreme power. This statement exhibits the true state of affairs, in which the church hid the scandal of its courts behind Elizabeth's skirts and took refuge in the favor she showed Whitgift and the prelates.

[1] Brown, *Life and manners*, art. 117.

[2] In 1572, Cartwright wrote an *Admonition to Parliament*, in which he objected to some of the details of the marriage ceremony. Whitgift's *Answer to the Admonition* led Cartwright to go into the subject more fully, as above.

[3] Cartwright, see Whitgift, *Works*, III, 267.

In the last decade of the century, there was any amount of pamphlet writing on the different religious questions of the day. Of all this, the Marprelate tracts have become the best known on account of their humorous and semi-literary character, which assured them a large number of readers; but there were also a great many less known books and tracts of the period by such men as Barrow, Perkins, Studley, Pye, Bradshaw, and others, who were opposed by an equal number on the bishops' side, the most important of whom was the great Hooker. By this time, the debate between Puritanism and the established church embraced the three large subjects of cermonials, doctrines, and church government; so that among so many disputed principles and practices, we find little reference to our particular subject. Hooker's *Laws of Ecclesiastical Polity* is the most exhaustive work in the whole period, but in continuing the Whitgift-Cartwright controversy on church government and jurisdiction, the writer uses such general arguments and illustrations that we get no further definite information on actual practices. Divorce is not mentioned at all, it being a detail too small to be considered, according to the scheme of the book.

There was, however, one important work which is valuable in giving concrete expression to much that was in the air. This is the *Christian Oeconomie* of William Perkins, a writer mentioned by Milton in his first divorce tract. The book was originally written in Latin in 1590 and was translated into English by Thomas Pickering in 1609. On the question of the nullification of marriage through some previously existing impediment, Perkins gives us more information than does any other Puritan writer. It is evident from what he says that the usual impediments were still in operation, and, in theory at least, were not opposed by the Reformed churches. In regard to divorce, he disagrees with the old Catholic principle that allowed it in the case of a man's entering holy orders,[1] but on the other hand, upholds in their broadest form the general Puritan grounds for granting it. These may be divided into four classes: (1) desertion, "when one of the married folkes, vpon a wilfull, and obstinate mind of their owne head, departeth from the other, without a iust, and necessary cause"; (2) malicious dealing, "when dwelling together, they require of each other intolerable conditions"; (3) long absence, opinions differing as to the extent of time; (4) adultery.[2] In all cases, according to Perkins, there should be no discrimination of sex. "Now in requiring of a diuorce," he says, "there is an equall right and power in both parties, so as the woman may require it as well as the man. . . . The reason is, because they are equally bound each to other, . . . prouided alwaie, that the man is to maintaine his superioritie, and the woman to obserue that modestie which beseemeth her towards the man."[3] In regard to the relations of church and state in causes matrimonial, it seems as if either authority could use disciplinary measures, that the church granted divorce, and that either church or magistrate might grant permission to remarry; but the discussion of these points is not full enough to show clearly either the practices of the day or the writer's views upon them.[4]

For a treatment of the Puritan attitude of this time in

[1] This was the logical outcome of the Puritan principle that a minister was in no way forbidden to marry, which was directly opposed to the orthodox doctrine.

[2] Perkins, *op. cit.*, p. 101 ff.

[3] *Ibid.*, p. 120.

[4] After discussing the case of desertion (*ibid.*, p. 105), he says: "After publike and solemne declaration made, the Minister vpon such desertion, may pronounce the mariage to be dissolued."

regard to church and state rights, we may turn to William Bradshaw's *English Puritanisme,* published in 1605. What he says here needs no comment. I quote only the most significant passages:

"All Ecclesiasticall actions invented & deuised by man, are vtterlie to bee excluded out of the exercises of religion."

"No Pastor ought to exercise or accept any Civill publique Iurisdictiō & authoritie, but ought to be wholly imployed in spirituall Offices & duties . . . And that those Civill Magistrats weakē their owne Supremacy that shall suffer any Ecclesiasticall Pastor to exercise any civill Iurisdictiō within their Realmes, Dominiōs, or Seigniories."

"The spirituall keyes of the Church . . . are not to be put to this vse, to lock vp the Crownes, Swords or Scepters, of Princes & ciuill States, or the ciuill Rightes prerogatiues and immvnities, of ciuill subiects in the things of this Life."

"The Civill Magistrate . . . hath and ought to haue Supreāe power over all the Churches within his Dominions, in all causes whatsoever."[1]

On the smaller question of divorce itself, the opposing parties came to blows, so to speak, in the last decade of the century. Since the Puritans admitted the validity of the old impediments, with certain modifications, the question of marriage after divorce — that is whether the separation should be merely *a mensa et thoro* or divorce in the modern sense of the term — now became the chief ground of debate. The ensuing controversy found expression in the more general marriage books, as already mentioned, and in sermons, as is shown by those of Bunny and Dove;[2] but does

[1] Bradshaw, *op. cit.*, pp. 1, 17, 25, 32, respectively. A full synopsis of this book is given in Neal, II, 55 ff.

[2] Bunny, in the preface to *Of Divorce,* written in 1595, mentions three sermons in which he opposed remarriage after divorce. Dove, in a sermon preached at St. Paul's Cross in 1601 and published the same year under the title *Of Divorcement,* takes a similar attitude.

not seem to have been a field for special writing in England, despite the books of Bucer and Beza,[1] until Cardinal Bellarmino of Capua reopened the subject by a Latin pamphlet upholding the old Catholic attitude.[2] In 1597, John Rainolds, in his *Defense of the Reformed Churches, etc.*, replied in English both to Bellarmino's treatise and to "an English pamphlet of nameless author." This work was not published, however, until 1609, after the writer's death, because the Archbishop of Canterbury "thought it not meet to be printed, as containing dangerous doctrine, and breeding sundrie inconveniences, if any weary of wife or husband might, by committing adulterie procure freedome of marying whom they list." [3] The "nameless author" mentioned by Rainolds may have been John Howson, who published a "third treatise" in 1602, entitled *Uxore dismissa propter Fornicationem aliam non licet superinducere.*[4] This was answered by Thomas Pye first in English and then in Latin in 1603.[5] Howson's treatise was republished in 1606 together with an anonymous *Tractatus modestus et Christianus* in defense of Howson *contra reprehensiones T. Pyi.*[6] In

[1] Bucer, *De Regno Christi*, 1557; Beza, *Tractatio de repudiis et divortiis*, 1569.

[2] I have not been able to locate this tract nor to discover any further information concerning it. It is merely mentioned by Rainolds.

[3] From the letter to Pye (see below, n. 6).

[4] On the other hand, were Howson the "nameless author," we should expect Rainolds' tract to have been written in Latin, since Howson's was, instead of in English.

[5] This tract by Pye does not seem to be extant in either version. Watt mentions an *Epistola ad Jo. Howsonum contra novum ejus Dogma de Divortiis Judaeorum*, which may be the one in question, but I have not been able to locate it.

[6] The edition of 1606, entitled *Uxore dismissa, etc.*, contains, beside the two treatises mentioned, a letter from Rainolds to Pye, which is valuable for its information concerning dates etc., and also one from Gentilis to Howson, in Latin, in which the writer gives his judgment

1610, Edmund Bunny published his *Of Divorce, etc.*, written in 1595, in which he supports the opposition of the established church to remarriage. In the "Advertisement to the Reader," Bunny gives some interesting sidelights on the times. Of the controversy in hand, he says that it was one "as wherein divers of great learning have already dealt," but he does not mention any by name. He says also that the practice of divorce and remarriage was by no means unusual. A few years before the writing of the treatise, there had been "of one family (but indeed, one of the greatest in those parts) or therevnto appertaining, about fowre several persons, and those of some note besides, who had thē so gotten divorce, & were married againe. And besides those (who, it may be, had else where mo fellowes also, than that heady course any waie deserved) an other there was of more speciall reckoning thā they, who so got divorce against his wife also, & married an other." [1] Speaking of a treatise on the opposite side of the question, he says: "True it is, that many of the learned haue beene, and yet are, of that opinion, & accordingly haue interpreted, and yet doe, such Scriptures as they haue conceived to appertaine therevnto: but it is as true withal, that as many of the learned againe, if not far mo, haue beene, and are, of other opinion, and haue otherwise vnderstoode, & yet doe, those Scriptures aforesaid." [2]

It is not worth while to go into the arguments produced by the opponents in this controversy to support their respective beliefs. The basis of contention, as one sees from Bunny's remarks, was, as usual, Scriptural interpretation and patriarchal authority. The subheading of Rainolds'

of Pye's book. In the note to the reader preceding this letter, there is mentioned a reply to Pye by Dove, entitled *Doctoris Pyi impium dogma.* This also seems to be non-extant.

[1] Bunny, *op. cit.*, "Advertisement," ¶ 2.

[2] *Ibid.*, ¶ 9.

treatise against Bellarmino, if the opponent's name were changed to suit each occasion, represents the substance of the argument in all cases: "how he depraveth Scriptures, misalleageth fathers, and abuseth reasons, to the perverting of the truth of God and poisoning of his Churche with errour." The attention drawn to the question of remarriage by this controversy resulted, in 1603, in the passage of a new canon, to the effect that "parties shall not marry during the lifetime of both and parties must give good and sufficient security that they will not break this agreement." [1] This canon, however, had little or no effect in preventing remarriage, for as Godolphin points out, by forfeiting the security, one satisfied the law and was free to do what he liked.[2]

III. The Final Deadlock

At this point, about 1610, and upon these propositions, — the general one of church government and the particular one of divorce in its various aspects — the Puritan reformers and the bishops of the established church stood face to face, hurling ineffective arguments back and forth until the fall of Laud in 1641. During this time, the contention was more for power than for principles, as both sides realized that the establishment of the latter depended upon the possession of the former. While Laud controlled the courts and exercised a censorship over the press, there was little printed expression of opinion; but from the close of his power until Parliament itself censored the press in 1643, controversy ran wild.[3] I have before me one pile of books labeled "Prynne and Opponents," another "Saltmarsh vs. Ley, etc.," and another "Smectymuun Controversy," and

[1] Canon 107.

[2] See below, p. 87, n. 1.

[3] Of course, there was unlicensed printing before and after this period of two years, but not very much; nor were the publications so definitely upon controverted topics.

I could lay my hands on many more; but all these must be passed over with the comment that they simply continue the debate of civil and ecclesiastical authority and have very little to say on the subject we are following.[1] In 1642, there was passed an act "for the utter abolishing and taking away of all archbishops, bishops, their chancellors, commissaries . . . together with their names, titles, jurisdictions, offices, and functions, and the having or using of any jurisdiction or power." This act ended, officially at least, the authority of the bishops until the Restoration.

For the final opposing opinions and the actual practice of divorce in this period, we must refer once more to the domestic books. Here we find that there is no change on the part of the established church, but that the Puritans have gone even further than previously from the old Catholic ideas, in narrowing the grounds for the nullification of marriage, and have departed from the more liberal principles of the German Reformation, by narrowing the grounds for divorce. For the latter, they admit only adultery and desertion, and for nullification, only the Levitical degrees of relationship. The stand in regard to nullification was due, perhaps, to the fact that the Star Chamber in 1601 had reëstablished the law of 32 Hen. VIII, ca. 38, by which the impediments to marriage were limited to those expressed in "God's law." [2]

[1] The reader should not get the impression that church government and matrimonial jurisdiction were equally the leading issues of the day. By 1642, church government was probably the chief subject in the field of controversy; next to this came questions of doctrine. Marriage and divorce were minor points in the discussion of the former of these topics; and one might read far into the writing of the time without finding mention of either, as is evidenced by the fact that many of the books and pamphlets discussed above have not been previously examined.

[2] See above, p. 62.

We have already examined, at least briefly, the controversy waged over the question of divorce *versus* separation. Our more general conduct books continue the same arguments, neither side yielding ground. The second edition of Whately's *Bride-bush*, in 1623, seems to be the last Puritan book before the censorship of the press to uphold these principles in full.[1] Here, in addition to the subject of adultery, the two recognized forms of desertion — actual departure from the home and refusal of the marriage right — are discussed at some length, and divorce with remarriage is allowed in either case, no distinction in regard to sex being made.[2] Although the Puritans narrowed the grounds for the nullification of marriage, the established church clung to the Catholic practices. Milton says on this point: "It [marriage] was thought so sacramental that no adultery or desertion could dissolve it; and this is the sense of the canon courts in England to this day, but in no other reformed church"; again, "Divorce for adultery and desertion, as all churches agree but England, not only separates, but nullifies, and extinguishes the relation itself of matrimony"; and again, "We know it [marriage] dissoluable for adultery and for desertion by the verdict of all reformed churches."[3] The *Answer to the Doctrine and Discipline*, citing Coke as authority, gives for the nullification of marriage *causa precontractus*, *causa frigitatis* or *impotentiae*,[4] and *causa minoris aetatis* or *impubertatis*.[5] Separation *a*

[1] Gouge's *Domestical Duties*, c. 1626, allows divorce for adultery and for desertion due to difference of religious beliefs, but it does not treat either very fully.

[2] Whately, *op. cit.*, chaps. 1 and 2.

[3] Milton, *Prose Works*, I, 344, and II, 133, 141, respectively.

[4] Frigidity and impotency are synonymous terms as here used. It was this that Milton referred to as "natural frigidity."

[5] *Op. cit.*, p. 2 ff. The Levitical degrees seem to be taken for granted. Although the causes here cited were doubtless those most often plead,

mensa et thoro continued to be granted by the established church for certain causes,[1] and in the case of the desertion of a Christian husband by a heretical wife, remarriage was allowed. Thomas Ridley, writing in 1607, says, "The causes whereupon Divorces grow, are Adultery, deadly hatred one toward an other, intolerable cruelty, neernesse of kindred and affinitie in degrees forbidden, impotencie on the one side or the other." [2] Godolphin, writing in 1678, exhibits practically the same state of affairs, and adds, "Touching the kinds and effects of Divorce, whether Divorce *a vinculo Matrimonii* or separation *a Mensa & Thori*, with the causes thereof; the Divines and Lawyers are of different Opinions, and each of these divided among themselves." [3]

Opposed to this confusion of impediments, separation, divorce, and whatnot, as administered or misadministered, by the established church courts, we may set the clear-cut

it is evident from legal treatises of the time that all the earlier ones were still in operation.

[1] This separation was the door of opportunity to all who wished to obtain an actual divorce, as the terms of it failed to prevent remarriage. The canons of 1603 attempted to put a stop to its abuse by requiring security against remarriage, but this did not help matters. Godolphin, in his *Repertorium Canonicum*, p. 495, gives the following legal opinion on the point: "By enjoyning such security to be given, and such Bonds to be taken, This seems to be a Penal Canon, viz. pecuniarily Penal; whoever therefore breaks the Law incurrs the penalty, and whoever suffers the penalty, doth answer and satisfie the Law, which before he had infring'd."

[2] Ridley, *A Viewe of Civile and Ecclesiasticall Law*, p. 11. Ridley makes no attempt to distinguish between the different kinds of divorce, and for this reason his information is of little help to us. On p. 72, he includes "by consent" among the means of obtaining a divorce. I have found "mutual consent" mentioned in several books; it is usually spoken of as not a proper cause for divorce, which together with Ridley's statement seems to indicate that divorce of some kind was sometimes obtained on this ground.

[3] Godolphin, *Repertorium Canonicum*, p. 501.

and definite statements of the Puritan divines as drawn up by their assembly in c. 1643 and published in 1651:

"Marriage ought not to be within the degrees of consanguinity or affinity forbidden in the word, nor can such incestuous marriages ever be made lawful by any law of man or consent of parties. . . .

"Adultery, or fornication being committed after a contract being detected before marriage, giveth just occasion to the innocent party to dissolve the contract; in the case of adultery after marriage, it is lawful for the innocent party to sue out a divorce, and after the divorce, to marry another as if the offending party was dead.

"Nothing but adultery or such wilful desertion as can no way be remedied, by the Church or Civil Magistrate, is cause sufficient of dissolving the bond of marriage, wherein a publike, and orderly course of proceeding, is to be observed, and the persons concerned in it not left to their own wills, and discretion in their own case." [1]

But aside from books of a strictly domestic nature, there were many others which treated of marriage, woman, and family life from every angle and in every style. These were popular books, too, both those which were somewhat literary and amusing and those which were purely utilitarian and dry. Moreover, debates were still raging, both in and out of print, on practically every question that the previous century had raised. In our particular field, we find the pros and cons of remarriage after divorce, the marriage of the clergy, marriages made without the parents' consent, the legal status of children in cases of divorced parents, and even "whether a man may beat his wife." If we add to the books here suggested all those of purely literary and religious character, as well as the many marriage sermons, by men like Hall, Gataker, Whately, and Donne, we may get some idea of the quagmire in which human nature, imprisoned by text, dogma, and precedent, yet ever and anon breaking forth into license and sin, was strug-

[1] *The Late Assembly of Divines Confession of Faith*, p. 263.

gling for life and the pursuit of happiness. "When I remember," says Milton, "the little that our Saviour could prevail about this doctrine of charity against the crabbed textuists of his time, I make no wonder, but rest confident, that whoso prefers either matrimony or other ordinance before the good of man and the plain exegence of charity, let him profess papist, or protestant, or what he will, he is no better than a pharisee and understands not the gospell." [1]

As Milton says, the pamphleteers and writers of domestic books who touch upon the subject of matrimony, with a few exceptions, argue as if they were trying to settle a hypothetical question rather than to remedy a burning evil in their own midst. But at the time that the assembly of divines was about to struggle with the problem, two writers, from different walks of life and from opposing sects, entered the field to discuss the situation as it actually existed and from the point of view of living needs instead of that of Hebrew history and Roman Catholic interpretation of the Scriptures.[2] These were Daniel Rogers, an orthodox divine,

[1] Milton, *Prose Works*, I, 340.

[2] One of the most important books of the time, *De Jure naturali et Gentium*, from the pen of the learned John Selden, written in Latin with frequent quotations from Greek, Hebrew, Assyrian, and other languages, and mentioned by Milton in his first divorce tract, can hardly be included among our books on divorce, because, as the title indicates, it is concerned not with English conditions but with primitive customs and ancient laws. These do, to a certain extent, uphold Milton's views, as he fervently asserts; but the argument "as it was in the beginning, is now, and ever shall be" is scarcely tenable. On account of the importance of the book, I quote the most important passage on the subject of divorce:

"*Nequi enim separari aut dividi nequibant conjuges, seu Matrimonium dirimi, nisi ex singulari aliqua legis permissione, seu repudii causa; neque communis consensus (quo ex veteri Jure Caesareo distrahi Matrimonia scimus) necessarius erat, ut dirimiretur. Neque individua dici potuit vitae consuetudo quae aequo Jure a marito pluribus communica-*

and John Milton, an Independent layman. The similarity of their views seems to be mere coincidence, but the causes of it were identical — existing conditions. Rogers in his domestic book *Matrimoniall Honovr*, in 1642, appealed to human nature in general by portraying the honor and beauty of the marriage state as it should exist; Milton in his *Doctrine and Discipline of Divorce*, in 1643, appealed to Parliament and the assembly in particular by portraying the evils and hideousness of marriage as it too often did exist.

Of the former, we may stop here only for a quotation, in which we may see Milton's ideas of compatibility of mind in husband and wife, expressed from a different point of view, in a chapter on "Consent."

"Love being the noble groundworke, this [consent] the sweet building upon the former foundation: both making up marriage, to grow to an happy frame and building, which who so behold, can no other judge, but that those parties are well met, and dwell commodiously. . . .

"This then is the point, that both married persons ought studiously to maintaine this grace of mutuall consent, as a maine peece of that, which must maintaine the honour of their marriage. . . .

batur. Quemadmodum vero ex veteri Jure Caesareo distrahabantur Matrimonia, alia quidem consentiente utraque parte, pactis causam, sicut utriqui (ut verba sunt Justinianii) placuerit, gubernantibus, alia vero per occasionem rationabilem quae etiam Bona gratia *vocabantur, alia citra omnem causam, alia quoque cum causa rationabili (cui libertati sanctiones tam Caesareae etiam quam Pontificiae haud parum derogarunt) ita ex Jure Naturali ab ipsis rerum primordiis communi citra ullam omnino causam ea distrahi fas fuisse volunt Magistri. Idque pro libitu tam uxoris quam viri, quod etiam, ex praescriptis aliquot causis, Jure Caesareo olim permissum est. Adeo ut pactum matrimoniale heic non aliud haberetur quam Sociorum contractus, qui eo usque stabilis manet dum in eodem consensu utrinque perserveratur, & renunciante societati alterutro solvitur. Ita, sive viro sive uxore matrimonio renuntiante, solutum aiunt fuisse contractum, velut divortio plane legitimo." Op. cit.*, Lib. V, cap. vii, p. 567.

"Oh, thou sweet amiablenesse and concord, what may not be said of thee? Thou art the offspring of God, the fruite of Redemption, the breath of the spirit: Thou art the compound of contraries, the harmony of discords, the order of Creation, the soule of the world: without which, the vast body thereof would soone dissolve it selve by her owne burden, as wearisome to it selfe, and fall in sunder by peacemeale from each other." [1]

So far Rogers is speaking in general, but further on he becomes more particular and strikes upon the very element which Milton emphasizes most of all.

"This consent must be in the speech and language of them both: Its true generally, but in this point specially, That speech is the discoverer of the mind: Looke what the abundance of the heart is, that will vent it selfe at the mouth. . . . Yea, the speech of each to other should bee (without flattery) as the glasse, to behold each other in. As face answers to face in the water, so doth man accomodate himselfe to his friend (saith Salomon). how much more the husband and wife to each other? They should even resemble each others frame and temper (in the Lord) with all ingenuity. As the beames do represent the Sun, in her heat and light: so should the sweet carriage of the wife, argue the body which gives her influence, even her husbands virtues." [2]

This is far prettier and more dignified than Milton's treatment of the same subject, though it lacks the force of the latter's sound and fury. But Rogers goes no further; he merely exhibits and eulogizes the qualities which go to make a successful marriage and leaves the subject there. Of divorce he has nothing to say.

Milton chose the psychological moment to hurl his "doctrine of freedom" in divorce matters at the head, or heads, of the English nation, which was fairly wallowing in the slough of despond over the questions of church, state, and personal liberty. The official overthrow of the bishops took

[1] Rogers, *op. cit.*, p. 184 ff.

[2] *Ibid.*, p. 189.

place in 1642, but the bill effecting it did not take the power of jurisdiction from the church, and the bishops did not lose the name and dignity of office until 1646. "In this interval," says Neal, "there was properly no established form of government, the clergy being permitted . . . to govern their parishes according to their discretion."[1] On June 12, 1643, the famous assembly was appointed for the consideration "of all things necessary for the peace and government of the church." This assembly convened on July 1, and within a month of this date, Milton's tract *The Doctrine and Discipline and Divorce* appeared.[2] Before the assembly had time to get more than well started, Milton brought out a second edition of the tract dedicated "to the Parliament with the Assembly."[3] The dedication contains a strong appeal to those in power to take some action to remedy the marital evils of the time.

"You it concerns chiefly, worthies of parliament! on whom as on our deliverers, all our grievances and cares, by merit of your eminence and fortitude, are divolved. . . . Ye have, now, doubtless, by the favour and appointment of God, ye have now in your hands a great and populous nation to reform; from what corruption, what blindness in religion, ye know well; in what a degenerate and

[1] Neal, II, 503.

[2] Thomason's date of Aug. 1, 1643, seems to be now pretty generally accepted, despite Philips' statement that the tract was first conceived about Michelmas of that year. In Appendix B, below, I discuss this matter of date in full. In the same place, I attempt to overthrow Philips' further statement, and all later theories built upon it, that the tract was written because Milton himself wished to obtain a divorce from his wife.

[3] The second edition appeared [Feb. 2], 1644. It differs greatly in size and general make-up from the first. It is one-third longer, is divided into books and chapters, contains references to authorities not mentioned before, and is prefaced by the dedication mentioned above. My remarks, however, except where noted, apply to both editions.

fallen spirit from the apprehension of native liberty, and true manliness, I am sure ye find; with what unbounded license rushing to whoredoms and adulteries, needs not long inquiry."[1]

Milton's tract is too well known to need any detailed analysis here, but as several of the issues of the period culminated in it, it is necessary to look for a moment at the more important doctrines advocated. Although Perkins is the only previous writer mentioned in the first edition of the tract, it is certain that Milton was familiar with the general arguments on all sides of the question and with the conditions which led to the stagnant and corrupt state of marital society and jurisdiction thereupon. *The Doctrine and Discipline* was and still is considered revolutionary; but the truth is that it does not contain a single point which was not either previously advocated or actually in practice, although certain principles are emphasized more than they had been before. The one usually taken as Milton's chief contribution to the controversy is the famous proposition that "indisposition, unfitness, or contrariety of mind, arising in nature unchangeable, hindering and ever likely to hinder the main benefits of conjugal society, which are happiness and peace," should be recognized as a just and sufficient cause for divorce. That this principle was already current is shown by Erasmus' mention of "*disidium animorum*" among the impediments to marriage;[2] by the gloss made by the Reform divines on *Deut.* 24, 1, in their *Annotations of the Books of the Old and New Testament*, where it is stated that to the usual causes of divorce "are added by some, barrennesse, madnesse, stubbornnesse, reproachfull insolence toward her husband, which is an uncleannesse of the minde, or any other thing which dispose him rather to loath them

[1] Milton, *Prose Works*, I, 336.
[2] See above, p. 9, n. 2.

than to love her;"[1] and by the comments of Perkins and Ridley already quoted.[2] There can be no doubt, however, that such "uncleanness of the mind" had never before been boldly proclaimed. Nevertheless, as a ground for divorce, it was but a logical result of the Puritan attitude towards marriage, according to which matrimony was instituted for the mutual blessing and benefit of husband and wife instead of for the procreation of children and the avoidance of sin, as the older writers upheld.[3] This idea of marriage as a conjugal society of happiness and peace rather than a "prescribed satisfaction for irrational heat," to use Milton's phrase, is indeed the basis of the whole treatise, and every argument, whether in support of the new doctrine or in opposition to the old, takes its source from this conception. The Puritan writers before Milton had tended towards emphasizing mental and spiritual satisfaction in marriage rather than mere physical, but they failed to see the fallacy of their position in allowing divorce for only adultery and desertion. This Milton points out. "Among Christian writers touching matrimony," he says, "there be three chief ends thereof agreed on: godly society, next civil, and thirdly, that of the marriage-bed. Of these the first in name be the highest and most excellent, no baptized man can deny; . . . but he who affirms adultery to be the highest breach, affirms the bed to be the highest of marriage, which is in truth a gross and boorish opinion, how common soever." [4]

[1] This work is entered in the *Stationers' Register* Oct. 31, 1643. This is, of course, after the publication of Milton's tract, but it cannot be supposed that such a voluminous work — two large tomes — could have been accomplished in the time between the two dates. There is a possibility that the note may have been inserted in consequence of Milton's argument, but this is unlikely, especially as the authors of the *Annotations* had no sympathy with his religious principles.

[2] See above, pp. 80, 87.

[3] For a full discussion of this difference in attitude towards marriage, see below, p. 119 ff.

[4] Milton, *Prose Works*, I, 367.

Since the practices of church and state were, as I have shown, in a complete muddle in regard to divorce jurisdiction, Milton wastes no time in attacking existing conditions, but instead uses their contradictions and corruptions as a foil for the new doctrine he has to advance. In this way they are mentioned continually, — no distinction being made between those of the old Catholic canons and those of the recent Puritan agitation — but they are always subordinated to the main issue of the tract, which is constructive rather than destructive. Milton's whole attitude towards the canon law is shown in the heading of his third chapter, "The ignorance and iniquity of the Canon Law, providing for the right of the body in marriage, but nothing for the wrongs and grievances of the mind." Again, of the evil and confusion of the time in affairs matrimonial, he says, "All of which we can refer justly to no other cause but canon law and her adherents." Of the old separation *a mensa et thoro*, he remarks in passing, "And this I observe that our divines do generally condemn separation of bed and board, without the liberty of second choice."[1] Divorce for "spiritual adultery," "which is so much controverted," he admits, as of course he would have to for the sake of consistency at least. Divorce for plotting by one party against the life of the other, to which "the canon law and divines consent," he admits also. In regard to the impediments annulling marriage, he expresses himself only to oppose the emphasis laid by canon law upon sexual impotency.

Except in insisting upon divorce for incompatibility of temper, to apply the modern phrase, Milton does not go beyond the views of the more radical Puritan writers in any respect. As we have already seen, the two chief points where these differed from orthodox doctrine, were the equality of man

[1] Milton, *Prose Works*, II, 54.

and woman in divorce suits, which had been advocated by the more liberal thinkers ever since the Reformation, and the practice of self-divorce, which I have been at some pains to show continued to be used to date among the Independents. On the first of these points, Milton goes into neither detail nor argument, but the subtitle of his tract, describing it as restoring divorce "to the good of both sexes," shows clearly that he meant to place husband and wife upon the same iooting before the law, although he writes entirely from the man's point of view.[1] Indeed, this was one of the objections raised against the tract by the anonymous answer, in which the reader is instructed to take notice "that all his Arguments, to prove a man may put away his wife for disagreement of minde or disposition, except it be his Argument from *Deu.* 24. 1. they prove as effectually, that the Wife may sue a Divorce from her Husband upon the same grounds."[2] The second point, that of private divorce, is given considerable attention towards the end of the tract. It was quite evident to Milton, as it must be to us, that the logical outcome of the long dispute between church and state rights and of the abolition of the ecclesiastical courts, was the restoration of jurisdiction in marital affairs to the civil authority. But, although the Independents and other

[1] Nevertheless, Milton runs into inconsistencies on the subject of women's rights in divorce matters. Despite the fact that in general he upholds the Puritan doctrine of equal rights for both sexes, he evidently discriminates against the wife in saying that "the absolute and final hindering of divorce cannot belong to any civil or earthly power, against the will and consent of both parties, or of the husband alone." (*Prose Works*, II, 53.) On the other hand, in translating Bucer's book, he passes over Chapter XXXIV, entitled "That it is lawful for a wife to leave an adulterer" with the remark that "this is generally granted, and therefore excuses me the writing out." But certainly his proposed private divorce either by consent of both parties or by that of the husband alone, discriminates against the wife.

[2] *Answer to the Doctrine and Discipline*, p. 13.

non-conformists favored such restoration of power to the civil courts in the case of most of the matters involved, they differed from their more orthodox brethren in persistently upholding that marriage and everything pertaining thereto was entirely a personal and private affair, with which neither church nor state had anything to do except to witness the event. We have already noted Milton's statement in regard to marriage.[1] His platform for divorce is quite consistent with this in its opposition to both civil and ecclesiastical jurisdiction. In concluding his argument on this point, he says, "Shall then the disposal of that power return again to the master of family? Wherefore not, since God there put it, and the presumptuous Canon there bereft it? This only must be provided, that the ancient manner be observed in the presence of the minister and other grave selected Elders." [2]

With *The Doctrine and Discipline*, the long controversy culminated. The advanced doctrines of the most advanced thinker of the time, as herein expressed, were received, on the whole, as the crabbed textuists and the carnally minded people of that day would naturally be expected to receive them, the attitude of the former being as exasperating as that of the latter is disgusting. Although Milton says that the tract was "held by some of the best among reformed writers [to be] without scandal or refutement, though now thought new and dangerous by some of our Gnostics," and that others thought it had "of reason in it to a sufficiency,"[3] there can be no doubt that the general church-going public was both scandalized and incensed, at least by the doctrine or divorce for "indisposition, unfitness, or contrariety of mind." The tract was answered by an

[1] See above, p. 60.

[2] Milton, *Prose Works*, II, 61.

[3] *Ibid.*, II, 112, 115.

anonymous writer from the orthodox standpoint in 1644,[1] was stigmatized in a sermon before Pariiament as wicked and deserving to be burnt, and was condemned, along with certain others, by Featley as advocating "most damnable doctrines."[2] The most authoritative opinion expressed against it was that subscribed to and published, in 1647, by certain ministers of London under the title of *A Testimony to the Truth of Jesus Christ,* in which they declare their "detestation and abhorence" of Milton's divorce for "indisposition, unfitness, or contrariety of mind."[3] It may be worthy of mention that in this tract neither his principle of equal rights for man and woman nor his advocacy of private divorce is criticized, and a marginal note directs the reader to "peruse the whole book."

Meanwhile Milton had come to his own defense by translating passages from the second book of Bucer's *De Regno Christi* in 1644,[4] which expressed the extreme liberal views of the German Reformers, but did not touch upon the subject of private divorce or go quite far enough generally to justify Milton altogether in saying, "I hope this will excuse me with the mere Englishman to be a forger of new and loose opinions." In the following year, he published his *Tetrachordon,* in which he follows the suggestion of some of his friendly critics and discusses at length the "four chief places in Scripture concerning nullities in marriage." In

[1] *An Answer to a Book, Intituled, The Doctrine and Discipline of Divorce.* This *Answer* is directed against the first edition of Milton's tract only, and replies merely to the first part of that. The principle of private divorce is therefore not mentioned.

[2] Featley, *The Dippers dipt,* f. B2 *b.*

[3] *Op. cit.*, p. 19. In the same paragraph, the ministers condemn also the doctrine expressed in *Little Nonsuch,* a slight and none too serious tract, anonymously published in 1646, which advocated the marriage of kin, after the example of the first people upon earth.

[4] Under the title of *The Judgment of Martin Bucer, etc.*

this tract he takes every opportunity to reiterate and amplify the principles of his *Doctrine and Discipline* for divorce on mental rather than physical grounds. In the same year, 1645, he replied to the "nameless author" above mentioned, in a short tract called *Colasteron,* but this work adds nothing of interest to the controversy.

What were the actual conditions of divorce legislation and jurisdiction from this time to the Restoration, it is impossible to determine accurately. The writer of the *Answer* to Milton's tract, quoting Coke as authority, defines divorce as a "sentence pronounced by an Ecclesiasticall Judge, whereby a man and woman formerly married, are separated or parted";[1] but as already noted, it does not seem possible that the church or any of its officers could have held court for divorce cases at this time. Private divorce doubtless existed to some extent among the Independents, and among others the word of the local pastor may have been deemed sufficient. Cromwell's act of 1653 was the first official expression of any kind during this period. Despite Milton's efforts to have divorce by private act established as the recognized legal method, Cromwell wisely decided to steer a more conservative course and to put the matter into the hands of the civil magistrates; but though this act appoints officials to decide cases, it gives no intimation of what were the acknowledged grounds — if, indeed, any existed — for their decisions. The bill reads:

"That the hearing and determining of all matters and controversies touching Contracts and Marriages, and the lawfulness and unlawfulness thereof; and all Exceptions against Contracts and Marriages, and the Distribution of Forfeitures within this Act, shall be in the power, and referred to the Determination of the Justices of the Peace, in each County, City or Town Corporate, at the General Quarter Sessions; or of such other persons to hear and determine the same, as Parliament shall hereafter appoint."[2]

[1] *Op. cit.*, p. 2.

[2] Scobell, II, 238.

Although nothing seems to have been done to form a legal and authoritative code of rules or principles on which such controversies and exceptions might be based, the appointment of the justices of the peace as judges in these matters was a long step in advance. But, of course, the Restoration overturned all this, and conditions reverted to those of the early part of the century, except for the fact that by 1700 divorce by special act of Parliament became possible to the wealthy. Since then England has muddled along in her usual way, and even the reforms of 1857, the first since Cromwell's time, left divorce affairs in a state that can hardly be thought satisfactory.

CHAPTER IV

THE DOMESTIC CONDUCT BOOK

I. The Type and its Origin

The origin of the domestic conduct book in England cannot be accurately determined. Priority for native writing in this field may be claimed on the evidence of Wiclif's brief treatise (if indeed Wiclif wrote it [1]) entitled *Of Weddid Men and Wifis and of Here Children also,* but as this was not printed until the nineteenth century, it is difficult to say whether or not it had any influence in the establishment of the genre, which did not take place for a hundred years after Wiclif's death. At this time, the first books were of foreign origin, although earlier interest in domestic affairs is evidenced in England by writing on morals, manners, and so forth, especially in books for the instruction of children, and was doubtless one of the causes for the translation of continental works. But after the establishment of the type, English writers soon entered the field, and although foreign books continued to be translated, the continuation and development of the writing of books concerning domestic affairs may be said to have been almost entirely a native product. In its most complete form, a book of this type contained four principal subjects: (1) discussion of the marriage state from religious and secular standpoints, (2) the legal elements involved in contracting matrimony, (3) mutual relations of husband and wife, (4) the govern-

[1] It is ascribed to Wiclif on the ground of its presence in a volume which Archbishop Parker, in the sixteenth century, believed to contain only tracts of Wiclif's composition. No other evidence on the question seems available.

ment of the family, including housekeeping, the upbringing of children, the management of servants, and general household economics. The ultimate sources of all these books were the New Testament (especially the teachings of St. Paul), the classics, and the church fathers.

Wiclif's treatise, but twelve pages long in its present form, is divided into five chapters, which may be summarized: (1) the two kinds of marriage (*i.e.* that of God and his church and that of man and woman), (2) the domestic elements in human wedlock, (3) the common duties of husband and wife, (4) the relations of parents and children, (5) duties and dangers in family life. The book lacks any discussion of the contract and ceremony of marriage, the grounds of divorce or annulment, and the care of the house and servants. Similarly, no one of the first group of domestic books presents a complete model for the type; hence the selection and combination of the important features of earlier works were the particular contributions of sixteenth century English writers and their foreign contemporaries from whom they translated, to the development of the genre. The latter, taken altogether, covered practically all of the different elements of the field, and in two cases at least [1] seem to have set the form for the English writers.

Among the very earliest books printed in England, we find the first on the family. This is Caxton's *Boke of Good Manners*, translated from the French of Jaques LeGrand in 1487 and republished at least four times before the century was out. The treatise, 118 folio pages in all, is divided into five books, which contain general instruction, or moralization, on the life of man and on his various professions. The first is on the seven virtues and some of the corresponding vices; the second on church people and clerks; the third on the lords temporal; the fourth on "thestate of the

[1] LeGrand's and Bullinger's.

comynalte and of the people"; the fifth on the transitory character of life and the coming of death. Of these, the fourth alone concerns us, and of it, only certain chapters. It runs to twenty-six pages; the chapter on matrimony is but three, and those on household affairs but a little more than one each. The complete contents are as follows:

I. Of Rychemen and how they ought to gloryfye in theyr rychesses.
II. Of the state of pouerte whyche ought to be agreable.
III. Of the state of olde age wherin a mā ouȝt to be vertuous.
IV. Of the state of yonge peple & how they shold gouerne them.
V. Of the state of maryage. & how it ouȝt to be mayntened.
VI. How wymmen ought to be gouerned.
VII. How virginite & maydenhede ouȝt to be maynteyned.
VIII. Of thestate of wymmen wydowes.
IX. How seruaūtes ouȝt to be mayntened in theyr seruyce.
X. How they that ben of euyl lyf dyen ylle.
XI. How fader and moder ought to teche theyr chyldren.
XII. How chyldren owen obeyssaūce & honour to their parents.
XIII. Of thestate of marchaunts.
XIV. Of thestate of pylgryms.
XV. How dedely synnes desyren deth.

Here we find eight chapters whose subjects have place in practically all later domestic books and which indeed form the greater part of them. These are the fourth, fifth, sixth, seventh, eighth, ninth, eleventh, and twelfth. It is evident that the arrangement of subject matter here is very poor; nevertheless, the substance, though briefly expressed, and the treatment also, is typical of this whole species of book. The fifth chapter is the most important one for us. On account of the rarity of the book and the importance of its subject and style, I am led to quote from it at some length. The passage below contains all that is essential.

"Mariage is ordeyned for to haue lygnage. and for to loue eche other. And therfor thappostle seynt poul in his fythe chapitre admonesteth the wedded men sayeng ye men loue your wyues as Jhūs Cryste loueth his chyrche. And to this purpoos valere in his iiij boke the v chapytre recyteth how a man named graceus lonyd[1] his wyf named Corneylle so moche that he wold deye for to gete helthe of his wyf. he recounteth also how Cuplacius herd saye that his wyf was deed. And thēne he smote hym self in the breste with a knyf and requyred to be with her. . . .[2] Semblably also the wymmen owen to loue theyr husbondes/ And herof we haue example as valere recounteth in his boke aforfaid. how Julia the doughter of Cezar seeyng the Robe of hir husbond spotted wyth blood was soo troubled that for sorowe and henynes/ her chyld that she had withiñ her bely was destroyed. . . . After he recyteth of the doughter of Cathon named Porcia seeyng her husboud brutus to be slayn/ she demaunded a knyf to slee her self also/ And by cause that none wold delyüe to her no knyf. she toke brennyng cooles. and put them in her monthe & ete them doñ in suche wyse that she deyde by a right marueyllo? manere. . . .[2] And it is good to knowe how in mariage after the doctours. thre thynges ought to be/ that is to wete fayth. loyalte/ lygnage & sacrament/ By fayth and loyalte is gyuen to understōde that neyther of the parties maryed ought not to trespace with his body but to kepe it to his partye/ For as thapostle saith in his fyrst epystle to the Corynthyeus/ the body of the man is bylongyng to the wyf. And the body of the wyf to the man. that is to understonde in mariage/ And as seynt Ambrose saith in his exameron. god made eue of the syde of Adam/ in signefy...ñce that in mariage a man and woman ought to be all one body one self thyng. And me semeth that the partye that forfayteth his maryage/ dooth a yenst the lawe of nature/ For the storke hath suche forfayture in abhomynacōn of storkes to flee hym or her that so forfayteth. lyke as Alexander recoūteth in his boke of nature of byrdes. And me semeth it is a grete abhomynacion to see in many maryages so lytyl fayth and loyalte as now is. But I byleue that one of the causes emonge the

[1] Evidently a misprint for louyd. Confusion of *n* and *u* often occurs in the book.

[2] Other stories omitted.

other is. that the maryage be not duely maad. but for money. or other euyl cause Thēne it is noo merueylle that the maryage contynue not well syth the begynuyng therfor the kynge lygurgis wolde and ordeyued in his Royāme that the virgynes and maydens shold be wedded without to haue gold or syluer to thende that the maryage shold not be made of couetyse. lyke as pompeus recyteth in his iij boke/ And valere in his vij boke the first chaytre recyteth how one demānded somtym of a phylosopher named themystodes how and to whome he shold marye his doughter. that is to wete to a poure man or to a ryche. The whiche ansuerde. that he ought not to demānde pouerte ne richesse. but the bounte and the vertues of the mā. More ouer in maryage ther lyeth right grete aduys. and not onely for parantage but also for to Mayntene it/ And to this purpoos speketh Theophraste dystyple of Arystotle/ in his boke that he made of maryage · in whiche he saith. that a mā ought more to beholde the bounte of the woman than the beaulte. and yf thou demānde whiche is better to take a fayr woman or a foule he ansuerde. that it is an hard thyng to kepe a fayr woman the whiche many men desyre. And it is a grete payne to loue the foule one whiche many despyse. alleway yf she be good the goodnesse shal kepe her beaulte. And yf she be not fayr. it is none hard thyng to loue her that is of right good wyll. for naturally & resonably more ought the bounte to be praysed than the beaulte. Moreouer in maryage is moche to be suffred. singulerly yf bothe parties be not wyse. For men ben ofte suspecyonno? of theyr wyues/ Therfore ought a woman to be symple and good. & not onely of her body. but also of her maynten and maners/ For in spekying. in beholdyng. ne in conuersace she ought not doo ony thyng. by whiche ony other myght thynke or Juge in her ony euyll. . . . The men also that purpose to marye oughten to aduyse and beholde the condycōn of her that thay desyre to haue to wyf. But many ben deceyued by cause they take them in the age of xij yere or ther aboute. and thēne what they be/ noman may wete ne knowe. For as the comyn prouerbe saith/ how seeth a chylde. seeth no thyng/ Also in maryeng hym self. one ought to here many speke For loue and carnal affeccyon blyndeth the understondyng. and maketh a man fauourable to Juge. whan he is surprysed of suche loue. therfore a mā ought to byleve more another than hym self." [1]

The chapters on women, servants, parents, and children, although short, formulate the nature of the instruction found in all later books on family affairs. The woman should fear and obey her husband and should not wear gaudy clothes or attempt to improve her complexion.

"A woman ought to haue resonably two condicōns. that is to wyte/ shame of repreef/ and drede of disobeyeng of her partye. . . . Semblably ben they that poppe them self & make them to seme fayr for to brynge other to synne/ And it is grete merueylle how they presume to deffeate and altere that whiche god hath made/ & moche lewde is the woman the whiche weneth to make her more fair than god hath made her." [2]

Servants owe their masters honor, truth, faithfulness, obeisance, diligence, and patience. Parents should teach their children good manners and the doctrines of the church.

"[Children] owen tobeye to theyr parents lyke as thappostle saith to the Ephesiens the vj chapytre. Filij obedite parentibus vr̄is/ That is to saye. ye chyldren obeye ye vnto your parents. . . . More oủ the chyldren ought to loue parfyghtly theyr fader and moder. and in nede socoure them lyke as sápion dyde. the whiche put hym self in peryll of deth for to saue his fader/ And also Eneas for to delyuer his fader passed by the myddys of his enemyes." [3]

The importance of the subject matter of this short treatise is self-evident. It may be noted that one element of the typical family book is lacking, that is, marriage from a legal point of view. This is supplied in full by William Harrington's *Cōmendacions of matrymony*, which was not only the first book of the kind of entirely English origin but also the first which made marriage and married life its whole subject and treated it with something like satisfactory com-

[1] Caxton, *op. cit.*, cap. V.
[2] *Ibid.*, cap. VI.
[3] *Ibid.*, cap. XII.

pleteness. It was published in 1528 and was probably reprinted but twice.[1] The gap between this book and Caxton's does not seem so great when we consider the small number of books published in those years; nevertheless, I do not find any evidence of a connection between the two except the general subject matter. Harrington's book is not long, being only forty-two pages,[2] but it is extremely meaty, and on the subject of the form of the marriage ceremony and the legal requirements and impediments of matrimony, it contains more definite information than all the others put together. It is divided into four parts: the lawfulness and godliness of matrimony, the method of lawfully contracting it, the impediments, and some general rules for the conduct of the family. Parts two and three are especially instructive, but as the essential points of each have already been quoted and discussed,[3] further mention here is unnecessary. The fourth section contains rules for the conduct of married life, but it is too brief and of too general a character to be of value except as exhibiting this feature of the typical domestic book. It recommends (1) love, peaceful dwelling, faithfulness (adultery being a cause for separation *a mensa et thoro*); (2) mutual help and economy in household affairs; (3) the proper upbringing of children and the observance of religious practices. As the "commendations" given in part one contain the substance, in brief, of many later books, it may be worth while to quote the most important.

[1] Ames' *Typog. Antiq.* (ed. 1810–19), III, 105, describes an undated edition by Jno. Rastell. The copy I have used is by Jno. Skot and seems to be totally unknown. Redman reprinted the book later.

[2] See bibliography for size and number of pages of books mentioned in this chapter.

[3] See above, pp. 39 ff. and 72 ff., respectively. On account of the importance of part two, I quote at greater length from it in Appendix C, below.

"Many thynges ben fonden as well in the olde lawe as in the newe, whiche dothe gretely cōmende ye state & ordre of matrymony. Fyrst in ye olde lawe it is cōmended of the dygnyte of ye maker therof whiche was almyghty god him self. The place where it was made which was paradyce. The tyme of ye makynge therof whiche was the tyme of innocensie afore there were ony synne/ the antyquite of it/ for it was afore all other ordres. The contynuaunce of it/ for it hath ben contynued frome ye begynnynge of the worlde in euery lawe/ in euery maner of people/ in euery Cyte and in euery tyme. . . . In the newe law it is cōmended and confirmed by oure sauyoure cryste. . . . Also in that yt is ordeyned to be one of the. vii sacramentes of holy chyrche. . . . For it betokeneth fyrst the unyte whiche is bytwyxte god and the nature of man . . . Secondely it betokenethe the unyon of Cryste to his chyrche catholycall. Thyrdely it betokeneth ye unyon of Chryste to mannes soule." [1]

The next book to appear in English was a work entirely devoted to the government of the household, neglecting the ceremony of marriage altogether. This was Richard Whitford's *A werke for housholders*, published first in 1531, and reprinted in 1532, 1533, and 1537.[2] It is a small book, fifty-six pages, to which is added a "breue and shorte monicyon or counseyle of the cure and gouernaunce of a household," translated from an epistle of Bernard Sylvester, seven pages in length. This book is of an intensely religious character, its rules for the conduct of the household being, for the most part, directions for prayer and an explanation of the creed and the commandments. For this reason, it is not strictly of the type we are following, but it seems worth a passing notice as showing the combination of household and religious affairs in a type of book which soon became prevalent but which we shall have to omit from our study hereafter. Whitford's work, though not divided into sections,

[1] Harrington, *op. cit.*, f. Aii *b*, ff.

[2] *D.N.B.* gives 1530 and 1538.

may be summarized: (1) the proper employment of the day, including prayers upon rising, "some certeyn occupacyon that may be profytable, and euer to auoyde ydlenes ye mother and nurse of all synne & euyll," and a review of the day with prayer upon retiring; (2) text and explanation at some length of the Lord's Prayer, the creed, the ten commandments (two of which are omitted and others confused), the principal sins, the five wits, and the works of mercy; (3) a form for confession of sin, which should be approached "with a meke & sobre countenaunce and behauyour (For it is no laughynge game)," the confession being a rehearsal of the seven deadly sins performed in full; (4) a table of the principal things in the life of Christ.

Of all this, the declaration of the ten commandments is the only part we need stop for, and here I will merely set forth a few passages which are interesting for one reason or another. The first commandment includes a short discussion of witchcraft, in which the difficulty of convincing "simple people" of its evil is quaintly described. "Syr," they say, "we meane well/ and we do byleue well & we thy̅ke it a good & a charitable dede to hele a sycke persone/ or a sycke beest/ and trewth they saye/ but yet it is neyther good ne charytable to heale them by unlawfull meane."[1] Under the second commandment, the discussion of which rambles far from its original subject of swearing, we find some interesting notes on the discipline of children. The following naively penitential verse is given for the child to recite at the end of the day:

"Yf I lye/ backebyte/ or stele
Yf I curse/ scorne/ mocke/ or swere
Yf I chyde/ fyght/ stryue/ or threte
Then am I worthy to be bete
Good mother or maystresse myne

[1] Whitford, *op. cit.*, Cii.

Yf ony of these nyne
I trespace to your knowynge
With a newe rodde and a fyne
Erly naked before I dyne
Amende me with a scourgynge." [1]

Nevertheless, Whitford maintains, children should be corrected "with a mylde and softe spirit," and should be informed that "you do the coreccyon agaynst your mynde/ compelled thervnto by cōscience/ and requyre them to put you no more vnto suche labour & payne. For yf thou do (say you) you must suffre parte of the payne with me and therfore you shall now haue experience and profe what payne it is vnto us both." [2] The third commandment, on keeping the Sabbath, warns the reader against "suche vanytes as cōmunely ben vsed/ that is to saye/ berebaytynge & bulbaytynge/ fodball/ tenesplayng/ bowlynge" and the "unlawfull games of cardynge/ dycyng/ closshynge/ with suche other vnthryfty pastymes/ or rather losetymes." [3] Under the sixth commandment, on the avoidance of adultery, there is an interesting comment upon private unwitnessed contracts of marriage. "It is a great ieopardy therfore," says Whitford, "to make ony suche contractes/ specyally amonge them selfe secretely alone. . . . And bycause the chyrche can not openly knowe that thynge that was spoken and done in pryuyte/ they bē thought and supposed so to lyue as lawfully in maryage." [4]

The second part of the book, translated by Whitford from Sylvester, is a treatise of practical advice of a general nature, particularly for a farming household, in the style of the *Proverbs* of Solomon. "Trust hym rather for thy frende/ that somwhat doth for the: than hym that dothe offre hym selfe: sayenge. I am youres in all I can and may.

[1] Whitford, *op. cit.*, Dii.
[2] *Ibid.*, Dii *b*.
[3] *Ibid.*, Div.
[4] *Ibid.*, Eiii *b*.

For in wordes is great plenty of frendes"; or again, in a different strain, "Make your byldynges rather for nede than for pleasure. For the appetyte of buyldynge for pleasure shal neuer haue nede/ tyll pouerte teche wytte somwhat to late. Sel not vnto great persones/ but rather for lesse vnto ye lower persones." [1]

We must now turn to several books of continental authorship, two of which preceded both Harrington's and Whitford's. As these two were not translated into English until some time later and do not seem to have influenced either of the books just discussed, I have delayed consideration of them until this point. The first is Vives' *De Institutione Foeminae Christianae* in 1523. The author was a Spaniard but was also identified with England. He had already received a fellowship from Oxford in 1517, and upon the publication of his book, he visited the country and was made Doctor of Civil Law by the same university. The second work is that of Erasmus, who after several visits to England, published at Basel his *Matrimonii Christiani Institutio* in 1526, a book of considerable importance, although I have found only one mention of it in any later writing.[2] Among these continental books, I must include, for the sake of convenience, the one classical example that was trans-

[1] Whitford, Hii and Hii *b*.

[2] Becon and Milton both refer *en passant* to Erasmus' views on marriage and divorce. Becon mentions both the *Annotationes in Novum Testamentum* and the *Matrimonii Encomium*. Milton mentions two books, without naming them; one of which must be the *Institutio*. Erasmus' *Matrimonii Encomium*, 1518, translated into English by Richard Taverner under the title of *A ryght frutefull Epystle, etc.*, c. 1536, is worth mention only because it seems to have escaped notice altogether in the biographies of Erasmus. It is merely a personal letter to a cousin urging him to marry. The bare facts of its publication may be found in the *Bibliotheca Erasmina* published by the Bibliothèque de l'Université de l'État (Gand, 1893). See also *D. N. B.* under Taverner.

lated into English. This is Xenophon's work, translated by Gentian Hervet in 1532 under the title of *Xenophon's Treatise of an Houshold,* the original of which was known to Vives and mentioned by him in the introduction of his *De Institutione.* The last foreign book of this period is Bullinger's *Christen state of Matrimonye,* translated under that title from the German by Coverdale in 1541.[1] Of the originals of these four books, it is difficult to say whether they had any influence or not, but my own opinion is that they had practically none at all.[2]

Erasmus' *Matrimonii Christiani Institutio* was never translated into English and seems not to have been republished even in Latin until 1650. It is, nevertheless, a very thorough study of the office and nature of marriage, consisting of 442 pages, but it slights the domestic side of the institution, discussing only the general relations of husband and wife. The impediments to marriage are treated at great length.[3] Erasmus takes the classics and the Christian emperors rather than the church fathers as general authorities on matrimonial affairs, but his views do not seem to differ greatly from those of Catholicism.

Vives' book was translated, under the title of *Instructions of a Christian Woman,* by Richard Hyrde in 1540, and was republished twice in 1541, and in 1557, 1585, 1592, besides an undated edition somewhere within this time. It consists of 310 pages. In the preface, which is addressed to Queen Catherine, Vives described the book as one

[1] I have not been able to find any mention of the original, nor to ascertain its title or date; but see below, p. 114, n. 1.

[2] Mention should be made somewhere of the fact that Thomas More touched upon marriage in his *Utopia.* He recommends a greater freedom of divorce, by allowing it to be obtained by common consent of husband and wife; but his discussion of marital problems is too brief (a few sentences only) to be of any importance. I have seen no references to it in later books.

[3] See above, p. 9, n. 2.

"of the information and bringing vp of a Christian woman: a matter neuer yet entreated of any man, among so great plentie, and variety of wits and writers. For Zenophon and Aristotell giuing rules of house-keeping and Plato making precepts of ordering the common weal, spake many things appertayning vnto the womans office & duty: & S. Cipri, S. Hierome, S. Ambrose, & S. Augustine, haue intreted of Maids, & Widows, but in such wise, that they appere rather to exhort and counsaile thē vnto some kinde of liuing, than to instruct & teach them." [1]

The book is a practical treatise of every phase of woman's life, divided into three parts, dealing with maids, wives, and widows respectively; but with the exception of two chapters, entitled "What the wife ought to do at home" and "Of Children, and the charge and care about them," the instruction is devoted to woman alone rather than to the family or the home.

The translation of Xenophon's little household work, made in 1532 by Hervet at the instance of Geoffrey Pole, was, like Vives' book, popular enough to run into further editions in 1534(?),[2] 1540, 1544, 1554, 1557, 1573, and 1592. It is but 105 pages and discusses household matters only, but being the first book in English entirely on housekeeping, it is important in directing attention to marriage as a state of life rather than as a single act. The form is that of a dialogue within a dialogue, in which Socrates, reporting a conversation with Ischomachus, instructs Critobulus as to domestic and farm economics. The chief features of household government, as described by Ischomachus, are the woman's duties within the house, and the man's duties

[1] Vives, *op. cit.*, p. 1.

[2] There is some doubt as to whether there was an edition in 1534. Ames mentions one such, but he may be referring to the 1544 edition, which has the date 1534 on the title page but the correct one in the colophon at the end. See also *D.N.B.*

without, in the care of the fields and workmen and the study of husbandry. Marriage itself is not discussed at all, except in the relationship of husband and wife, and this, together with the fact the household described is that of a simple Greek husbandman, removes the book to some extent from the type we are investigating.

Of the continental books, Coverdale's *Christen state of Matrimonye*, from Bullinger's original, in 1541, is by far the most important both for its content and its influence. The extent of the latter is suggested by the fact that seven more editions of it appeared by 1575.[1] Bullinger discusses all the important points treated by LeGrand and Harrington,

[1] There are several peculiar circumstances connected with this book. Foxe (*Acts and Mon.*, IV, 679) mentions the *Christian state of Matrimony* as prohibited by ecclesiastical proclamation in 1531. This mention is misleading, as the original proclamation (see Wilkins, *Concilia*, III, 720) gives the title as *Oeconomia Christiana*, which, if it refers to Bullinger's book at all, must be taken to indicate the original version, since there can be no doubt that Coverdale's translation first appeared in 1541. (In the same list, is given *Matrimonium Johannis Tindall*, which if ever published, has been since lost sight of. It is not mentioned in biographies of Tindale, nor is it included in the 1573 edition of his complete works.) *The Christen state of Matrimonye* became confused with *The Golden Book of Matrimony*, 1542, attributed to Becon. The truth is that the two are really the same book in different dress. Becon wrote a preface for the *Christen state* (after its first appearance), and some printer changed the name of the book and advertised Becon as the author in order to increase its sale. In this disguise, it was published in 1542, 1543, and 1546; in its proper form, it appeared in 1541, twice in 1543, twice in 1552, and in 1575. (See Ames, *Typog. Antiq.*, I, 497 ff.) There are some variations in the different editions. Becon's own book, *The Boke of Matrimony*, must not be confused with this one.

Bullinger's book gives considerable evidence of a connection with the divorce of Henry VIII. The following sentence seems to refer directly to the royal case: "What is the cause of all this dissention, cruel persecution, tyrrany, cruel laws . . . but only the blind ignorance of unlearned rulers, which measure all things after their own fond fleshy and although his book presents little that is new and lacks some of the definite information given by Harrington, it goes into the various aspects of matrimony in greater detail and at greater length than any of its predecessors. The discussion of domestic life occupies at least one-third of the author's attention and establishes this section as a feature of this type of book in somewhat the importance it deserves; and although the legal and ceremonial aspects of the subject still occupy more than their proper share of the whole, it seems fair to say that the full form and content of the typical family book are here first established. Altogether, it runs to 156 pages, the substance of which may be epitomized as follows: (1) eulogy of marriage and general explanation of domestic life, with warning to parents not to force their children to marry against their will or before they reach a proper age; (2) tables of consanguinity and affinity with remarks thereupon; (3) general advice in regard to cleanness of life and avoidance of carnal sin; (4) account of the marriage ceremony and feast, with warning against cxcess; (5) household relations of husband and wife; (6) housekeeping, servants, children, education, and apparel; (7) divorce. On the whole, this treatise is one of the most broad-minded, unbiased, and modern in principle of any before Perkins' *Christian Oeconomie.* Marriage is defined as the "yoking together of one man & one woman/ whom god hath coupled according to his worde/ with the consent of thē both/ from thence forth to dwell together/ . . . to the intente that they maye bring forth childrē in the feare of him/ that they maye auoyde whordome/ and that (according to gods good pleasure) the one maye helpe & confort the tother." [1] A mate is to be chosen for true riches of

affections . . . and would have their own carnal wishes to stand in the stead, yea, rather to be above God and his lawyers."

[1] Bullinger, *op. cit.*, f. iii *b*.

mind, body, and temporal substance; "yf beside these/ thou fyndest other greate riches (bewtye and such like giftes) and comest godly and honestlye by them/ thou hast the more to thanke God for." [1] Seven chapters are devoted to the affairs of the household, in which much sensible advice is contained. In the one on cohabitation, it is pointed out that mutual love and forbearance are necessary, that the husband is the head of the house, and that the wife should be obedient to him. The following chapter gives suggestions for the maintenance of love and faithfulness on the part of both. Two chapters are devoted to housekeeping, one to children, and one to the conduct of maidens. The English primers are recommended for the instruction of children, after which they should study Latin and Greek authors, "noble histories," and "the tongues," and should read and memorize parts of the Bible. Travel is spoken of as beneficial to young men.

For the sake of convenience, we must mention here two somewhat later translations of continental writings. One is *The Commendation of Matrimony* by David Clapham from the Latin of H. C. Agrippa, in 1545; and the other, *The office and duetie of an Husband,*[2] by Thomas Paynell from the Latin of Vives, in 1553. The former is a very small and unimportant book and needs no further notice. Vives' book, 410 pages, a companion volume to his *De Institutione,* is a pretty solid and thoroughgoing presentation of married life in all its aspects; for, despite the title, it discusses the whole subject and even gives more attention to the wife than to the husband. Nevertheless, there is

[1] Bullinger, *op. cit.*, f. xivi.

[2] The date of the original is not known. Wood, who includes Vives in his *Oxonienses*, did not know this book at all. A description of it may be found in Brydges, *Censura Literaria*, IX, 25. The date of the translation is settled in the article on Paynell in *D.N.B.*

practically nothing new brought forth, and the value of the book is greatly decreased by faulty arrangement and constant digression. The chief feature of interest is that, although the writer was undoubtedly a member of the Church of Rome, the book does not present the low ideal of marriage held generally by that body. On the contrary, Vives' attitude is broad and temperate and his ideals are high; he even goes so far as to emphasize the importance of mental rather than physical agreement in marriage. The greater part of the book is on married life, although it opens with the usual stereotyped praise of matrimony and advice on the choice of a wife.

Meanwhile, the divorce case of Henry VIII and Catherine had excited almost world-wide controversy, which had started as early as 1528. This, however, was largely confined to the question of marriage with a deceased wife's sister and the power of the Pope in dispensing with the recognized impediments to marriage.[1] The general position of the Church of England and its relations to Rome were, as has been shown, at this time somewhat obscure. In order to place these clearly before the world, the King, having accomplished his immediate project, caused to be compiled two books, in which he took occasion to set forth authoritative views on matrimony as held by the established church. These are *The Institution of a Christian Man*, popularly known as *The Bishops' Book*, in 1537,[2] and *The Necessary Doctrine and Erudition for any Christian Man*,[3] sometimes known as *The King's Book* from the fact that he personally

[1] An account of this controversy and the English writing concerned in it, is given in Appendix A, below.

[2] Wilkins, *History of Divorce and Remarriage*, p. 136, dates this book "about 1543–4." There can be no doubt, however, that 1537 is the correct date.

[3] The substance of both of these books is given in Blunt, *Doctrine of the Church of England.*

revised it, in 1543.[1] The latter was simply a recasting of its predecessor into a less ecclesiastical form by the Convocation of Canterbury. Popularly, it was the more important of the two, as is shown by the fact that it ran into at least seven editions in the year of its publication,[2] but the *Institution* was considered by the King and the church as the more authoritative. This treatise was compiled by a royal commission of the two archbishops, the nineteen bishops, eight archdeacons, and seventeen other doctors of divinity and law, and was intended to serve as a handbook for the clergy of the realm from which to instruct the people. It was translated into Latin and sent by the King to the Diet of Spires in 1543–4 to represent the principles of the Church of England. The section devoted to matrimony, only twelve pages in length, represents it exactly as it was held to be by the Church of Rome, except for the Pope's powers of dispensation, and may be taken as expressing the attitude of the established church from then on, except that by the Articles of 1552 marriage was excluded from the number of sacraments. Despite the brevity of treatment, most of the usual points in regard to matrimony are discussed, viz.: (1) the dignity and value of marriage, (2) the original command of God that his people marry and his warning against trespassing within the forbidden degrees, (3) marriage as signifying the union of God and man and of Christ and the church, (4) Christ's blessing upon marriage and his decree as to divorce,[3] (5) the parts of marriage, which are the outward contract and the inward blessings

[1] Ames (*Typog. Antiq.*, I, 441) mentions an edition of 1542, but says that the book was amended and enlarged in 1543. By the edition of 1542, he must mean the *Institution*, since all other evidence points to 1543 as the year of the first appearance of the *Necessary Doctrine*.

[2] For further account, see Neal, I, 23 ff., and Blunt, p. xiv.

[3] Matt. V, 32, and XIX, 9, allowing divorce (i. e., *a mensa et thoro*) for fornication only.

and comforts, (6) admonition and advice on married life, (7) the nature of the bond, providing that a lawful marriage cannot be broken but that one discovered to have been unlawfully contracted is null and void *ab initio*,[1] (8) the education of children. It is evident that this book shows no originality either in form or substance, but the authority under which it was published, its purpose as a handbook for popular instruction, and the number of editions its revised form ran into, show at once its great importance in current thought. In later writing, however, I find no mention made of it, but this may be accounted for by the fact that the church fathers and the great Biblical scholars of the German Reformation remained the ever-present authorities on ecclesiastical matters, and almost no other writers are ever referred to.

II. Puritan and Romish Attitudes towards Marriage

With the Bullinger-Coverdale book, the formative period of our type comes to an end. In those which follow, we find no new elements of any importance, although greater detail of treatment is present in many. Heretofore, I have made no effort to classify the books considered in accordance with the wider religious movements of the time, but it is evident that different viewpoints are expressed in them.

[1] Wilkins in his discussion of this book (*Hist. of Div.*, p. 137), quotes merely the passage that "the bond of lawful marriage is of such sort that it cannot be dissolved or broken, but by death only." This by itself is misleading, as it gives no clue to the existence of the further passage providing for the annulment of marriage due to former impediments, in which it is definitely expressed that "The Church may and ought to divorce the same persons so unlawfully contracted, and declare that such matrimony is unlawful, and the bond thereof to be of no strength or efficiency, because it was never good from the beginning." Blunt, p. 201.

Harrington, for instance, is thoroughly Catholic, even to the extent of considering marriage a sacrament, and his whole treatment is from this point of view. Bullinger, on the other hand, represents consistently the German reform ideas, which his translator upheld. A point of controversy between these two churches which we have not noted as yet was in regard to the marriage of priests. The Reformers held that marriage was entirely an honorable state, quite equal with the virginal life, and that therefore the entrance into holy orders was no reason to exclude a man from it; so they favored the marriage of the clergy, especially as the sexual vileness of the lives of many of them would be thus remedied. But the Catholic Church and the Church of England held to the belief of celibacy and preferred to wink at existing immorality among the clergy. Historically, the thing went through rather a ridiculous course. Edward VI passed a decree allowing priests to marry, whereupon many former mistresses as well as many reputable women became wives; but Mary revoked this decree and compelled the priests not only to put aside their newly-made wives but to confess publicly that they had been living in adultery; and Elizabeth also refused to legalize the marriage of priests but overlooked the practice when it occurred. At any rate, the question was greatly debated at the time and has place in many of the domestic books, as well as being the entire subject matter of considerable other writing. But as this dispute is somewhat aside from our real interest, we cannot stop for further discussion of it.

The attitudes of the opposing parties in this question originated in their different conceptions of the marriage state, which affected all later writing in the field, the Puritans following the German ideas, and the Church of England those of Catholicism. The supporters of the latter, although they extolled marriage at great length, took the attitude that it was a kind of necessary evil for the propagation of the race; the Puritans, on the other hand, regarded it rather as an honorable and natural society of man and woman, of which children were the proper result but not the prime cause. We find the new attitude in the writings of both Tindale and Coverdale, but Becon, writing about 1562, seems to be the first to point out the difference between the orthodox and the radical conceptions.[1] After extolling the dignity and honor of the marriage state and lamenting the abuses which it had suffered, he says:

"But amonge all these aduersaries and enemies of Matrimonye, the Romanishe Bishoppe . . . maye not be passed ouer with silence: whiche . . . hathe moste filthely corrupted, mangled and defiled all the misteries of God, of his holy worde, and blessed Sacramentes: yet the moste holy state of godly Matrimony hathe he moste vilely and moste wickedly enbased, caste downe and made almoste of no reputation. No Turke, no Jewe, no Saracen, no Infidell, no Ethnycke, no Heathē, no Miscraūt, no, no Devill hath at any time so vilely and so wickedly taughte and written of this blessed state of honorable wedlocke: as thys wicked Bishop of Rome and his adherentes have done." [2]

Although Becon's language here may seem a little extreme, he had good grounds for his statements. The early church fathers were almost unanimous in their condemnation of marriage,[3] and even when the purity of it was admitted,

[1] This difference of attitude toward marriage accounts to a large extent for the difference in the way woman was regarded, the Puritan conception being much the higher. See below, pp. 170–171.

[2] Becon, *Boke of Matrimony*, in *Worckes*, Pt. I, f. cccccIxxv. The evidence in proof of these statements, as Becon says in another place, "woulde not a litle not only corrupt the ayre but also offend the eares and myndes of the godly readers." Becon's own ideas of marriage are given below, pp. 126–127.

[3] Milton says on this point: "It was for many ages that marriage lay in disgrace with most of the ancient doctors, as a work of the flesh, almost a defilement, wholly denied to priests, and second time dis-

it was with a tone of apology or depreciation. The words of St. Paul, "It is better to marry than to burn," expressed the usual justification for marriage, when one was given. St. Augustine could justify it only for the propagation of the race. Tertullian, a married man himself, went so far as to proclaim that marriage must be eschewed although the race perished in consequence. During the sixteenth and seventeenth centuries, the attitude of the Church of England was exactly that expressed in the LeGrand-Caxton book: marriage was for three causes, — first and most important, the begetting of children, second, the avoidance of carnal sin, and third, mutual help and comfort. Catholics, in their turn, were quite ready to condemn the Puritan ideas. The Council of Trent anathematized those who claimed that "the marriage state is to be placed above the state of viginity, or of celibacy, and that it is not better and more blessed to remain in virginity, or celibacy, than to be united."[1] In England we find similar expression. Nicholas Harpsfield, writing in Queen Mary's time of conditions under Edward VI, says: "Then was the heretic Jovinian's old lesson renewed that the religious and virginal chaste life and the life of married men should be alike rewarded. Then were Wicliff's pestilent heresies concerning marriage revived. . . . And it was one of the errors and heresies of John Wicliffe . . . for the marriages of priests and other religious persons, which were made lawful by

suaded to all, as he who reads Tertullian or Jerom may see at large." *Prose Works*, I, 344.

[1] For references to books on this subject and brief notes thereupon, see Howard, I, 329. John Donne says that the Catholic teachers "injure the whole state of Christianity, when they oppose marriage and chastity as though they were incompatible, and might not consist together." *Works*, IV, 22. He also discusses at some length the attitudes of Catholic and Protestant churches in Sermons LXXXI and LXXXII, *ibid.*

act of parliament."[1] Similarly, even as late as the reign of James I, when the marriage of priests was again permitted by law, a writer makes the statement, "Heluidius stands condemned by S. Hierome and the other Catholike Doctors, for equalling the merit of marriage, with the merit of virginitie, which heretical doctrine all the Doctors of Protestancie do also eagerly maintaine."[2]

The books which follow Coverdale's up to the middle of the seventeenth century, are almost entirely from the Puritans, who, being the aggressors in the general reform controversy, maintained their cause against the established and royally-protected church only by continued agitation. In the domestic books, however, there is little controversial writing, this being confined almost entirely to the question of divorce, as before noted. Indeed, we find that from this time on less and less attention is given to the legal and ceremonial aspects of marriage, and that the social or household side of it is more and more developed, until in such books as *Carters Christian Commonwealth,* Gouge's *Domestical Duties,* and others, the former subject is either omitted altogether or but very slightly touched upon. The tendency of the Puritans to ignore or to avoid discussion of the annulment of marriage through impediments, also lessened the attention to the legal side of marriage by removing the largest field for explanation and debate that had ever encumbered the question.

The cause of the Puritan writing seems to have been more a sincere effort to reform the evil practices of the time than a desire to wage a war of words upon the Church of England, although the latter element contributed. It is diffcult to tell from the writings of religious persons, especially from those of the straight-laced Puritans, just what the social

[1] Harpsfield, *Pretended Divorce,* p. 274.

[2] O. A., *The Uncasing of Heresie,* p. 49.

conditions of England were; but it seems pretty clear that marriage was not looked upon then as it is now as the pleasantest and most profitable form of life. There were several causes for this. First, a marriage was seldom of the young people's making, but was arranged and often performed for them by their parents before they came to years of discretion and many times while they were infants in arms, as has been already shown.[1] The family books all contain a discussion of whether or not children should marry without their parents' consent, and are pretty well agreed that they should not, even though they were of age. Through contracts foolishly made by children or ambitiously made for them by their parents, much unhappiness and many unsuitable marriages occurred. Thus, the marriage state itself was actually, on the average, not nearly so happy as it is today. Secondly, according to orthodox ideas and teaching, married life was worldly and imperfect at best; and from the point of view of public opinion, a single life of immorality was not only not condemned in the slightest, but was openly extolled; so that between church and laity, marriage had little ground to stand on as a worthy institution. Thirdly, if we may judge from the entire literature of the period, except that based on the ideals of the Italian Renaissance, woman, either by nature or training or both, was not a little inferior to man; so that the average man preferred an occasional mistress to a permanent wife.[2]

Passages illustrative of these points may be found in practically all the domestic books of the time, as well as in other writing. One author, candidly comparing married and single life, says:

"He therefore that would know the difference betwixt the married, and the single life, shall neither finde the one to be absolute good, nor the other to be altogether euill: but herein he shall

[1] See above, p. 14, ff.

[2] For discussion of this point, see below, Chap. V.

see the difference chiefely to consist, that the inconueniences of the one may be remedied when a man wil, the miseries of the other remaine vncurable; which as they are many, so it is not possible to recken them vp." [1]

Becon, both in the preface written for Coverdale's book and in his own *Boke of Matrimony*, devotes a good deal of space to existing conditions. We have already noted his ideas on the influence of the Catholic Church.[2] On the results of the forced marriages among noblemen's children, he has the following interesting passage:

"This kinde of marryeng hath euer bene detested. . . . And not without a cause. For whan they come once vnto the perfection of age, and see other whome they coulde finde in theyr harte to fansie and loue better, than many of them beginne to hate one another . . . and curse theyr parentes euen vnto the pitte of hel for the coupling of them together. Than seeke they all means possible to bee diuorced one from another. But if it bee so, that they remayne styll together, what frowning, ouerwharting, scolding, and chiding, is there betwene them, so that the whole house is filled full of those tragedies eue vnto the toppe. . . . What a wycked and hellyke life is this! The baser sorte of people seeth this vnquiet life, that is vsed among the Gentilmen and theyr wyues, . . . than go they home, and if anye thinge (bee it neuer so lytle) displeaseth them, streight they are together by the eares with their wiues, so that shortly after the whole towne is in a rore. . . . What is the orygynall cause of all these tragicall and bloudy dissencions, but only the couetous affection of those parentes whyche for lucres sake so wickedly bestow theyr children in theyr youth and yoke them with such as they can not favoure in theyr age." [3]

[1] *A Discovrse of the Married and Single Life*, f. A8 *b*.

[2] See above, p. 121.

[3] Becon, *Worckes*, Pt. I, f. cccccl xiiii. Compare the sentiment expressed in *How a Man may Choose a Good Wife*, I, 1:

> "This 'tis to marry children when they're young,
> I said as much at first, that such young brats
> Would 'gree together e'en like dogs and cats."

Bullinger, on the immorality of the time, says:

"Amonge other greuous synnes & shameles blasphemies/ which in this last euell and perelous tyme haue sore increaced (helas therfore) & preuayled into a great nõbre. This is not the leest. I meane aduoutrye with shameles whordome/ and all maner of unclẽnesse in vayne wordes and unchaist workes. All this now commeth/ because that such vyces beare nomore theyr owne right names/ and therfore doth no man esteme them as they are in them selues and in the sight off God. The bloudy murtherer . . . is called a good bold mã of his handes. . . . To be dronkẽ/ is to be mery/ To commytte whordome/ is called as much as to exercise the worke of a man. . . . To cast our vnclenly wordes/ and to synge vayne songes off ribawdry/ is called good pastyme. yee in many places (the more pite) it is come so farre/ that these & such like vyces are coũted no synne/ nether is ther any thyng rekened for synne in a maner saue onely to talke of god and his trueth."[1]

Becon, in his point of view toward marriage, seems to be the most modern and least sordid of all the religious writers. His definition of the institution comes like a breath of fresh air into a cattle shed.

"[Matrimony is] an hie, holye and blessed order of life, ordayned not of man, but of God, . . . wherein one man and one woman are coupled and knit together in one fleshe and body in the feare and loue of God, by the free, louinge, harty, and good consente of

[1] Bullinger, *Christen state*, "Author to Reader," ¶ 1. This condition of immorality continued long after Elizabeth's time. Thomas Heywood, writing in 1624, says, "It followes next in course, that I should define vnto you, what these prostitutes and common women are; but what need I trouble my selfe so farre, when in these corrupt daies almost euerie Boy of fifteene or sixteen yeres old, knowes what a strumpet is, better by his own practise than I can illustrate to him by all my reading." *History concerninge Women*, p. 287. Similar passages may be found in other books, such as Barnaby Rich's *Faults, Faults* and *Roome for a Gentleman*, Stubbes' *Anatomie of Abuses*, etc.

them both, to the entent that they two may dwel together, as one fleshe and body of one wyl and mynd in all honesty, vertue and godliness, and spend theyr lyues in equal partaking of all such thinges as god shal send them with thankes geuynge." [1]

This is the key-note of Becon's *Boke of Matrimony*, a work of 115 folio pages, published about 1562.[2] He had already considered matrimony and family life to some extent in his *Catechism*, a voluminous treatise on almost every phase of human existence,[3] and had touched upon the duties of the various members of the family in his *Principles of Christian Religion*. Considerable attention is given in the *Catechism* to the conduct of men in different walks of life — landowners, rich men, servants, beggars, and men of the various professions — and also to household affairs, in which the duties of husbands, wives, parents, children, widows, young men, maidens, servants, and old people, are considered in some detail. The household instruction occupies fifty-eight pages in the *Catechism*, whereas, in the *Boke of Matrimony*, it is reduced to just about half, the reader being referred to the earlier treatment.

[1] Becon, *op. cit.*, f. DCxvi. Compare this with Milton's definition: "Marriage is a divine institution, joining man and woman in a love fitly disposed to the helps and comforts of domestic life." *Prose Works*, II, 143. Milton had already said, "God in the first ordaining of marriage taught us to what end he did it . . . to comfort and refresh him [man] against the evil of solitary life, not mentioning the purpose of generation till afterwards, as being but a secondary end in dignity, though not in necessity." *Ibid.*, I, 343.

[2] No one seems to have made any attempt to ascertain the dates of Becon's different works. The earliest extant edition of the *Boke of Matrimony*, which was written during his prolonged illness, seems to be that contained in his *Worckes*, published in 1564.

[3] The catechism was a very popular form of instruction book in this period, and all of them contain points of interest. The instruction, however, was almost entirely religious, and seldom descended to everyday life sufficiently to give us information on the practices of the time.

The *Boke of Matrimony* we may take as our typical domestic book in its completest and best balanced form. It is divided into four parts: (1) the excellence and dignity of marriage, (2) what matrimony is, from different standpoints, (3) for what it was instituted, (4) the conduct of the family. Internally, each part is not so well balanced, but a proper sense of proportion seems to have been universally lacking in writers of these books. The only one of the four parts which I have not treated to some extent already, is that on family life. We may consider it a fair representative of like discussions in other domestic books. Indeed, the similarity of all such treatises is so great that one wonders what moved the different writers to repeat over and over that which had been said so often before. Speaking generally, we may say that, except for greater detail or more extensive illustration, the household section of the domestic book remained the same in content and point of view from start to finish, and that to read one is to read all. The reason for this is obvious: the original authority, that is the Bible, was the same for all, and no controversy of interpretation had arisen in this field among the fathers of the church. Without clinging too closely to Becon's arrangement of his material, we may summarize this section of the typical book as follows: (1) mutual duties of husband and wife — to love each other, to beget children, to live chaste; (2) duties of husband to wife — to act as guide, philosopher, and friend, to provide for her, to defend and help her; (3) duties of wife to husband — to serve him in subjection, to be modest in speech and apparel, to have charge of the house and its management; (4) duties of parents to children — to bring them up in godly wise, to settle them in an occupation and in marriage; (5) duties of children to parents — to be subject and obedient; (6) duties of masters and mistresses to servants — to protect and be kind to them; (7) duties of servants — to be obedient and faithful. In some books, the discussion of domestic relations is more full than this, there being in addition special chapters on maids, widows, and stepmothers. The woman usually receives the greater part of the instruction, in accordance with the popular principle of the time that she was, as Touchstone said, "an ill-favored thing but mine own," or, as R. C. put it, "though she be by nature weaker than he [the husband], yet she is an excellent instrument for him."

III. Later Domestic Books

For the light they throw on Milton and on the early seventeenth century writers in general, it seems worth while to trace the course of the domestic conduct books as far as 1643, although, as I have already stated, they show very little development during this time. By way of preface to this period, it may be well to remark that both new books and new editions of the old continue without break, and, excepting a very few,[1] without any effects from other literary influences. One would expect that the two types of Italian book illustrated by the *Principe* and the *Cortegiano* would have exerted a strong influence in our field; but, although both of these works were translated and imitated in the period, they do not seem to have affected the domestic book as a whole in the slightest, and although they were popular among aristocratic circles, it is doubtful if they were read by our authors.

The eighth and ninth decades of the sixteenth century witnessed a considerable amount of publication in the field of domestic literature. James Chillester's translation of Boaistuau's French rendition of the Latin work of Tigu-

[1] These are treated separately later on, pp. 140–141, 143–144. See also Chap. VI.

rinus Chelidonius, under the title *A most excellent Historie of . . . Christian Princes*, in 1571, concludes with a chapter on marriage and shows a combination of the interest of the family book and the book of the *Principe* type. John Fit Jonn's *A Diamonde Most precious*, in 1577, "Instructing all Maysters and Seruaunts how they ought to leade their lyues," touches only one side of the domestic book. Somewhat longer and more inclusive works are: Dudley Fenner's *The Order of Household*,[1] in 1584, *The Schoole of Beastes*, translated by J. B. from the French of Pierre Viret, one of the French-Swiss Reformers, in 1585, Hans Dekin's translation in c. 1588 of Herman V's handbook for his people under the title *A briefe and plaine declaration of the duety of maried folkes, etc.*, *The Housholders Philosophie*, translated by Thomas Kyd in 1588 from the Italian of the poet Tasso, the anonymous *A Display of Duty*, in 1589, and three apparently non-extant books, R. W.'s *Order of Matrimony*, in 1580, S. S.'s *Brief Instructions for Families*, in 1583, and Charles Gibbon's *Compendius Form of Domestical Duties*, in 1589.[2] All of these are rather small books (except, perhaps, the non-extant ones), and contain nothing new in the way of subject matter.[3]

Two books of this time devoted entirely to the relations

[1] This forms the third part of Fenner's *The Artes of Logike and Rhetorike*.

[2] The last three titles are taken from Watt, who also mentions *A Modest Means to Marry*, translated in 1568 by N. Leigh from the Latin of Erasmus. I can find no other reference to Leigh anywhere, and no such book by Erasmus ever seems to have been heard of.

[3] The fact that several of these books are translations from continental works, may seem to invalidate what has been said of the lack of external influences upon the English domestic book; but it must be noted that these are not only small and ephemeral in themselves but also that they do not seem to have influenced in turn the later and more important books of the type.

of parents and children are *The Christian man's Closet*, translated in 1581 from the Latin of Bartholomew Batty by William Lowth, and *A Bartholmew Fairing for Parentes* by John Stockwood in 1589. The former is in the form of a dialogue between three men and a woman, and treats pretty thoroughly of the upbringing, education, and duties of children. Stockwood's book is concerned entirely with the marriage of children, in which he claims, on Biblical authority, that they should submit entirely to their parents' dictates.

"The question here [he says] is not, what children in regarde either of age or wit are able for to doo but what God hath thought meet & expediēt. . . . For there are many children found sometimes far to exceede their fathers in wit and in wisedome, yea and in al other gifes both of mind & body, yet is this no good reason that they should take vpon them their fathers authoritie." [1]

Such was the logic of the time.

The books between 1570 and 1590, it may be noticed, are all rather brief and not in any sense as weighty as either Bullinger's or Becon's. In the next decade, however, we find several of both length and thoroughness. The first is William Perkins' *Christian Oeconomie*, written in Latin in 1590 and translated by Thomas Pickering in 1609. Perkins was a man of both sense and learning, and his book is one of the best planned, best balanced, most practical, and most informing of the whole series. In the table of contents to his *The Golden Chain*, "oeconomics," or family government, is described as one of the sacred sciences which are "handmaids to the Science of Theology"; and this represents his attitude to his subject, which he treats from a reasonable

[1] Stockwood, *op. cit.*, p. 82. Stockwood says further that marriages made by children without parental consent were legally void. He is wrong here, unless he means only children under age.

and charitable point of view rather than from the dogmatic attitude of the textuists. Marriage is first explained and extolled; then the legal aspects are discussed, with a consideration of what persons are fitted to marry and what forms should be gone through with; and lastly the relations and duties of the members of the household are concisely set forth.[1] All things considered, this book is far more satisfactory than any of its predecessors. It is of convenient length for practical use, being 175 pages, and it impresses the reader as presenting the true conditions of the time without any attempt to further the views of any one sect.

Two other good books appeared about the same time. One was *A Preparative to Mariage,* in 1591, by Henry Smith, whom Brook calls "the first preacher in the nation." According to the title page, this treatise was developed from a marriage sermon. It discusses most of the usual points but is poorly proportioned and absolutely without order or arrangement. Domestic relations are summarized thus:

> "The dueties of marriage may be reduced to the dueties of man and wife one toward another, and their duties towarde theyr Children, and their dueties towarde their seruants. For themselues, sayeth one,[2] they must thinke themselues like two birdes, the one is the Cocke and the other is the Dam: the Cocke flieth abroad to bring in, and the Dam sitteth vpon the nest to keepe all at home . . . for the mans pleasure is most abroad and the womans within."[3]

The other book, which is quite similar on the whole to those of Perkins and Smith, is *A Godly Form of Hovseholde Gouernement,* by R. C. [Robert Cleaver?], in 1598 and republished in 1600, 1603, 1612, and 1630. This book, the writer says,

[1] The table of contents of this book is given in Appendix D, below.

[2] This story occurs also in Dekyn's book, f. B8 *b*, and may have been taken from it.

[3] Smith, *op. cit.*, p. 46.

is partly original and partly gathered from preceding works. Its various sources are unimportant, but even a casual reader will notice that whole passages are lifted from Smith's *Preparative.* R. C.'s was the longest book yet written, running to 392 pages, but its material is poorly arranged. The point of view is, on the whole, broad and lenient. Of family government, it is said:

"A wise husband, and one that seeketh to liue in quiet with his wife, must obserue these three rules. Often to admonish: Seldome to reprooue: and neuer to smite her. . . . The husband is also to vnderstand, that as God created the womā, not of the head, & so equall in authoritie with her husband: so also he created her not of Adams foote, that she should be troden downe and despised, but he tooke her out of the ribbe, that shee might walke ioyntly with him, vnder the conduct and gouernment of her head." [1]

Three other works may be briefly dismissed. Charles Gibbon's *A Work worth the Reading,* in 1591, has two chapters on the relations of parents and children, but as a whole is not a domestic book. In his discussion of the marriage of children, Gibbon upholds the belief that the affections of the children should be of more weight than the wishes of the parents. The anonymous *Order of Household Instruction,* in 1596, seems to be non-extant.[2] There is a very brief treatise, *Duties of Husband and Wife,* undated, annexed to R. C.'s *Godly Form* and perhaps written by him, but it is of no importance.[3]

[1] R. C., *op. cit.*, p. 201. The same statement and illustration, in somewhat different wording, occurs in Perkins' *Christian Oeconomie,* p. 125, in Griffeth's *Bethel,* p. 289, in the anonymous *A Curtaine Lecture,* p. 170, and in one of Donne's sermons, *Works,* IV, 29, where it is attributed to St. Jerome. So much sameness of subject matter and treatment is there in these family books.

[2] It is mentioned by Watt.

[3] The book *Of Mariage and Wiuing,* a controversy between Tasso, the poet, and his cousin Hercules, the philosopher, translated into

The course of the domestic book during the first half of the seventeenth century is somewhat obscured by the many contemporary works of various kindred types all centering around the subjects of marriage, married life, and divorce. Some of these have already been mentioned in preceding chapters, and others will be taken up later; but all such must be omitted for the present in order that we may follow our narrow stream into the larger and more confused current. As suggested above, these other influences seem to have left the narrower stream unaffected.

The family books of this period contain practically the same subject matter as their forerunners, except for the omission or curtailing of the discussion of the entrance into matrimony, and approach the subject, on the whole, in much the same way. It will be sufficient, therefore, to pass them by in review as briefly as possible. Swinburne's *Treatise of Spousals*, already referred to many times, was written about 1600, but as it treats of spousals only, further mention of it is unnecessary. William Vaughan's *The Golden Grove*, 1599, republished in 1608, contains one section on marriage. Beside the usual contents, Vaughan presents a new classification of marriage, according to which he represents it as being of four kinds: (1) of honor, that is, between man and God, as in the case of the Virgin Mary with the Holy Ghost or of Christ with the church; (2) of love, that is, the union of an honest man and an honest woman; (3) of toil, in the case where a man chooses a woman for her riches only; (4) of grief, the union of two wicked persons.[1] Joseph Hall's *Salomons Diuine Arts*, in 1609, devotes one section to oeconomics or household government, in which he discusses family affairs, omitting mar-

English by R. T. in 1599, can hardly be classified with the family books. For further notice of it, see below, p. 144.

[1] A similar classification is made in Griffeth's *Bethel*, p. 255 ff.

riage itself altogether, by stringing texts together, with words of his own interpolated, in a style unequaled by Sancho Panza.[1] It contains nothing of interest. In 1610, Edward Topsell published a volume of three sermons entitled *The House-holder,* in which he says in the preface "are many sweet flowers, many profitable trees or Plantes, and many faire growing seeds." The last sermon contains some instruction of a definite kind, particularly for farm life; the others are merely moral discourses. Robert Snawsel's *A Looking Glasse for maried Folkes,* in 1610, a dialogue between four women and one man, is almost as good as a play and has real literary qualities, but its purpose seems to be utilitarian rather than artistic. Its entire subject matter is the relationship which should exist between man and wife, especially the treatment that wives owe their husbands. A book concerned altogether with the relations of parent and child was translated by John Budden in 1614 from the French of Peirre Ayrault, under the title of *A Discovrse for Parents Honour and Authoritie.* In this, the opposite view is taken from Gibbon's, as the author, in a kind of supplication of distressed parents, argues that in the question of their marriage, children should have nothing to say whatever.

The book of domestic duties reached its culmination in the second quarter of the seventeenth century. Although the household alone had previously been made the subject

[1] The following description of the scarlet woman is too good to lose: "By the abundance of the sweetnesse of her speech (Pr. 7. 21) shee caused him to yeeld: and with the flatterie of her lippes she intised him; and straight wayes hee followes her as an oxe goeth to the slaughter (Pr. 7. 22) and as a foole to the stockes for correction (Pr. 7. 23) till a dart strike through his liuer, the seate of his lust: or as a birde hasteneth to the snare, and knoweth not that it is against his owne life: thus shee doeth and when her husband returnes, shee wipeth her mouth and saith, I haue not committed iniquitie." *Op. cit.,* p. 158.

of several works, these were for the most part very slight. At this time, however, we have a number of important books, some of which we must consider for a moment at least. These are: William Whately's *A Bride-bush*, 1619 and 1623, Alexander Niccholes' *A Discovrse of Marriage and Wiving*, 1620; William Gouge's *Domestical Duties*, second edition in 1626, third in 1634 [1]; *Carters Christian Commonwealth*, by Thomas Carter, 1627; Matthew Griffeth's *Bethel*, 1633; Daniel Touteville's *Saint Paul's Threefold Cord*, 1635; the anonymous *A Curtaine Lecture*, 1637; Daniel Rogers' *Matrimoniall Honovr*, 1642; William Dyke's *A Discourse on Matrimony*, 1642; and Thomas Page's *Demonstration of Family Duties*, 1643. The last two seem to be non-extant.[2] Niccholes' and Touteville's we may also drop without further notice, as they contain nothing of interest. Carter's book, bearing the subtitle of *Domesticall Dutyes deciphered*, a treatise of 275 pages, is on the family alone, taking up in separate chapters the duties of husbands, wives, parents, children, masters, and servants. Whately's book is concerned entirely with the duties of husband and wife, which are divided into the greater and the lesser, the classification being based on whether or not the failure in any one was sufficient cause for divorce. This book, 220 pages in length, is perhaps the most thorough of all as far as it goes, but it is evident that it covers but one phase of family life. Besides its thoroughness, it has the merits of being excellently planned and written from the point of view of practical common sense rather than from the authority of the Bible and the classics.

[1] I am unable to ascertain the date of the first edition.

[2] Dyke's book is mentioned by the *Stationers' Register*, Feb. 25, Page's by Watt. Another book, *A Discovrse of the Married and Single Life*, anonymous, 1621, is merely a coarse and silly diatribe against women.

Gouge's *Domestical Duties* and Griffeth's *Bethel: or, Forme for Families* may fairly be said to exhaust all previous sources and authorities in their treatment of family life. Both are large works, the former running to 368 folio pages, and the latter to 528 pages quarto. Although both are chiefly concerned with the domestic side of marriage, there is a discussion in each of the contract of matrimony from a practical standpoint. The impediments are confined by both writers to the Levitical degrees, but Gouge strongly condemns the marriage of impotent or diseased persons. He also states that divorce is allowable for adultery and for desertion due to religious differences; Griffeth condemns adultery and other vices but does not touch the subject of divorce. A short consideration of the double standard of morality occurs in both books, in which the authors agree that faithlessness on the part of the wife causes greater evils to the family; but on the magnitude of the sin itself, they disagree, Gouge holding that it is the same for both sexes and Griffeth maintaining that the woman sins the more. Gouge's book is superior in both arrangement and general treatment, and is further enhanced by a table of contents, an index, and cross references. The first part, comprising one fourth of the whole, is an exposition of those parts of the Scriptures from which the later teachings of the book are drawn, and obviates the overloading of the following sections with Biblical texts, a fault which is only too noticeable in Griffeth's work. Moreover, like the books by Perkins and Whately, it is most sensibly written and argued, and impresses one as being based not only on the Scriptures but also on the practices and thought of the time, whereas Griffeth's work resembles more some of the previous hashings and rehashings of ancient dogma. For the word *Bethel* on the title page, Griffeth substitutes *God's building* in the body of his book; and it is his intention to show how a family should be constructed into some such form. Gouge, on the other hand, is more concerned with giving practical instructions for family life along the best human lines.[1]

Daniel Rogers' *Matrimoniall Honovr* is interesting for several reasons. It was written by a minister of the Church of England; like Gouge's book, it is an exposition of life rather than the Scriptures; it is extremely human in its attitude, kindly towards the much abused weaknesses of mankind, and respectful towards people whose beliefs differed from the author's own. Were it not for the fact that it covers but a small part of the field, although 389 pages in length, it would surely outrank all others of the type. Rogers discusses only two main subjects, the honor of matrimony and the duties of husband and wife, but digresses at times to speak of parental consent to child marriages, of contracts of marriage, and, in an appendix, of chastity and the lack of it. The chapter on contracts contains much information, but nothing that has not been already noted, except that on the subject of the marriage of cousins germain, the writer says: "I observe of late time many more Divines to encline to the affirmative, then formerly have done; and some of them . . . that they do write for it, and have determined the marriages of some in this way."[2] Rogers himself upholds the Levitical degrees but does not mention other impediments. Divorce and the annulment of marriage are not discussed at all. The book is particularly free from Scriptural references (there is about one per page) and even more so from allusions to the classics and the church fathers. On the whole, the style is the most pleasing and the least pedantic of all

[1] In order that the reader may have a complete idea of the domestic book, I give in Appendix D, below, outlines of the contents of those by Perkins, Gouge, and Griffeth.

[2] Rogers, *op. cit.*, p. 111.

the books we have considered. At times there is real beauty of a naive kind, as in the passages already quoted [1] or in the following one on the "gracefullness" of the wife:

"Let thy pleasing influence breake through all opposition and sorrowes, as the Sunne breakes through the thick mist, or darke cloudes, yea although eclipsed in part, yet shine in part, and let a glimmering appeare; remember, thou art a true friend, made for the day of adversity. . . . Every base bird (while summer lasts) will chirp and chitter: But to sing upon a bare bow, or thorne bush, when the leaves are gone, and the cold winter approacheth, this argues a wife truely gracefull, truly amiable and cheerfull, and (next to the Soule's peace with God) is the greatest content under the Sunne." [2]

IV. The Domestic Book as Literature

As has already been intimated, the domestic book is utilitarian rather than literary, and whenever a passage of some artistic merit occurs, such as the one just quoted from Rogers, it is, like water in the desert, refreshing but seemingly out of place. A few sporadic works make usefulness subservient to art; but before mentioning these, it will be well to note the stylistic features of the more typical book.

Perhaps the most noticeable of these is the use of Biblical texts and Biblical, ecclesiastical, and classical authority and illustration. In Fenner's *Order of Household,* texts occupy more space than the explanation of them; on the other hand, some books are almost free from texts as well as from precepts and anecdotes from the classics and church fathers. A generous sprinkling of all three is found on the average page, the proportion depending on whether the writer is accustomed to argue on the basis of authority and precedent or on that of common sense and expediency.

[1] See above, pp. 90–91.

[2] Rogers, *op. cit.*, p. 315.

Many writers vary the monotony of their prose by introducing verses translated from Greek and Latin authors. The translations are usually clumsy, but occasionally there is one with considerable naive grace.[1] For illustration, writers went also to the animal world. Viret, for example, in *The Schoole of Beastes,* draws all his lessons in household economy from this source, which he divides into three species, — (1) ants, conies, grasshoppers, and spiders; (2) pigeons, swallows, partridges, hares, and hedgehogs; (3) the Halsion (a "Byrde of the Sea"), "phyces," the lamprey, the tortoise, the sea-calf, and the crocodile. Much of this pseudo-naturalism, like Lyly's, is taken over from classical sources, Ovid being a favorite. The amount of such illustrations, like that from the Scriptures and the classics, varies greatly, in some books being practically absent altogether. The more ecclesiastical writers preferred to take examples from their own stock in trade.

The dialogue form was employed to add variety, which it usually failed to do, inasmuch as the writer, without changing his character or point of view, merely shouted through different masks. This was not so in every case, but at best the debate resolved itself into a puppet show in which the author pulled all the strings. In only one or two instances is the nature of these dialogues taken from the Italian *conversazione.* The devise is, of course, much older than the Italian Renaissance, having come into England through the classical dialogue and the French débat and more directly at this time through the dialogues of the church fathers. The former, especially the dialogues of Plato, Cicero, and Seneca, was, I think, a greater influence among these books than either the older French or English

[1] Viret, *Schoole of Beastes,* Niccholes, *Discovrse of Marriage and Wiving,* and Heywood, *History concerninge Women,* contain some of the best of these.

or the contemporary Italian. The similarity to the classic type is seen in the use of various speakers merely to draw out the opinion of the one man who leads the discussion and who alone has any character or anything to say. Thus the style failed to be affected to any extent by the device, and remained practically the same as when the writer spoke in his own character without taking the trouble to dodge about in different make-ups. The only really successful exception to this, outside of those where the purpose of the work is avowedly artistic rather than utilitarian, is Snawsel's *Looking Glasse for maried Folkes,* where each speaker has a distinct character and distinct ideas. A passage on the proper way for a wife to treat her husband may be worth quoting:

> "Eulalie [the well-spoken]. When he lookt at any time very sad, & there were no fit time to speak to him, I would not thē laugh & daily with him, and play the tom-boy . . . but I put vpon me a sad countenance, and lookt heauily. . . . So it beseemes an honest wife to frame herselfe to her husbands affections. . . And if at any time he were stird, I would either pacify him, with a gentle speech, or giue way to his wrath. . . . This course also I tooke; if he came drunken home, I would not then for anything haue giuē him a foule word, but I would cause his bed to be made very soft and easie, that he might sleepe the better, and by faire speeches get him to it.
>
> "Margerie [a proud malapert]. Here are fetters for the legs, and yoakes for the neckes of women: must they crouch on this manner to their currish and swinish husbands? If I had such an one, as he behaued himselfe like a swine, so would I use him like a beast." [1]

When the writer faced a real rather than an imaginary opponent, his style was likely to become much more vivacious; but this seldom took place in these books. The Church

[1] Snawsel, *op. cit.*, f. D *b*.

of Rome was the usual opponent when there was one, but the lack of personality and personal criticism in this case rendered opposition to it much less vigorous than other contemporary writing of more truly controversial nature.

As a rule, then, the style of the domestic book is pretty flat, pedantic, heavy. It reminds one of the atmosphere of a Puritan household: the author or father is tremendously serious, texts fly about, the fate of the family seems to hang momentarily in the balance, now and then there is a sally at those who would take Sunday to walk in the Mall, less often a softening of tone over some remembered incident; but on the whole life is earnest, if not real, for this household; God is watching overhead ready to descend in his wrath at the first slip by any one of its members from the narrow path, and the devil is waiting in ambush hoping to trip the unwary.

As I have already indicated, there grew up no literary genre on the subject of matrimony. Books in which the characters happen to be married, more general works on morals and conduct, and plays dealing with the subject, are not to be classified here. The residue are few in number, scattered as to date, and, except for a few satires, seem to have neither mutual relations nor common ancestry. Nevertheless, these should be mentioned briefly before we leave the field altogether.

As early as Middle English times, we find the subject of marriage entering literary fields. Passing by such allegorical poems as the *Wohing of ure Laverde,* which deal with the old idea of the marriage of Christ and the church, we find more than incidental interest in the subject shown in the story of Meed in *Piers the Plowman.* The treatment here, however, is too general to merit more attention. Chaucer makes considerable capital of marital affairs, and a number of the *Canterbury Tales* seem to have been designed to set forth the different contemporary points of view towards married life and the character of the married woman. The Prologue to the Wife of Bath's Tale, which introduces the group, is especially noticeable for its satire of the ecclesiastical attitude towards the institution. Barclay, in his *Ship of Fools,* devotes a few sections to the various evil practices connected with marriage, but these do not form any distinct part of the larger work. For over half a century after this, the subject occurs only in verse satires and as an incidental interest in other literary works — the drama for instance. The former are altogether on the hardships of married life and emphasize the evils suffered by one party from the brutishness of the other.[1] John Heywood's *A dialogue . . . concernynge two maner of maryages,* in 1561, alone shows a serious interest in the subject. Here, in a one-sided dialogue between a young man and an old, the latter, in recounting the history of two marriages — one of an impecunious but loving couple, the other of a poor young man and a rich old widow — shows the ill fate of both unions. It is in four-stress verse, irregular and uneven, rhymed in couplets. The most interesting literary feature of it is the use of old saws, of which it is a veritable storehouse. Tilney's *Flower of Friendship* shows very strongly the Italian influence, and is the most successful English court of love *conversazione* that I have seen. There were two editions in 1568 and another in 1571. This book, by Edward Tilney, afterwards Master of Revels to Queen Elizabeth, is a close imitation of the *Cortegiano.* The title signifies marital love, which Tilney understands to be literally the flower of friendship. In the first day's discussion, Master Pedro leads the dialogue, which turns upon how a husband should preserve this flower. On the second day, Lady Julia, who has been replaced by Aloisa

[1] For further account of these, see p. 163 ff. below.

as queen, leads a discourse on the duties of a wife. Vives and Erasmus are introduced as interlocutors, but neither has much to say. On the whole, the dialogue falls short of Castiglione's in having less exchange of opinion and less repartee and in the absence of the wisdom of a Bembo. A book by Tasso, translated by Thomas Kyd in 1588[1] under the title of *The Housholders Philosophie,* though similar in many ways to the *Cortegiano,* is not a conversation but a monologue in a typical Italian setting on the usual household subjects. The poet's ideal of marriage is better expressed in the dialogue with his cousin Hercules, entitled *Of Mariage and Wiuing,* which was translated by R. T. in 1599. Here, woman is apotheosized in Platonic love; marriage is apostrophized thus:

> "O sweete conioyning of loyall hearts, O dulcet union of our soules togither, O most louely nuptuall knot, O most chaste, pure and religious marriage yoake, who are rather a pleasing ease, and a most welcome delight to support and beare, then any hard weight or greeuous burthen to sustaine: rather a releeuing comfort that vpholdeth vs euery way, then a troublesome labour, that any way paineth us."

This is somewhat typical of the poet's part of the dialogue, which inclines towards cant and rhapsodizing. It is disconcerting to think that this writer was not married, and that his cousin, who villifies woman and marriage, was. Bacon wrote three essays which are worth mentioning here, *Married and Single Life, Parents and Children,* and *Friendship;* but these are too brief and empty to be of importance to us. The opening sentence from the first, "He that hath wife and children hath given hostages to fortune," is deservedly famous.

In the first half of the seventeenth century, we find more

[1] On the title page, only the initials T. K. are given, but the *Camb. Hist. Eng. Lit.,* V, 177, ascribes the translation to Kyd.

literature on the subject,[1] but still not enough to enable us to attach much importance to it. An anonymous Scottish poem, in 1603, *Ane verie excellent and delectabill Treatise intitulit Philotus*, reminds one of Heywood's dialogue. The title page gives its substance —"Qvhairin we may persave the greit inconveniences that fallis out in the Mariage betvvene age and zouth." It is a verse dialogue and may have been written as an interlude.[2] Patric Hannay's *A Happy Husband*, 1618, and R. B.'s *The Good Wife*, 1619, may be taken together.[3] Both are in verse, the former in heroic distich, well maintained, and the latter in seven-line stanzas. Both are on women, are fairly short, and are typical of the "character writing" popular at the time. The *Happy Husband* consists of two parts, directions for a maid as to how to choose a husband and her proper behavior after marriage. The poem is coupled by commendatory verses with Overbury's *A Wife*. *The Good Wife* is merely the usual description of what she should be.

Two amusing books of similar nature appeared in 1637 and 1640. The earlier is the anonymous *A Curtaine Lecture*,[4] the other is *Ar't asleepe Husband? A boulster lecture* by Richard Brathwait under the pseudonym of Philogenes Panedonius. The content of each represents what the husband has to submit to from his talkative wife after they

[1] It must be borne in mind that the divisions I am making between "literary" and "non-literary" works and between those which are on and off the subject, are purely arbitrary ones. It is impossible to divide the wheat from the tares accurately on either basis, but some attempt at classification must be adopted for obvious reasons. Books which combine the subject in hand with other interests, as well as those which but touch upon it, are discussed in Chapter VI, below.

[2] It is mentioned as such in the *Camb. Hist. Eng. Lit.*, III, 138.

[3] *The Good Wife* was contributed to the 1619 edition of the *Happy Husband*. R.B. is Richard Brathwait.

[4] The dedication of this book is signed T. H., which has been taken to stand for Thomas Heywood.

have retired for the night, but the former contains also a treatise of the ordinary kind on the duties of the wife. The frontispiece of each represents a belligerent looking wife sitting up in bed and pointing an authoritative finger at her husband, who is evidently trying to sleep. From her mouth issue the words, "*Vera praedico*," to which he replies "*Mulieri ne credas*." The second part of the *Curtaine Lecture* and the entire *Ar't asleepe Husband?* are typical jest books composed of "all variety of witty jeastes, merry tales and other pleasant passages," those of the latter claiming the classics, Ariosto, Tasso, Boccaccio, Barclay, and others as their sources. The original point of view is lost somewhere, as most of the stories are on the characteristics of womankind, particularly her failings. Most of them are fabliau and exemplum tales; often the vulgar subject matter of the former is used with the moral purpose of the latter. The dedication to *Ar't asleepe Husband?* gives promise of a style which is not fulfilled in the book but is perhaps worth quoting for itself. It is addressed by the author "To his Dainty Doxes."

"Dainty fine Creatures, — I will not sweare, in good faith you be; But — if in your censure you prove sweet to me, I little care, believe't how sowre you be. One thing I must tell you, the World ha's a strange opinion of you: But let this not trouble you: for the most of those that sojourne in it, are Walking Pictures, or Puppy Motions. So you live without Scandall, let the Constable of the Ward snore, and Diogenes walke all the night o'er with his Candle. Though he finde Works of lightnesse in Houses of Darknesse, Single Skirmishes in blinde Alleys, Backstayres and Long Entries: whole bunches of Cornucopia in his new found Europia: Cleave you like Ticks to your own, preserve your renowne, and sing Hey downe a downe, to the honour of the towne. Thus, neither to all, nor to many, but to very-very few, and those of that Crue, who are loyall and true, bids Musaeus — Adiew." [1]

[1] Brathwait, *op. cit.*, f. a3.

CHAPTER V

CONTEMPORARY ATTITUDES TOWARDS WOMAN

I. Ecclesiastical

It would be difficult to find in the whole of our period a single book of religious or moral nature touching upon woman in which it did not appear that she was, if not wholly weak and sinful, at least far inferior to man. The more lenient writers admitted that there were a few exceptions to this rule; but until Puritan ideals came to have some influence, the average characterization represented woman as at best but a "necessary evil" for the propagation of the race. "A Good Woman (as an old Philosopher observeth) is but like one Ele put in a bagge amongst 500 Snakes, and if a man should have the luck to grope out that one Ele from all the snakes, yet he hath at best *but a wet Ele by the Taile;* and he that wedds himself to one fair and dishonest, he wedds himself to a world of misery, and if one beautifull and never so Vertuous, yet let him think this he wedds but a woman, and therefore a necessary evil." Bishop Aylmer, in a sermon before Queen Elizabeth, admitted that some women were superior to some men, but claimed that the majority were far otherwise. "Women are of two sorts, some of them are wiser, better learned, discreeter, and more constant than *a number* of men; but another and a worse sort of them, and *the most part,* are fond, foolish, wanton flibbergibs, tatlers, triflers, wavering, witless, without council, feeble, careless, rash, proud, dainty, nice, talebearers, evesdroppers, rumour-raisers, evil-tongued, worse-minded, and in every way doltified with the dregs of the devil's dunghill." [1] The

[1] Neal, I, 478.

writer of the *Answer* to Milton's first divorce tract thinks to crush the argument that marriage was first constituted for "solace and comfort in gifts of the mind" by saying that if such had been the case, "then it would have been every wayes as much, yea more content and solace to Adam; and so to every man, to have had another man made to him of his Rib in stead of Eve; this is apparent by experience, which shews, that man ordinarily exceeds woman in naturall gifts of the mind." [1] The writers who take a more charitable view towards womankind usually do so in a tone of condescension resulting from a consciousness of their own superiority. "Man," says one, "hauing that diuine Image of God, and smelling something of the celestiall Carrecter of whom he tooke his beginning, is not onely dreadful to the moste furious and proudest beastes vppon earthe, but further he hath a preheminence and authoritie ouer the woman (a creature moste noble nexte to him selfe of all others)." [2]

It would take us too far afield to attempt to account for the origin of the conception of the inferiority of woman. In the history of evolution, it was doubtless the result of her physical weakness. In the sixteenth century, her mental inferiority was certainly a result, wherever it existed, of the fact that not only had the education of woman been wholly neglected in the past, but even in the so-called "woman's sphere," she was always under the authority and direction of her husband. But a still greater inferiority, or rather a belief in it, was ascribed to the sex. This was moral weakness. There can be no doubt that the belief in woman's physical and mental limitations is far older than Christianity, but that she was morally weak seems to be the particular contribution of the early church fathers to the unjust and undignified conception in which womankind

[1] *Answer to Doctrine and Discipline*, p. 12.

[2] Chelidonius, *A most excellent Hystorie*, p. 183.

was held during the middle ages and later times. This attitude is more important than may at first appear, for the judgment of the church, disseminated through at least the male portion of Europe and England, prevented any chance of the betterment of woman through education. Thus, by being thought weak and fit only to obey, she was robbed of any chance of becoming either strong or intelligent.

The causes of this belief in woman's lack of moral strength in sixteenth century England, connect very closely with the interests and movements we have been studying. These causes are two: the conception of marriage as merely a means of propagating the race and of avoiding promiscuous sexual indulgence (particularly on the man's part), and the teachings of the church — drawn chiefly from the book of *Genesis* and the apostles' commentaries thereupon — that it was the woman who by her fall first brought sin into the world.[1] It is, perhaps, hardly fair to blame the origin of these two doctrines upon the Christian church, as both existed to some extent before Christ's day; but the persistency with which the early church fathers clung to them and magnified their importance for the benefit, or detriment, of future generations, and the tenacity of the mediaeval ecclesiastics' grasp upon them, despite the fact that they are unsupported by the teachings of Christ, render their ultimate origin of little or no account.

We have already seen what was the attitude of the Roman Catholic Church towards marriage even as late as Elizabeth's time.[2] This attitude sprang from two related causes, the supposed sinfulness of marital intercourse and the evil nature of woman. St. Chrysostom speaks of woman as a "necessary evil, a natural temptation, a desirable calamity,

[1] The fact that Adam was made first and Eve second, she from Adam but he from divine materials, was also made much of in the case against woman.

[2] See above, p. 120 ff.

a domestic peril, a deadly fascination and a painted ill." [1] But if the nature of woman was one of the ills of the marriage state, conversely the low repute in which marriage was held served for centuries to tarnish the reputation of woman.

The doctrine of woman's responsibility for the existence of sin in the world was well established by Augustine's time; indeed, the book of *Genesis* would suggest that it had existed from the time of its writing, but it seems not to have been made much of until the early fathers began their textual criticism of the Bible. As a result of Eve's part in the downfall of her noble spouse, many early commentators could not conceive the possibility of her possessing a particle of the divine nature, of which Adam was the human personification; and a debate of one thousand years' duration ensued over the question of whether or not woman possessed a soul. Feminists today may congratulate themselves upon their early progenitors, for from the opening of this debate at the Council of Macon in 585, when fifty-nine bishops took part, the weight of argument seems to have continually favored the affirmative. "Christian women were therefore allowed to remain human beings in the eyes of the clergy, even though considered very weak and bad ones." [2] Although by the end of the sixteenth century, this exalted position was granted to women, they were nevertheless held firmly in leash by textual chains, as if they were a race of Amazons, who once having bested man — in the apple episode — were still likely by some Machiavellian policy to accomplish a similar *coup d'état.*

The Bible was ransacked to provide such texts. The writings of St. Paul and St. Peter proved to be the most profitable mines, the best passage of all being in St. Paul's *Epistle to Timothy.*

[1] Hill, *Women in English Life,* I, ix.

[2] Gage, *Women, Church and State,* p. 56.

"In like manner also, that women adorn themselves in modest apparel with shamefacedness and sobriety; not with broidered hair, or gold, or pearls, or costly array;

"But (which becometh women professing godliness) with good works.

"Let the woman learn in silence with all subjection.

"But I suffer not a woman to teach, nor to usurp the authority over the man, but to be in silence.

"For Adam was first formed, then Eve.

"And Adam was not deceived, but the woman being deceived was in the transgression." [1]

As a sample of what we find over and over on each of these texts and many similar ones, we may take a passage from a sermon on the last, preached by John Brinsley and afterwards published (1645) under the title of *A Looking-Glasse for Good Women.*

"*Adam was not deceived,* viz. not *immediately* by the *Serpent:* So was the *Woman* deceived, giving eare to Satan, speaking in and by the Serpent, she was deceived; but so was not *Adam* deceived: Deceived indeed he was; but it was by means of the *Woman,* handing those suggestions unto him, which she had received from the Serpent: withall, soliciting, and inticing him; to whom he yielded, partly, *Ex amicabili quadam benevolentia,* out of a loving and indulgent affection towards her, and so was overcome, even as *Sampson* was by his *Delilah* and *Solomon* by his *Wives.*

"These two last Resolutions (being in effect one and the same) we may safely pitch upon. *Adam was not deceived,* viz. so as the Woman was deceived: not *firstly,* not *immediately,* so was the Woman deceived; and being so deceived, she was the *Instrument to deceive her* Husband: So it followeth; But *The Woman being deceived, she was in the Transgression.*" [2]

[1] St. Paul, *op. cit.,* II, 9–14. The first verse still occurs in the marriage service of the Church of England. See also St. Paul, I *Cor.* II, 7, and *Ephes.* V, 22–24; and St. Peter, *First Epistle General,* III, 1.

[2] Brinsley, *op. cit.,* p. 3. This kind of stuff continues for fifty pages.

II. Domestic and Courtly

The writers of domestic books take practically the same attitude towards woman as that held by the church, and base their directions for her conduct upon ecclesiastical teachings. The most complete brief for the case of the Bible *vs.* Woman that I have seen occurs in a book of this type.

> "Two reasons [for woman's subjection to man] may be given: the one from the law of creatiō; the other from the law of Penalty, following disobedience. For the first, The man (we know) was the first created, as a perfect Creature, and not the woman with him at the same instant, as we know both sexes of all other Creatures were contemporary: not so here. But, after his constitution and frame ended, then was she thought of. Secondly, she was not made of the same matter with the man equally; but she was made and framed of the man. . . . And thirdly, she was made for the mās use and benefit, as a meet helper, when no other creature besides her was not able to do it. . . .
>
> "The second warrant hereof is penall. . . . For, since she would take upon her as a woman without respect to the order, dependence, and use of her creation, to enterprise so sad a business, as to jangle and demurre with the divell about so waighty a point as her husbands freehold, and of her own braine to lay him and it under her foot, without the least parlee and consent of his . . . so that, till she had put all beyond question, and past amendment, and eaten, she brought not the fruit to him to eate, and so, became a divell to tempt him to eate; therefore the Lord strips her of this robe of honour, accursing her with this penalty." [1]

Some writers, not being restrained by Scriptural authority, use the subject of domestic life to vent their spleen against woman. Thus we sometimes find passages such as the following: [2]

[1] Rogers, *Matrimoniall Honovr*, p. 254 ff.

[2] See also quotations below, pp. 163–164.

"Deponares hauing tasted the martirdomes of marriage, said, that there were but two good dayes in all the life of mariage, the one was the wedding day, and the other the daye that the womā dieth, for that on the day of mariage, there is made good cheare, the Bride is fresh and new, and all new things are pleasaunt. . . . The other day that he saith is good, is the daye wherein the woman dieth, for that the beast being deade, deade is the poyson, and that by the death of the woman the husband is out of bondage. In confirmation whereof, there is recited a pretie historie of a noble Romaine, who the day after his mariage . . . was verye pensiue and sorowfull, and being demaunded . . . what was ye occasion of his sorrow, seeing that his wife was so faire, rich, and come of a noble progenie: shewing them his foote, he stretcheth out his leg, saying, My friendes, my shooe is newe, faire and well made, but you know not where about it doeth hurt and grieue me." [1]

But although the woman is reminded in the domestic book of her inferiority and subserviency to her lord and master, it is always recommended that he treat her with kindness and honor. Still, even in this view of the husband's attitude, the wife's mental and moral weakness is not lost sight of. Brinsley says: "A last respect due unto the Woman in regard of her weaknesse is . . . giving honour unto her. Honour, not as from the inferior to the superior; but honour as to the weaker vessel. Which consisteth chiefly in three particulars. 1. In hiding their weaknesse. 2. In defending them against injuries. 3. In providing what is meet for them. All these wayes nature teacheth us to put honour upon the less honorable parts of the bodie, as the Apostle tells us, I *Cor*. 12.23. And all these wayes both Nature and Grace should teach Husbands to give honour to their wives." [2] In return for this good measure

[1] Bouaistuau, *Theatrum Mundi,* p. 136. The former of these stories occurs also in Nixon, *The Dignitie of Man*, p. 111; the latter in Milton, *Doctrine and Discipline, Prose Works*, II, 57.

[2] Brinsley, *A Looking-Glasse for Good Women*, p. 47.

of honor, pressed down and overflowing on three separate counts, women should look to their husbands "euermore to reuerence them, and to endeuour with true obedience and loue to serue them, to bee loath in any wise to offend them: yea, rather to bee carefull & diligent to please thē, yt their soule may blesse them. And if . . . the wife shall anger or displease her husband . . . she ought neuer to rest, vntill shee hath pacified him, and gotten his favour againe. And if he shall chance to blame her without a cause . . . yet shee must beare it patiently, and giue him no vncomely or vnkinde woordes for it: but euermore looke vppon him, with a louing and chearefull countenance, and so rather let her take the fault vppon her, then seeme to bee displeased." [1]

Although a great deal of attention was given in the domestic books to woman and her duties, practically no books were written for the instruction of women alone before the first part of the seventeenth century, except such as deal with specific subjects, like cookery, dairying, housekeeping, etc. Vives' book, already mentioned, is the chief exception here. Among a number of works written for the instruction of young people, particularly on the subject of marriage, I find only one addressed to girls. This is *A goodlie advise . . . touching mariage* by Andrew Kingsmill, a very short treatise appended to his *A Viewe of mans estate.* It was written in 1560, but was not published until 1574, after the writer's death. Vives' *Instruction,* as translated by Hyrde in 1540, is a full treatment of woman from birth to death, but contains little that is not to be found in the more general books of family life. These, as well as the many so-called *Catechisms,* devote several chapters to the various phases in the life of a woman, among which are discussed particularly the maid, the married woman, and the widow. Practically

[1] R. C., *A Godly Form of Hovseholde Gouernement,* p. 214.

all treat of the first two, some include the third, and some add chapters on stepmothers and old women.

Becon, in his *Catechism*, has given perhaps the fullest account of maidenhood, which is supplemented by a similar but shorter discussion on his *Boke of Matrimony*. The former gives nine duties to be observed by maids.[1] First, they must fear and serve God. Secondly, they must obey their parents. Thirdly, they should avoid idleness, "out of ye which springeth all mischefe, as pride, slouthfulnesse, banketting, dronkenshyp, whoredome, adoultry, vain communication, bewraying of secretes, cursed speakings &c. to auoid these pestilences, it shall become honest and vertuous maides to geue them selues to honest and vertuous exercises, to spinning, to carding, to weauing, to sowing, to washing, to wringing, to sweping, to scouring, to bruing, to bakinge, and to all kinde of labors withoute exception, that become maides." Fourthly, besides idleness, maids must eschew "the runninge about vnto vain spectacles, games, pastimes, playes, enterludes &c." Fifthly, "forasmuch as nothing doth so greatly hinder ye good name and fame of maids, as keeping cōpany with naughty packs, & persōs of a dissolute & wanton life, . . . therefore shal it be requisite that al godly maids do refrain thēselues from keping cōpany with light, vain & wanton persons: whose delite is in fleshly and filthy pastimes, as singing, dauncing, leaping, skipping, playinge, kissing, whoring &c." Sixthly, "that they be not full of tonge, and of much babling. . . . Except the grauity of some matter do require, that she should speak: or els an answer is to be made . . . let her kepe silence. For there is nothinge that doth so much commend, auaunce, setforthe, adourne, decke, trim, and garnish a maid, as silence." Seventhly, "forasmuch as maides no les then yonge menne after they come ones to xiiii yeres of age, are so desirous to

[1] Becon, *Worckes*, Pt. I, f. cccccxxxi ff.

be maried, . . . notwithstanding suche vntimely mariages are not to be commended . . . it shalbe conuenient for al honest maides, if they tender the health and cōseruation of their bodies . . . that they labor to the vttermost of their power to suppresse that luste and desire in them." Eighthly, "seeinge that . . . maides desyre nothinge so greatly as galante apparell, and sumptuous raiment . . . it shall not be vnfytting, that all honest and godly disposed maydes cōtent them selues with comely and semely apparell . . . according to the doctrine of the gospell." Finally, when they come to marry, they should "presume not to take in hand so graue, waighty and earnest matter, nor entangle them selues with the loue of anye parson, before they haue made their parents, tutors, frendes, or suche as haue gouernaunce of them priuye of their entent, yea and also require their both councel and consent in the matter." This set of rules is perhaps the fullest given anywhere, but most of them occur more briefly stated in other similar books. One thing which Becon omits but which is particularly interesting, is the warning sometimes given to young girls against reading "naughtie ballets" and "vaine romances." Vives has the fullest list of the latter, which he calls ungracious and full of filthiness: "in Spaine, *Amadise, Florisande, Tirante, Tristane,* and *Celestina;* . . . in France, *Lancelot du Lake, Paris & Vieuna, Ponthus and Sidonia,* and *Melucine;* in Flanders, *Flori and White Flower, Leonel and Cenamour, Curias and Floret, Primus and Thisbe;* in England, *Parthenope, Genarides, Hippomadon, William and Melyour, Libius and Arthur, Guy, Beuis,* and many others." [1]

[1] Vives, *Instruction,* f.D. Vives is a forerunner of Cervantes in the ridicule he heaps upon such romances. He says: "What delight can there bee in those thinges that be so plaine and foolish lies? One killeth twenty himselfe alone, another killeth thirty, another wounded with a

The duties of the married woman have already been set forth to some extent and require no more than a brief summary here. Besides obedience and submission to her husband, those most frequently mentioned are: chaste living, the avoidance of gaudy apparel, jewels, and cosmetics, the ordering of the household so far as its master allowed her control, the suckling of her babies, and some part in the teaching of her children. How far she had authority within the house is a point upon which there seems to have been no definite expression, and it was doubtless thought of and practised as a personal matter between the individual husband and wife.[1] Becon comes as near as any to a definite statement, where, in a passage describing the things a young girl should learn for her future service in life, he enumerates "spinning, cardinge, weuing, sowing, milking, chese, and butter making, gouerning of an house, dressing of meate and drink, and such like." Without these acquirements, Becon continues, "all beauty, favour, personage, nobilitye richesse, galant aparel, and whatsoeuer can be reckned more wherein womē do most of al glory, is nothinge else, then a

hundred woundes, and left dead, riseth vp againe, and on the next day made whole and strong, ouercommeth two Gyants and then goeth away loaden with gold and siluer, and pretious stones, mo thē a Gally would carry away. What madnes is it in folkes, to haue pleasure in these books? Also there is no wit in them, but a few wordes of wanton lust: which be spoken to mooue her minde with whome they loue, if it chance she is stedfast. . . . Nor I neuer heard man say that he liked these bookes: but those that neuer touched good books. And I my selfe sometime haue read in them, but I neuer found in them one steppe either of goodnesse or wit." *Ibid.*, D *b*.

Bullinger, on the same subject, says: "[the books of] Robyn Hode/ Beues of Hampton/ Troilus/ & such lyke fables do but kyndle in lyers lyke lyes and wanton loue/ whyche ought not in yought wyth theyr fyrst spettle to be dronkē in/ lest they euer remayne in them." *Christen state*, f. lxxv *b*.

Ascham's disapproval of the literature of romance is well known.

[1] But see p. 237, n. 1, below.

ringe in a swines snowte."[1] No wonder Vives says, "Great sadness of behauiour and arayment is required in a wife."

The widow was given less attention in the domestic book than either the maid or the married woman, and her duties may be briefly stated. If she was old, she should "be occupyed aboute matters of God and about busynesses of the congregation"; if young, she should keep out of trouble. The belief that a young widow was more attractive and in greater danger from men than a maid, seems to go back to St. Paul's time; but whether this attitude in the sixteenth (as well as in the twentieth) century is entirely the result of the apostle's teachings or is founded upon fact, is a question that we cannot go into here. At any rate, according to Vives, a young widow should lead a cloistered life, and if she went abroad at all, she should be accompanied by "some good and sad woman" and should avoid the company of men, especially friars and priests. On the other hand, some writers, following the advice of St. Paul to young widows, would have them marry again as soon as possible and thus avoid the "daunger of everlasting damnation"— it being thought practically impossible for a young widow to live chaste — "for how lyghte, vayne, trifeling, unhonest, unhousewifelike, younge widowes haue ben in all ages, and are also at this present day, experience doth sufficiently declare."[2] It is interesting to note that of the seven chapters given by Vives to the subject of the widow, three are devoted to her behavior towards her deceased husband.

The references above to woman in her various spheres, to her relation to man, and to the attitude of at least the religiously-minded towards her, represent one side of the pic-

[1] Becon, *Worckes*, Pt. I, f. DCLxxvi *b*. See also the list given in the *Catechism*, p. 155, above.

[2] *Ibid*, f. cccccxxix. Cf. the widow in Dunbar's *Tua Maryit wemen and the wedo* (see below, pp. 164–165).

ture of woman of the sixteenth and seventeenth centuries. I have gone into this in some detail as this point of view seems to have been neglected heretofore and to be at present quite overshadowed by the numerous discussions of the Renaissance idea of woman, which predominated among the courtly writers of Elizabeth's reign. The influence of Platonism as revamped in the Italian Renaissance is well enough known to obviate the necessity of my discussing it further.[1] Indeed, it is quite too well known, for students of the period, being saturated with the conception of woman as found in Italian literature and Italian court life and among the imitators of both in England, seem not to have realized sufficiently that woman as here portrayed is as fictitious as the love expressed for her in the average Petrarchistic sonnet. We should fall into a similar error were we to maintain, on the other hand, that the books we have been examining represent the true state of man's regard for woman, and that the Platonistic poetry and *Cortegiano* type of prose writing represent mere conventionalized dreams of fair women. Each attitude, we may say now, was a pose, the one resulting from the authority of the Scriptures, and the other from that of Plato and the Italian Renaissance. How sincere the writers in these two fields were, it is difficult to say; but at least it is safe to believe that each school was to some extent true to an imagination ingrown upon dogmas that seemed to express actual life, although the authors themselves may not have been fortunate, or unfortunate, enough to have so experienced it, except perhaps momentarily. In many cases, however, the writer must have been conscious, at least at times, that he was a hypocrite and that his productions were mere vapories of an over-religious or an over-sentimental state of

[1] For a treatment of this subject, see Einstein, *The Italian Renaissance in England.*

mind. The spectacle of John Donne, for instance, on Sunday preaching the subjection and inferiority of woman to a newly married couple, and on Monday apotheosizing his mistress in extragavant metaphors, will hardly tempt the fair-minded reader to accept him as a trustworthy witness for either the prosecution or the defense of womankind.[1] Similarly, John Knox, who denounced women as "weak, frail, impatient, feeble, foolish, inconstant, variable, and lacking the spirit of council," was twice married, was all his life surrounded by women, was co-respondent in the alienation of Mrs. Bowes from her husband and twelve children, and was accustomed to write in letters to those absent such sentiments as, "Dear sister, if I should express the thirst and langour which I have had for your presence, I should appear to pass measure. . . . Yea, I weep and rejoice in remembrance of you."[2] And Milton represents not only the popular ideal of woman in *Paradise Lost* but also the Petrarchistic one in his sonnets to the ladies of his Italian journey; and despite the difficulty he describes in his divorce tract of choosing a "sweet conversing soul," seems to have been unable to live without at least some makeshift for such a mate. The point here is more important than may at first appear, as it results in obliging us to accept only *cum magno grano salis* the testimony of all who have any axe to grind, be it sentimental, religious, or otherwise.

III. Commendation and Satire

However insincere the attitudes of moralists and courtiers towards women may have been, it is clear that the reign of Elizabeth did a great deal in awakening serious men to

[1] Donne himself in early life made a clandestine marriage with Anne More and was dismissed from office as a result.

[2] Stevenson, *John Knox and his Relations to Women*, in *Familiar Studies of Men and Books*, p. 383. The whole essay is instructive.

the importance of woman and her sphere. We find examples of books illustrating this fact as early as the middle of the century, as in the case of David Clapham's translation of Agrippa's *De Nobilitate & Praecellentia Foeminei Sexus*, in 1542, Thomas Elyot's *Defense of good women*, in 1545, William Bercher's *Nobylytie off Wymen*, in 1559, and two poems, Gosynhyll's *The Prayse of all women, called Mulierum paean*, in 1541, and Edward More's *Defense of women*, in 1560. But not until the beginning of the next century does there seem to have been anything like a development of a literature in praise of woman or in exposition of her affairs. A book quite similar to Elyot's, except that it is not in dialogue form, is *A Womans Woorth, defended against all the men of the world*, "proouing them to be more perfect, excellent, and absolute in all vertuous actions than any man of what qualitie soeuer." The title page also informs us that the work is by "one that hath heard much, seen much, but knowes a great deal more"; and the dedication is signed by Anthony Gibson, who says that he has translated the treatise from the French of a "friend and fellow servant to her Majesty." This book was published in 1599. Among the books of less pretentious titles but more utilitarian character and greater real worth, may be mentioned *The Excellency of good women*, in 1613, and *My Ladies Looking Glasse*, in 1616, both by Barnaby Rich, Thomas Heywood's *Nine Bookes of Various History concerninge Women*, 1624, and *Nine the Most Worthy Women of the World*, 1640, Brathwait's *The English Gentlewoman*, 1631, T. E.'s *The Lawes Resolvtions of Womens Rights*, 1632, and Samuel Torshell's *The Womans Glorie*, 1645.

A word will suffice for each of these. The first of Rich's two small books is sufficiently described by its subtitles — "The honour and estimation that belongeth vnto them, The infallible markes whereby to know them." The *Look-*

ing Glasse is merely one of the many books on the evils and immorality of the time, and deals as much with men as with women. Thomas Heywood shows his interest in woman both in his plays and in the books before us. The *Various History* is a folio volume of 466 pages, divided into nine books on various feminine types, the first eight of which contain histories and anecdotes of particular women of fame, almost all from ancient history, and several essays of a general nature on woman and her characteristics. The ninth book is made up entirely of such essays. The volume on the whole is a veritable storehouse of historical, traditionary, and fictitious stories, and contains a considerable amount of verse both original and translated. It does not, however, throw much light upon the contemporary English woman. The *Nine Most Worthy Women* presents history only, in the form of the lives of three famous Jews — Deborah, Judith, and Esther; three Gentiles — Boadicea, Penthesilaea, and Artimesia; and three Christians — Elphreda (daughter of Alfred the Great), Margaret (wife of Henry VI), and Queen Elizabeth. The *Lawes Resolvtions* by the unknown T. E.[1] is entirely a legal work, and although uninteresting for us, is particularly important in showing the increased recognition of woman's position in civil affairs. It is a thorough treatise of her rights before the law. The *Womans Glorie* is an ordinary conduct book for women, her "glorie" consisting in properly filling her part in the family. Brathwait's *English Gentlewoman* represents the culmination of the writing upon women. It is a book of some 240 pages devoted entirely to feminine interests. Its chapters treat separately apparel, behavior, complement, decency, education, fancy, gentility, and honor. From these headings it may be seen that the work is a general one of manners and conduct rather than, like Vives' *Instruction*, one concerned with the different stages and con-

[1] The British Museum Catalogue suggests Thomas Edwards.

ditions of woman's life. Mention is made of Vives' book and also of Erasmus, from which fact, as well as from the recurrence of certain anecdotes, we may believe that Brathwait knew to some extent the domestic books of the period. He mentions also the Italian type of courtier and lady, and shows himself familiar with the Italian point of view by ridiculing the contemporary love poetry. Although he is a little too much saturated with the ecclesiastical idea of female humility, advising the gentlewoman that "the way for you to ascend is first to descend," he presents on the whole a very sane picture of woman as she should be, and one not greatly different from the English ideal of today.

Despite these books in commendation of the gentle sex, less complimentary writing continued, reminiscent of the time when woman figured in literature principally as the object of satire. In 1637, an anonymous writer says: "In turning over the leaves of some both moderne and foreigne writers, I have met with so many satyricall invectives aimed directly against it [the feminine sex] and some of them so pathetically bitter, that I am halfe perswaded they had forgot themselves to have been borne of mothers." [1] It may have been this author's misfortune to have run across *A Discovrse of the Married and Single Life*, or Hercules Tasso's part of *Of Mariage and Wiuing*. Both of these treatises, like Bansley's *Pryde and abuse of women* (1540-50), are such diatribes against womankind that one is inclined to class them with those Torquato Tasso speaks of as "too too ridiculous." The parting shot from the former is, "Yet let mee aduise thee, that with thine eyes shut, thy nose stopt, thy fist closed, & thy stomack armed, thou will take thy wife as a medicine of Rubarbe." [2] Hercules Tasso concludes:

> "(Friend) marry when thou please, yet thou shalt find
> Thy wife bad alwaies, and but vse her ill

[1] *A Curtaine Lecture*, p. 5.
[2] *Op. cit.*, p. 115.

And she is worse, but vse her well and kind
She is worser then, and so continue will:
Yet is she good (if she but once would die)
But better, if she packt before thy selfe,
But best of all, if she went speedily,
Leauing behind to thee her hoorded wealth."[1]

But neither these two books nor others of similar nature can be called satire; they are invective pure and simple. Nevertheless, there was satire on the subject of woman, especially the married woman, just as there had been ever since Chaucer's day and before that. This is found everywhere except in religious books and prosaic household directories, such as many we have been studying. The origin of the genre, which was contemporary with Chaucer, seems to have been in France and took the form of warnings against marriage, as in such a piece as *Les quinze joyes des Mariage*, which afterwards became the groundwork for Dekker's *Bachelars Banquet*. Chaucer himself, although inclined to poke fun at the sex, was certainly on the side of its defense in the so-called marriage group of the *Canterbury Tales*. His successor, Douglas, said of him that he "was ever, Got wait, wemenis friend," and it is reasonable to believe that his attitude in the tales told in reply to the Wife of Bath and in the *Legend of Good Women* was a sincere one. Nevertheless, Chaucer's championing of woman partook somewhat of the nature of a weather-cock on a gusty day. The Wife of Bath is representative of a succession of female Bluebeards, of whom she may have been the prototype. *The boke of Mayd Emlyn*, c. 1530, contains the most extended portrait of such a character, to whom may be likened the adventuress in the *Twelve mery gestys of one called Edyth* and the widow in Dunbar's *The Tua Maryit wemen and the wedo.* Married life came in for more direct satire in ballads

[1] Tasso, *op. cit.*, f. G4.

such as *A Complaynt of them that be to soone maryed*, *The Payne and sorowe of euyll Maryage*, and many from the prolific pen of Martin Parker, as well as in a few less ephemeral works like Dunbar's *Tua Maryit wemen*. In the whole of this group, the satire on women is incidental to the accounts of married life and the warnings against it. Dunbar's poem, like *The Schole-howse of women*, written in reply to Gosynhyll's *Prayse of all women*, presents marriage and its hardships entirely from the woman's point of view. In the former, the widow advises the afflicted wives, after listening to their tales of woe, to make the best of their bad bargains by consoling themselves, as she had done, with "othir bachilleris blyth blumyng in youth"; in the latter, a dialogue between an old gossip and a young wife, the elder, while appearing to council her friend in regard to her sufferings, plays Job's comforter by reciting the evils and weaknesses of womankind, with illustrations drawn from history and current jest-books. In the years 1560 to 1570, there was quite an outburst, which seems to have abated thereafter, of satirical poems against the married woman — *The Proude Wyves Paternoster*, *An hundred poyntes of evell huswrifrye*, *A Commyssion unto all those whose wyves be thayr masters*, *A Shrewde and Curste Wyfe lapped in Morrelles skin*, and others — but these contribute little that is new to the type.[1]

In all these would-be satires, in which the weapon employed is the bludgeon rather than the rapier, we find that, just as the courtier pretended to regard woman as the queen of love and beauty, and the sanctimonious writer looked upon her as the handmaid of the devil, or at best as a weak and sinning specimen of human kind, so the satirist assumed a conventional point of view and portrayed her from that aspect. The two things which women had been especially

[1] For further account and bibliography of satire against women, see *Camb. Hist. Eng. Lit.*, II, 437 ff., III, 98 ff. and 551 ff.

instructed to do, from the time of St. Paul onward, were to be subservient to their husbands and to avoid costly raiment.[1] Whether or not these warnings caused women to do exactly the opposite, so that the satire was directed against actual conditions, we cannot say, though one is inclined to doubt very much if such were the case; at any rate, these two points furnish the *casus belli* for by far the greater part of the satire against woman. Of course, her other occasional attributes were not neglected, such as jealousy, especially in the case of a woman married the second time, her propensity for continuous talking, her extravagance, her love of pleasure, her temper. It is noteworthy, too, that as St. Paul's words were directed against married women, so the satire is chiefly at their expense. Chaucer's Wife of Bath is an excellent example of these points. She had been married five times, having mastered the life and death of each of her husbands, she flaunted her gaudy apparel and lewd personality in the faces of her fellow pilgrims, and she told a story illustrative of woman's desire for sovereignty.

> "Women desyren to have sovereyntee
> As wel over hir housbond as hir love
> And for to been in maistrie him above."[2]

Descendants of the Wife of Bath may be found in English literature without break throughout Elizabethan times and beyond. In the middle of the century, "Walter Wedlocke" thus slyly defends woman's love of sovereignty:

"Surely the prehiminence that wyues doth couette at theyr husbands handes by vertue of that humour is none other, but onele to haue lybertie in three kynde of thynges, which is, to saye what they wyll, to haue what they wyll, and to do what they wyl, wherin

[1] These two warnings, hardly changed from their original Biblical phraseology, to this day form part of the marriage ceremony of the Church of England.

[2] Chaucer, Wife of Bath's Tale l. 182.

you know the husbande maye easely bere with them, and surely doyng so, they are the most quyet and comfortablest creatures, that euer were ordeyned for man."[1]

Before the introduction of the Italian and Spanish fashions in clothes, the greater part of both serious and frivolous writing against woman was directed towards preserving her subserviency and condemning her attempts at sovereignty. At this time, the only satire entirely against female attire that I have found was Lindsay's *Syde Taillis;* but with the coming of foreign and exaggerated styles of dress and the greater attention given to clothes by both men and women, satirical writing on such love of display received a fresh and powerful stimulus.

Despite the works discussed above, the greater part of the satire against women, especially in the latter half of the century, was incidental to some other piece of work, as it had been earlier in the case of the writings of Chaucer and John Heywood. For this reason, it is impossible to trace its history more closely here. At the beginning of the seventeenth century, running parallel with other writing on the subject of women, we find the genre coming to life again, and here the foibles of dress are dealt with to a far greater extent than formerly. Gosson's *Pleasant Quippes for Upstart Newfangled Gentlewomen*, in 1595, is a case in point, the title page of which describes it as a satirical poem against the "fantastical foreign Toyes daylie used in Women's Apparell." Dekker's *The Bachelars Banquet*, in 1603, is more inclusive, exhibiting the "humours" of women of different types and in different situations. This is the most thorough satirical treatment of women that I know of. The drama, in such plays as *The Taming of the Shrew*, *The Silent Woman*, and others, contributed its quota. The

[1] Wedlocke, *Image of Idlenesse*, f. Ei *b*.

years 1615–1620 saw two controversies on the subject. One was started by Joseph Swetnam [1] with *The Araignment of Lewde, idle, froward, and vnconstant women*, in 1615, which was answered in 1616 by the anonymous *Asylum Veneris, or a Sanctuary for Ladies, etc.*, in 1617 by Constantia Munda [2] with *The Worming of a mad Dogge: or, a Soppe for Cerberus the Iaylor of Hell*, by Ester Sowernam [2] with *Ester hath hang'd Haman, etc.*, by Rachel Speght with *A Mouzell for Melastomus, the Cynicall Bayter of, and foule mouthed Barker against Evahs sex*, and in 1620 by an anonymous comedy entitled *Swetnam the woman-hater, arraigned by women.* The replies are, of course, in defense of the sex. There is much humor in Swetnam's little book, and its popularity was great. Of the jealousy of women married a second time, he tells this story:

> "Another [man] hauing married a widdow, and within a while after they were married, she went out into the garden, and there finding her husbands shirt hang close on the hedge by her maides smock, she went presently and hanged herselfe for a iealous conceit that she tooke, and a merry fellow asked the cause why she hanged herselfe, and being tolde it was for iealousie: I would said he that all trees did beare such fruit." [3]

The second little passage of arms on the subject consisted of one book against women and two replies. These are: *Hic Mvlier: or, the Man-Woman; Being a Medicine to cure the Coltish Disease of the Staggers in the Masculine-Feminines of our Time; Haec-Vir; or, The Womanish Man: Being an Answere to a late Booke intitulit Hic-Mulier;* and *Muld Sacke: or The Apologie of Hic-Mulier: To the late Declamation against her.* All three books are anonymous and give the impression of being by the same writer. *Muld*

[1] Swetnam issued his book under the name of Thomas Teltruth, but his identity was known to the writers of the answers.

[2] Constantia Manda and Ester Sowernam are probably fictitious names.

[3] Swetman, *op. cit.*, p. 63. This is an old tale.

Sacke is dated 1620, and the other two are probably of the same year or very shortly before. The first is against the mannish woman; the second, being a dialogue, cuts both ways; the third is principally against foppish men.[1] There is not much wit in any of them — more invective than satire. There is good satire in the two jest-books above mentioned, *A Curtaine Lecture,* 1637, and *Ar't asleepe Husband?*, 1640; but space forbids further discussion of this subject.

IV. Historical and General View

In attempting to formulate an opinion of woman's position in Elizabeth's time, we shall get a fairer and more fundamental view by examining historical and biographical facts than by studying the writings of moralists, lovers, and satirists. These writers are helpful in furnishing detail and color to the picture and in distinguishing individuals from the mass, but history will give us a clearer idea of the general character of the woman of the day, to which the minor features, in one case or another, are to be attached. For whether the individual was a household drudge, a queen of love, or a Wife of Bath, she was first of all a woman, and as the philosopher characteristically observed, "but a woman."

There can be no doubt that previous to Elizabeth's reign woman was considered a very inferior creature. The neglect of her education, the conditions of marriage and divorce, the piggishness of the average home, and the scarcity of women of ability and prominence, all put this fact beyond

[1] The womanish man became an object of satire, as in Decker's *Gulls Hornbook* as a result of Italian foppery of dress and manners, in the same way as did the woman. A good deal of such satire was carried on in the drama, as in the case of the comedies of Jonson, Middleton, Marston and Field.

question. But conditions for the betterment of the sex began long before this time. Henry III was a great patron of the home and was influential in improving housing conditions.[1] Henry IV showed his interest in womankind by extolling the writings of Christine de Pisan, the well known champion of woman, and inviting her to his court. The works of Juliana Berners, the first English literary woman of fame, were widely read. Thomas More was a believer in female education, taking his ideas from Italy, and his daughters were said by Vives to "perfectly fulfill all the points of a good woman." [2] Queen Catherine, the wife of Henry VIII, after the abominable treatment she received at the hands of her royal spouse, became a national heroine in the eyes of those not under the King's thumb.[3] Before Elizabeth's reign, and to a greater extent during it, Italian books were imported, translated, and imitated, Italian architecture was introduced, Italian culture and court life were adopted as far as possible, and the Renaissance homage was paid, whether sincerely or not, to the women of nobility as well as to many others.

These facts are well known. Two others are worthy of attention. The one is the new and higher attitude toward marriage, as taught by the Reformers of Germany and their followers in England, particularly the Puritans, which has

[1] For early housing conditions and Henry III's patronage of architecture, see Sparrow, *The English House*, chaps. II and VII, respectively.

[2] Vives, *Instruction*, f. C5.

[3] Speaking of her, Vives says: "If suche incredible vertue hadde fortuned then, when honor was the rewarde of vertue, thys womā had dusked the brightnesse of the Heroes, and as a diuine thynge and a godlye sente downe from heauen, had bene prayed vnto in temples, although she lacke no tēples, for there can not be erected vnto her a more ample or a more magnificente temple then that, the whiche euery man among al nations marueylinge at her vertues, haue in theyr owne heartes buylded and erected." *Office and duetie*, f. Eiiii.

been sufficiently set forth in a previous chapter.[1] It is very doubtful whether the average man had ever undertaken matrimony for the two causes originally sanctioned by the church, — the begetting of children and the avoidance of sexual sin — but the ecclesiastical recognition among Protestant sects of the possibility of woman's occupying a higher position in matrimonial society than that of a mere instrument for carnal desires, is important in marking the beginning of the end of the degradation she had suffered at the hands of the church. The attempts to put woman on the same footing as man in matters of divorce, although unsuccessful, show also a tendency to regard her as an equal partaker with him in the state of wedlock. Nevertheless, despite these facts, the church as a whole consistently maintained the inferiority of woman and sought to instil into her an entire submission and obedience to her husband in all family affairs.[2] Moreover, wife beating continued to be practised under the sanction of the law.[3]

The second important factor in raising woman's position was Elizabeth herself. It will be remembered that the Reformers in England had been persecuted and driven into exile by Queen Mary. John Knox and his congregation had also been proscribed in Scotland by Regent Mary of Guise. The bitter opposition to the Reformers by Mary Tudor, Mary of Guise, and Catherine de' Medici in France, together with the fact that female rule in Europe was pretty generally considered an anomaly, led Knox to start a controversy against woman rulers in general. In accordance with the Biblical teaching already noted that women should

[1] See above, p. 120 ff.

[2] The marriage sermons of John Donne (*Works*, vol. IV) are excellent examples of the changing yet conservative attitude of the time on this subject.

[3] For discussion of this subject and writing thereupon, see Jeaffreson, *Brides and Bridals*, I, 317 ff

not hold positions of authority over men,[1] he attacked all queens in a pamphlet entitled *The first Blast of the Trumpet against the Monstrous Regiment of Women,* which was not long in "wakening all the echoes of Europe." But unfortunately for him, Queen Mary, against whom it was principally written, died the year of its publication, Elizabeth came to the throne as a patron of Protestancy, and the exiles on the continent trooped back to England to live under the protection of their female champion. This put Knox in an awkward situation. In addition, John Aylmer, afterwards Bishop of London, replied to the Scotchman's pamphlet with *An Harborwe for faithfull and trewe Subjectes against the late bloune Blaste, etc.*[2] The result of this controversy, which was more extended than the brief note here indicates,[3] was that Elizabeth secured more firmly than ever her place in the hearts of the people as a defender of the faith and a Portia come to judgment, and Knox was reduced to the ignominious position of having to eat his own words and swear allegiance. This he not only did, but showed in addition, by a series of textual quibbles, that his pamphlet did not attack Elizabeth's supremacy at all.

Besides appearing as a champion of Protestancy, although a bitter enemy to its more radical sects, Elizabeth occupied a position in literary England similar to that of Laura in the eyes of Petrarch or Beatrice in those of Dante. Even after her death poets and prose writers continued extravagant praise of her. Thomas Heywood writes in 1640:

"As the most famous Painter of his Time, Apelles, to frame the picture of one Venus, had at once exposed to his view an hundred

[1] St. Paul, I *Tim.* II, 12.

[2] Aylmer is another example of the inconsistency of writers on women. See his opinion of the sex expressed above, p. 147.

[3] For full discussion of this controversy, see Stevenson, *John Knox and his Relations to Women.*

of the most choyce and exquisite Virgins, of Greece, to take from one the smoothest brow, from a second, the most sparkling eye, [etc.] . . . so in the accurate expression of this rare Heroicke Elizabeth, should I peruse all the ancient, and Authenticke Histories, and out of them select the lives of the most vertuous Ladyes, for their rare and admirable endowments . . . (whether Piety, or Virginall purity; Beauty, and Bounty; Majesty, and magnanimity; Language, and learning; polliticke Governement, or practice of goodnesse; pitty of forraigne distressed nations, or indulgence over her owne Natives, &c.) Nay, what praecelling vertue soever, was commendable in any one particular, or all in general, may, without flattery be justly conferred on her." [1]

Nor were other ladies of fashion and attainments lacking. The three daughters of Sir Anthony Coke were as accomplished as Elizabeth herself, and surpassed her in marrying brilliantly, one becoming the mother of Francis Bacon. The classical learning of Lady Jane Grey is commented upon by Roger Ascham, who discovered her one day reading Plato in the original. Jane, Countess of Westmorland, the daughter of John Fox, was said to bear comparison with the greatest scholars of the age. Dorothy Leigh, one of the few woman writers of the time, published a volume, *The Mother's Blessing*, dedicated to Elizabeth, which ran to fourteen editions by 1629. Mary Sidney, afterwards the famous Countess of Pembroke, held a "court of love and learning" at Wilton Place, like those at Urbino and Ferrara, where many of the leading literary men of the day were to be found. She was probably the most thorough and most Italianate lady of Elizabethan England. But these women represent only the aristocracy of the country, and it seems to have been a principle of the age that such ladies might enjoy some privileges forbidden their humbler sisters.[2]

[1] Heywood, *Most Worthy Women*, p. 184.

[2] "Thus," says Stevenson, "Margaret of Navarre wrote books with great acclamation, and no one, seemingly, saw fit to call her con-

Moreover, one is inclined to distrust the roseate light with which these "great ladies" were surrounded by their admirers. The historian would hardly recognize Elizabeth from Heywood's picture of her or from Spenser's Gloriana or Lyly's Cynthia. The same may be said of the innumerable goddess-like mistresses of the time. Carew's Coelia appears as real in *To a Strumpet*,[1] when the poet lost his temper and exhausted his vituperative power, as she does in *A Rapture*, when she consented to "be kind." And at the other end of the scale from the sonnet sequences and similar poetry in praise of women, we have such malicious diatribes against the sex as have already been mentioned. Nevertheless, the position of women of learning and culture and the homage paid them, as well as the idealization of the less worthy members of society, cannot have failed to contribute in raising the general estimate of woman considerably above that of preceding periods.

The letters of foreigners furnish excellent evidence of the position of the English woman of the time. Many speak of her beauty, her charm, and her lavishness of dress; and although the subserviency of the wife to the husband is remarked upon, it seems agreed that she was allowed greater freedom than in other countries. Indeed, a popular saying on the continent was, "England is a paradise for women, a

duct in question; but Mademoiselle de Gournay, Montaigne's adopted daughter, was in controversy with the world as to whether a woman might be an author without incongruity. Thus, too, we have Théodore Agrippa d'Aubigné writing to his daughters about the learned women of his century, and cautioning them in conclusion, that the study of letters was unsuited to ladies of middling station and should be reserved for princesses. And once more, . . . we shall find . . . the Abbot of Brantôme claiming . . . a privilege, or rather a duty, of free love for great princesses, and carefully excluding other ladies from the same gallant dispensation." *Familiar Studies*, p. 332.

[1] Printed only in my article on Carew, *Mod. Lang. Rev.*, July, 1916, and there only in part.

prison for servants, and a hell for horses." One writer says, "The women there are charming, and by nature so mighty pretty, as I have scarcely ever beheld, for they do not falsify, paint or bedaub themselves as in Italy and other places; but they are somewhat awkward in their style of dress; for they dress in splendid stuffs, and many a one wears three cloth gowns or petticoats, one over the other." [1] The writer here was evidently fortunate in his acquaintances, as there is abundant evidence that the English woman was quite accustomed to falsify, paint, and bedaub herself after the Italian fashion. A Dutchman gives us a fuller account: "Although the women there are entirely in the power of their husbands except for their lives, yet they are not kept so strictly as they are in Spain or elsewhere. Nor are they shut up but they have the free management of the house or housekeeping. . . . They go to market to buy what they like to eat. They are well dressed, fond of taking it easy, and commonly leave the care of household matters and drudgery to their servants. . . . All the rest of their time they employ in walking or riding, in playing at cards and otherwise, in visiting their friends and keeping company . . . and all this with the permission and knowledge of their husbands." Further on, the same writer says, "The girls who are not yet married are kept much more rigorously and strictly than in the Low Countries." [2] In regard to the married woman's going abroad, Thomas Heywood upholds this foreigner's account. He condemns the French proverb for the conduct of women, "*La Femme in La Maison, et La Jambe rompue,* that is, let the woman be in the house and her legge broke," and approves rather the practice of "allowing both their features and fames a liberall freedome to undergoe any

[1] Keichel (1585), trans. in Rye's *England as seen by Foreigners,* p. 89.

[2] van Miteren, in Rye, *ibid.,* p. 77 ff.

publicke censure."[1] Thus the cloistered life of woman of feudal days had disappeared along with most of the false sentiment of chivalry. These descriptions manifestly deal only with women of the better classes, but a similar or perhaps greater liberty of the sex is shown to have existed among the working classes by the fact that the trade guilds were, for the most part, open to women as well as men.

"Poets in the Middle Ages had sung of woman as an angel, ecclesiastical asceticism had treated her as little better than a demon, but the men of the sixteenth century were of a different mould. They had something of the modern spirit, and looked upon woman as a being to share the common burdens and pleasures of life, not to be worshiped or shunned."[2] Sir Walter Raleigh gives an excellent expression of this attitude. In his *Instructions to his Son,* he writes in regard to the choice of a wife:

> "Have therefore ever more care, that thou be beloved of thy Wife, rather than thy self besotted on her; and thou shalt judge of her love by these two observations: first If thou perceive she have a care of thy estate, and exercise her self therein; the other, If she study to please thee, and be sweet unto the in conversation, without thy instruction, for Love needs no teaching. . . . Let her have equal part of thy Estate whilest thou livest, if thou find her sparing and honest."[3]

Nevertheless the Elizabethan ideal of woman, whether justly so or not, was considerably lower than that of today, especially than that of America. The model wife was a woman of moderate attainments only, and St. Paul's dictum, "I suffer not the woman . . . to usurp the authority over the man," expressed in one way or another, was a knell that was constantly rung in her ears. Perhaps Eve, in the latter part

[1] Heywood, *Most Worthy Women,* f. ** *b*.

[2] Hill, *Women in English Life,* I, 117.

[3] Raleigh, *Remains of Sir Walter Raleigh,* p. 85.

of *Paradise Lost*, where she appears as a real helpmate to her husband, presents the best contemporary picture of what it was thought, from the latter part of the sixteenth to the latter part of the seventeenth century, a wife should be.[1] A similar portrayal is found in Overbury's *A Wife,* which judging from its immense popularity,[2] seems to have had wide approval.

"Give me next Good, an understanding Wife
By nature wise, not learned by much Art.
Some knowledge on her side will all my Life
More scope of Conversation impart.

. . . .

A passive understanding to conceive,
A judgment to discern, I wish to finde.
Beyond that, all as hazardous I leave:
Learning and pregnant wit in Woman-kinde,
What it finds malleable maketh frail,
And doth not add more ballast, but more sail." [3]

Thomas Heywood upholds this point of view in his instructions to prospective husbands:

"Yet were it best a modest medium keepe,
Chuse neither compleate Shrow, nor perfect Sheepe,
I would have my wife neither tongue-tide quite
Nor yet all tonnge; so much as could accite
To affability and amorous prate
So much I'd haue her vse, and more I hate.

. . . .

[1] A good deal of nonsense has been written about Milton's supposed "low ideal of woman." It must be clear by this time that, although his ideal was lower than that of today, it was considerably higher than the average of his time.

[2] At least five editions of the poem occurred the year of its publication (1614) and ten more by 1632.

[3] Overbury, *op. cit.*, ll. 175 ff.

She of the two extreames, if you demand
With which I would be troubled, vnderstand,
I'd take the gentle beast, the harmelesse Sheepe,
Whose calmenes would not fright me from my sleepe."[1]

The author of *A Discovrse of the Married and Single Life* says on the point raised by Heywood, that some men "haue made it a great question, whether it were better for a man to marrie a shrew, or a sheepe, but hardly can it be resolued."[2] Again, Niccholes, writing on the choice of a wife, says that she should be "of sober and mild aspect, courteous behauiour, decent carriage, of a fixed eye, constant looke and vnaffected gate."[3] Such expressions may be found in almost all the domestic books. L. Wright puts it, "A woman that is silent of tongue: shamfast of countinance: vertuous qualities correspondent: is like a goodly pleasant flower . . . which shall be giuen for a good portion to such a one as feareth God."[4] John Donne says in one of his sermons that it would be a sin for one to love a wife as he does his mistress; and although he is evidently referring to the quality rather than the quantity of love, the statement is nevertheless evidence of the prevailing idea that a mistress was to be passionately idealized, whereas a wife was to be regarded as a natural and somewhat uninteresting, though none the less valuable, adjunct to every-day life. The poetry of the period raises the former to the gods; the prose instructs the latter how to walk upon earth.

1 Heywood, *History concerninge Women*, p. 236.
2 *Op. cit.*, f. A6.
3 Niccholes, *Marriage and Wiving*, p. 9.
4 Wright, *Display of dutie*, p. 22.

CHAPTER VI

WIDER RANGES OF DOMESTIC LITERATURE

I. More General Conduct Books

It is possible in a brief discussion only to indicate the many types of writing with which the books we have been studying heretofore are more or less intimately connected, and to suggest tentatively certain relations that seem to exist among them. As has been said already, the domestic book is not as a rule literary in character; nevertheless, certain tendencies toward conscious artistry often exist, and, as has been shown, examples of real literary merit are not altogether lacking. If we go further afield, to the conduct books of kindred nature, we find many that are distinctly literary; and in the recognized literature of the period, we may discover the influence of the increasing interest in domestic affairs and possibly that of the family book itself.

The culmination of interest in domestic life took place in the last quarter of the sixteenth century, at which time we may group around the household book such allied types as the book of manners, the book of moral reflection and allegory, the book of direction and advice to young people, and books following the models set by Machiavelli's *Il Principe*, Castiglione's *Il Cortegiano*, and Nenna's *Il Nennio*. Besides these, there were others on more specific subjects connected with domesticity and the conduct of life, such as cookery, household medicine, the education of children, the government of estates, gentlemen's callings (especially the practice of arms), recreations, the religious life of the family, the various phases and occupations of society, the pleasures of city and country life, and so forth. The last part of Elizabeth's reign has been described as a period when the English nation paused to take stock of itself. The literature of the time certainly exhibits a national awakening, and the more utilitarian writing shows equally the development of an individual self-consciousness. This attitude had been steadily growing in England with the increase of the practice of inquiry and thought in place of the acceptance of dogma: the Reformation was an important stimulus in this direction; the Renaissance brought the movement to flower. We cannot here go into the origin and development of even the more important types of books before us, but must content ourselves with a glance at the results therefrom.

Of the books which I have mentioned as culminating to some extent about the beginning of the seventeenth century, those on particular topics are too specialized, and those of the moral meditation and moral allegory types are too general and form too large a field, for our consideration. Of the others, the book of manners, the book of the courtier, and the book of princely conduct, are pretty well known. But there is another type of some importance, which, although akin to the three types just mentioned, seems to have escaped observation. This we may call, for convenience' sake, the book of honor or nobility. A typical volume of this class, while reflecting the ideas of the *Cortegiano*, is really nearer in nature to the book of moral philosophy, since it is concerned with the virtues which go to make up a gentleman, such as justice, temperance, friendship, education, etc., rather than with his qualifications as an ornament of the court. The usual conception of the gentleman of this time has been expressed thus: "The knight had been transformed into the courtier; and the 'virtuous and gentle discipline,' deemed requisite for him in his new sphere, was, for the most part, to be found in such regulations for external behaviour as are laid down in Castiglione's *Il Cortegiano*."[1] Such a statement obviously presents but half the case, for beside the transformation of the knight into the courtier, we find in the book of honor a presentation of him as the English gentleman, clad with "the armour of a Christian man specified by St. Paul, vi Ephes.," as Spenser expressed it.[2] An example of such a book, written before the *Cortegiano*, is Barclay's *Mirrour of Good Manners*, translated from the Latin of Dominicus Mancinus in 1523, which consists chiefly of discussions in verse of prudence, virtue, magnanimity, and temperance. The books nearest to this type in Italian literature are Nenna's *Il Nennio*, Muzio's *Il Gentiluomo*, and Giraldi's *Dialoghi della Vita Civile;* but the first two of these are concerned only with the question of what should constitute a nobleman, — whether birth, riches, or virtues of the mind — and the third is simply a reworking of the ethical philosophy of Plato and Aristotle. The Spanish writer Jeronomo Osorio, in his *Discourse of Civill and Christian Nobilitie*, as translated by William Blandy in 1576, comes nearer the type we are following, and treats briefly justice, courage, liberality, magnanimity, eloquence, and knowledge of men as virtues requisite for a nobleman, and justice, liberality, friendship, fortitude, and magnanimity as those of a Christian gentleman. The *Academie Françoise* by la Primaudaye, which was put into English in 1586 by T. B., combines the nobility type with some of the others noted, and includes discussions of such topics as virtue, vice, duty, prudence, friendship, education, temperance, fortitude,

[1] *Camb. Hist. Eng. Lit.*, III, 266.

[2] Spenser, *Letter to Raleigh*, prefatory to *Faerie Queene*. Graund Amour in Hawes' *Passetyme of Pleasure*, Youth in his *Example of Virtue*, and Spenser's own Red Cross Knight are all described as wearing the same Christian armor, and St. Paul's *Epistle* is expressly referred to in each case.

justice, etc. The continued popularity of this book in England is shown by the fact that the translation ran into six editions by 1618.

In England itself, we find a clear sequence of nobility books from Middle English times down. The best early example is, of course, Hoccleve's *Gouvernail of Princes,* which is almost entirely given up to the discussion of moral virtues, but the roots of the type go further back to such works as *Piers the Plowman* or even to the still earlier exemplum and virtue stories. We cannot say that this series was unaffected by foreign literature and foreign ideas, any more than we can say the like of any other literary development, but we may claim perhaps that the main stream was native.

In the last part of the sixteenth century, however, the Italian influence was so strong that the nobility book became combined with others, in a type which, gradually clearing itself of irrelevant matter, culminated in the book of "the complete gentleman."[1] Previous to this time, Elyot had entered the field with his *Gouvernour,* in 1531, in which some of the Italian ideas are combined with treatments of many of the moral virtues. A better example, however, of the combination of types is Humphrey's *The Nobles,* written first in Latin in 1560 and translated into English in 1563. Here, in addition to a great deal of general moral discourse, we have the usual Italian classification of nobility, on the grounds of

[1] The Italian books, especially those of the *Principe* and *Cortegiano* types, and the ideas contained therein, are fully discussed in Einstein, *The Italian Renaissance in England.* The more prominent English imitations, Elyot's *Gouvernour,* Humphrey's *The Nobles,* the anonymous *Institutions of a Gentleman,* and some others, are also noted. But the later books combining various types are entirely overlooked, as are also *The Covrt of ciuill Courtesie* by S. Robson in 1591, *Ars Avlica,* translated from the Italian of Lorenzo Ducci by Ed. Blount in 1607, and *The Honest Man,* translated from the French of N. Faret by Ed. Grimstone in 1632, which are all typical books of the *Cortegiano* class.

birth, wealth, and attainment, as in the *Nennio;* we have also a similarity to the *Cortegiano,* in the instructions given to the courtier; and finally, in the field of gentlemanliness, we have brief treatises of liberality, justice, temperance, continence, magnificence, apparel, the house, sports, the education of children, etc., perhaps modeled on the *Discourse* of Osorio, who is mentioned by name. A similar treatise is John Larke's *Flower of Vertue,* translated from the Italian of Fiore in 1565. A work which has little or nothing of the courtier but which represents a combination of the morality and nobility books, is Thomas Rogers' *Anatomie of the minde,* in 1576, one of the many "anatomies" of the time, some of which are distinct forerunners of Burton's famous *Anatomy of Melancholy.* Rogers' book is divided into two parts, the first on "Perturbations in Generall," which he defines according to Zeno's opinion as "conditions of the mind contrary to reason," for example, pleasure, ambition, lust, anger, love, fear, sorrow; and the second, "Of Morall Vertues," which is a typical nobility book, discussing first wherein felicity or nobility exists, — whether in mind, body, or estate — and secondly, the qualities or virtues of the mind, including those of Aristotle in addition to many others. The last named division of the work runs to some 250 pages and is the fullest treatment thereof that I have found. *The Blazon of Gentrie* by John Ferne, in 1586, illustrates a type of book which only just touches upon that we are following. It is, in the main, a treatment of the bearing of arms, the laws of combat, and kindred topics, together with a second part showing the ancestries of certain families and various interests connected with them. The first contains a discussion of nobility from a civil point of view, the professions of gentlemen, and some allied subjects. The whole treatment is presented in a dialogue between a herald, a knight, a divine, a lawyer, an antiquary, and a plowman, but this device to disguise expository writing was so common in English literature from earliest times down that we are unable to argue anything from the fact that it is here used.

So far, we have noted no discussion of marriage in these books of combined interests. The earliest example I have found which does include this subject is *The French Academie* of la Primaudaye. This work contains seven successive chapters on marriage and domestic affairs, which by themselves would make a typical family book. But in 1589, there appeared a book of native origin combining several of the types of the time and containing a treatment of marriage. This is L. Wright's *A Display of dutie,* "dict with sage sayings, pythie sentences, and proper similies." It consists of short, somewhat unrelated chapters, among which are discussions of idleness, fortitude, chastity, the duties of a subject to a prince, friendship, marriage, art, etc. The *Display,* however, is too slight to be of importance, except as the first native example of the type. In 1597, there appeared a book of similar nature by John Bodenham, the compiler of *England's Helicon,* entitled *Politeuphuia; Wits Commonwealth,* which was popular enough, for undiscoverable reasons, to run into ten editions by 1605 and ten more before the new century was out.[1] This rather small volume combines the interests of the morality, nobility, and domestic books, and, as the title indicates, treats of almost everything under the sun, the first chapter being on God and the last on hell. Each topic is presented very briefly by means of a general statement in italics, as a proposition for demonstration, followed

[1] The similar book *Wits theatre of the little World,* is included here. The compiling of these two books seems to have been done by Ling and Allott respectively, over whom Bodenham held some kind of editorship. (See *D. N. B.*) Both books are practically the same in content.

by quotations from the classics and references to the usual well-worn historical and mythical events. The book is absolutely without arrangement, and on the whole amounts to little more than a multitude of quotations and anecdotes gathered under different headings. A far superior, although less popular, work was William Vaughan's *The Golden Grove*, published in 1599, with a second edition in 1608. The author's prefatory description of this book gives a good summary of the three treatises which compose it: "If any man delight to haue himselfe shine with a glorious shew of vertue, I haue giuen him the toppes or moral behauior; if to haue his house and family wel beautified, I haue yeelded him diuers braunches for that purpose; if to haue his country flourish, I haue sent him deep-grounded stemme of policy." To speak more plainly, the three parts consist of a typical treatise of nobility, which discusses justice, truth, magnanimity, temperance, magnificence, courtesy, friendship, patience, etc., a typical domestic book, and a book of politics, — perhaps a distant follower of Machiavelli's — treating of such things as the duties of subjects, the functions of governmental bodies, the value of education, and other interests of a commonwealth. Each treatise is divided up into short chapters, 186 in all, so that in appearance the book is much like its predecessors, but in reality the topics are better chosen and better arranged.

In the seventeenth century, we find the above types continuing. Segar's *Honor Military and Ciuill*, in 1602, and Peacham's *Compleat Gentleman*, in 1622, only border on our field, the former being concerned chiefly with arms, combats, tournaments, orders of chivalry, etc., and the latter, after a discussion of the education of youth, with the various diversions and pleasures of a man's life. Similarly, Francis Markham's *Booke of Honour*, in 1625, is also off the track, as it deals with the different orders of nobility and the honor to which they are entitled rather than with the character of a noble or a gentleman. Barckley's *A Discovrse of the Felicitie of Man*, newly corrected and augmented in 1603, is a book more of moral philosophy than of conduct. It is an extensive treatise of some 600 pages, in which it is demonstrated that the true felicity of mankind lies not in pleasure, riches, glory, or virtue, but in the "grace of God," and that man's "*summum bonum*" is "to worship and glorify God in this life that wee may be ioyned with him in the life to come." The book is not so stuffily religious as this outline would indicate, and a great deal of attention is given to classical philosophy. Bryskett's *A Discovrse of Civill Life*, in 1606, which is a pretty slavish translation of Giraldi's *Dialoghi della Vita Civile*, is not greatly different in kind from Barckley's book, but the argument depends more on the Greek and Latin philosophers than on the teachings of the Scriptures. The subjects discussed also deal much more with actual life and less with abstractions, so that whereas the *Felicitie of Man* seems properly to be classed as a book of morality, the *Civill Life* is distinctly one of gentlemanly conduct. Burton's *Anatomy of Melancholy* is too well known to require more than a word, despite its importance in literary history. The title suggests a very narrow field of interest, but the author finds place within the book for discussions of many phases of the life of man.

But by far the best example of the culmination of the type is Richard Brathwait's *The English Gentleman*, published in 1630, with later editions in 1633, 1641, and 1652. This is a large book of 456 pages, divided into eight treatises entitled youth, disposition, education, vocation (including domestic life), recreation, acquaintances, moderation, and perfection. A glance at the index, in which over 200 separate items are mentioned, gives some idea of the completeness of the work. Each topic is thoroughly treated; the argument is based first on common sense and secondly on classical and scriptural authority; and the style of writing, though showing little conscious attempt at artistry, is clear, strong, and often spirited. The book concludes with a brief characterization of the English gentleman, summarizing in a few words each of the eight main divisions, which is worthy to be put beside the better known one of Sir Philip Sidney. The companion piece to the *English Gentleman*, entitled *The English Gentlewoman*, published in 1631, does for woman what *Gentleman* work does for man.[1] In 1633, the two were published in the same volume, and in this form make one of the most interesting books, from an extra-literary standpoint, of the century, and one which certainly deserves more attention than it has received.

Three other books may be dismissed with a word each. Rous' *The Art of Happiness*, 1619, republished in 1631, is a combination of the conduct and moral philosophy types. Stafford's *Gvide to Honovr*, 1634, is a small volume of practical advice in regard to man's various activities. R. C.'s *The Happy Mind*, 1640, is similar to the *Art of Happiness*, but contains in addition a treatment of the four "complexions," which may have been suggested by the *Anatomy of Melancholy*.

All of these books, dealing with life and human nature in their different aspects, like the typical domestic book, are utilitarian rather than literary; but the development of which they are a part and the ideas they express, without doubt had a distinct influence upon the purely literary work of the time. That which comes nearest them in kind is the moral allegory, and their influence here is greater than has heretofore been demonstrated. Take the *Faerie Queene* for example, of which it is usually said that Spenser took the twelve virtues, on which the poem was to be built from the

[1] See above, pp. 162–163.

neo-Platonists of Italy.[1] It is indisputable that Spenser's debt to the thought and literature of Italy was large. Beside the better known writings of that country, he may have known Piccolomini's *Institutione Morale;* he seems to have been a friend of Bryskett, the translator of Giraldi's *Vita Civile,*[2] and perhaps knew this work in the original; and he certainly was familiar with Nenna's *Il Nennio,* since he wrote a commendatory sonnet (though a very bad one) to Jones' translation of it. Considering his interest in this kind of writing, which his valuable letter to Raleigh fully testifies, it is only natural to suppose that he read the English as well as the Italian works. It is certainly pushing the Italian influence too far to make it entirely responsible for the writing of the *Faerie Queene,* since discussion of the ideas embodied in the poem was widespread in England, both in and out of print. An interesting feature which connects Spenser's moral philosophy with English rather than Italian thought and with one of the new ideas which I have tried to emphasize in this study, is his treatment of the virtue of chastity. This he casts to be played by a woman, which is in exact keeping with the teaching of the domestic books, in which the word is used in connection with woman only and in which the virtue is regarded as especially a feminine one.

[1] Jusserand, *Mod. Phil.,* III, 373 ff., has shown that Spenser spoke carelessly in saying that he took his twelve virtues from Aristotle, and that they came rather from Renaissance interpretation of the classics. He pitches upon Piccolomini and Giraldi as the chief sources, but his evidence here is far from convincing, especially as the conversation reported by Bryskett in regard to Giraldi's book has been shown to be fictitious.

[2] Erskine, *P.M.L.A.,* XXX, 837 ff., has overthrown the belief that the famous conversation between Spenser and Bryskett actually took place; however, he believes that the two were friends, as seems more than likely, and that Spenser took his conception of friendship as a virtue from Giraldi's original Italian.

Furthermore, Spenser's conception of chastity as a characteristic of the wife and mother, rather than of the virgin only, is in keeping with the new thought of the German and English Reformation and contrary to that of Catholicism, which held sway in Italy.[1] It is evident that the doctrines of the *Faerie Queene* came, for the most part, from the classics; but these doctrines were influenced and added to not only by Christian philosophy but by the new religious and moral ideas of the sixteenth century.[2] These two elements in Spenser's allegorical treatment of the English gentleman have been neglected by students of his work, probably because they have been ignorant of the English books discussed above and of the extent of English thought on the subject.

Of the less known moral allegories, space allows for mention of only three, which from their obvious connection with the books we have been studying, seem to stand out as particularly important.

An interesting book of purely moral conduct type was published in 1584 by W. Averell.[3] It contains three treatises, entitled *A dyall for dainty darlings, rockt in the cradle of securitie, A glasse for all disobedient sounes to look in,* and *A myrrour for vertuous maydes.* The main feature of each treatise is an exemplum tale of some length, inculcating the desired lesson. The style is typically Euphuistic, although lacking Lyly's lightness of touch. The opening of the first tale is as follows:

[1] Bacon, in his essay *Married and Single Life,* also speaks of chastity as a characteristic of the married woman. Contrast Spenser's and Bacon's conception of chastity with the earlier English usage of the term by Chaucer in the Prologue to the Wife of Bath's Tale, where it is consistently used as a synomym of virginity and an antonym to the marriage state. See also Donne's remark on the subject, p. 122, n. 1, above.

[2] Spenser himself refers to St. Paul's teachings. See above, p. 181.

[3] The book goes under the combined titles of the three treatises.

"There was within the famous Cittie of Constantinople, a Captaine ouer a certayne bande of Venetians, who, if he could as well, by wisdome haue gouerned his wiues infirmitie, as he could by pollicie conduct and rule his armie, his memorie had beene obscured with blotte of obliuion, and his wiues example drowned in the suddes of silence." [1]

A still more interesting volume is *Willobie his Avisa,* in 1594, which ran into four more editions by 1610. According to the "Epistle to the Reader," it was put out by Hadrian Dobell, who says that he found it among Willoby's papers.[2] It is this book which contains, in one of the commendatory verses, the first definite printed reference to Shakespeare, and also, in the poem itself, a character called W. S., whom some fond critics have taken for the bard of Avon himself, Avisa being the "dark lady." [3] The epistle has other references to contemporary literature in the sentence, "Although hee flye not alofte with the wings of Astrophell, nor dare to compare with the Arcadian shepherd, or any way match with the daintie *Fayry Queene* . . ." The poem itself, which runs to 74 cantos and 128 pages, represents the "true picture of a modest maid and of a chast and constant wife" under the attempts of various suitors to make love to her. But she remains true to her name, the letters of which stand for "*Amans vxor inuolata semper amanda.*"

"So thus she stands vnconquered yet,
As Lambe amidst the Lions pause,
Whom gifts, nor wils, nor force of wit,

[1] Averell, *op. cit.*, f. Bi *b*.

[2] The whole account of this publication is probably fictitious.

[3] See Grosart, Introd. to his reprint of the *Avisa;* also Fleay, *Life Shakes.*, p. 121 ff., and *Biog. Chron.*, II, 221 ff. This theory seems to me, like that built up on Milton's divorce tracts, a case of first putting the plum in the pie.

Could vanquish once with all their shewes,
To speake the truth, and say no more,
I neuer knew her like before." [1]

Spenser's imitators are well known and may be omitted here. But I must mention one small book of this class which seems to have been overlooked heretofore. This is *The Labyrinth of Mans Life* by John Norden in 1614. It is an allegory of the Spenserian type, but differs from the latter in that it is made up chiefly of moralizing on the part of the author and the characters and contains little action. One stanza of the author's prefatory verses is worth quoting for its references to contemporary writers.

"Chawcer, Gowre, the bishop of dunkell,
In ages farre remote were eloquent:
Now Sidney, Spencer, others moe excell,
And are in latter times more excellent
To antique Lauriats paralell." [2]

The book itself is in heroic couplets, an early example of their use. The verses given as the argument of the poem summarize both its story and its moral teaching.

"The Man that in the Cell of Silence sits,
Imports content, in his distastfull fits,
The Labyrinth, the worlds inconstancie,
The passionate Desert doth signifie.

True vertue doth the Lady represent,
The hag foule Enuy, alwaies malecontent:
Who what the Ladie, frames and rectifies,
She in despite, inchants, and vilifies.

Wherein the Authors purpose is to show,
Enuies assault, And Vertues counterblow:
How Enuie showes her most obsequious,
When she would circumuent the Vertuous." [3]

[1] Willoby, *op. cit.*, f. 62 *b*.
[2] Norden, *op. cit.*, f. A3 *b*.
[3] *Ibid.*, f. Bi *b*.

II. Domestic Drama [1]

As has already been noted, the drama was early used for satire against women and the marriage state in general. In the *Towneley Mysteries*, for instance, the merry devil Tutivillus is given the special office of denouncing women who talk in church; in the same cycle, the quarreling of Noah and his wife, due to the latter's shrewishness, forms an episode of some importance; and Joseph, previous to the flight of the holy family into Egypt, soliloquizes on the troubles of married life and warns the young people of the audience against entering into it. Among the moralities, the problem of the proper upbringing of children was occasionally touched on, as in *Nice Wanton;* and in a few cases, the state of matrimony itself was dealt with in plays presenting the evils of forced and ill-assorted unions and of marriages made by children against the will of their parents, as in *Juventus Pater Uxor* and *The Disobedient Child.* But the excursions of the morality into the field of home life for the purpose of instruction as to family relations, did not give rise to any series of moral domestic plays in later drama; for although there is evidence that some feeling existed even into James' reign that the stage should be used as a didactic medium and "so obtain the very end of poesy," — as Sidney put it — it is not possible to find more than a handful of plays in all fields combined that have any well-defined moral issue as their basis.

Despite this lack of moral intent, there can be no doubt that some of the plays put on were designed to present a

[1] By domestic drama I mean that dealing with family life. The occasional use of the term to refer to native plays or influences or to plays of middle-class life, is here disregarded altogether. For fuller information on plays mentioned, see Schelling, *Elizabethan Drama, 1558–1642.* A list of Elizabethan plays, telling where each is published, may be found *ibid.*, II, 538.

domestic situation or problem for the consideration of the public; such plays as *Arden of Faversham* and *A Warning for Fair Women* were even taken from actual life and dramatized as horrible examples of evil households. But among the many plays dealing with domestic relations of one kind or another, we are forced to admit that comparatively few were actually aimed to present or dicuss marriage itself or the allied interests found in the domestic conduct books. As a rule, the importance of the home in the drama of the time is chiefly that of a convenient setting for a plot which, although involving husband, wife, and perhaps children, is motivated more by outside agents than by actions or passions within the family circle. Moreover, in those plays where it is evident that the author had some serious intention to instruct, as in *How a Man May Choose a Good Wife from a Bad,* the lesson often fails of actual demonstration. Nevertheless, a number of plays remain which do present domestic conditions, and if indeed they are not motivated to any great extent by family relations, they at least offer marital problems for thought and discussion. The commonest subject presented in this connection was the situation produced in a family by an extraordinary wife, a creature who seems to have existed in but two types, the "complete shrew" and the "perfect sheep." In addition, we find the "horrible example" play of marriage at its worst, plays on the contention of parents and children in regard to marriage, and several triangle plays, like *A Woman Killed with Kindness*, wherein the author seems to have had a real feeling for the subtle possibilities of the domestic drama to portray the more intimate thoughts, feelings, and situations of human life. In as much as all these plays have a distinct connection, of subject matter at least, with general domestic literature and the ideas therein expressed, it will be worth while to glance briefly at some of the more noteworthy.

The first play in which the shrewish wife is more than episodic is the well-known comedy *Johan Johan* usually attributed to John Heywood, c. 1532. Here she is not only the central figure but the motive force as well, and the fun is chiefly at the expense of her too patient husband. Up to this time, the shrew is primarily a comic figure in the drama, with perhaps just a touch of the didactic; but about the middle of the century, we find, in *Tom Tyler and his Wife*, the same theme used in a semi-morality play. There is a certain amount of fun in this piece, but the final resolution is entirely serious, in which the wife is persuaded by Patience to try to live on more amicable terms with the world. The two plays *Juventus Pater Uxor* and *The Disobedient Child* make a still more serious use of the shrew in employing her as one of the chief elements in driving home a moral. Both plays are on the theme of the marriage of children against the wishes of their parents, in which the wife acts the part of nemesis, since the evils of both marriages are due largely to the fact that the brides turn out to be shrews. Thus what was originally a comic situation at the expense of the woman became a tragic and didactic one for the instruction of the man. The resultant plots might almost be said to be dramatizations of certain chapters of the domestic book, the husband's career illustrating the value of the warnings against forbidden marriages, and the unattractive character of the wife representing the evil results of the woman's flying in the face of St. Paul's dictum and usurping the authority over the man.

But with the decline of the morality play, the shrew, when forming the central figure of a drama, became rehabilitated as a comic character. In *The Taming of a Shrew*, the didactic element has given away altogether to the comic. The forbidden marriage motive is also absent, and the play resolves itself into the mere carrying out of the action suggested in the title. The single serious element occurs in Kate's final subjection to her husband and her speech explaining the reasons for her docility. Shakespeare's adaptation of this play under the almost identical title needs no further comment.[1] An important contrast between these two plays and their predecessors lies in the fact that, whereas the earlier ones were written for the instruction of the man in regard to marriage, their successors have no well-defined interest in marriage itself but merely aim to present an entertaining combat of wits. Thus, although the wife is the butt of the comedy, it may not be pushing a point too far to find an influence of the growing attitude towards woman in the fact that she holds an equal part with the man and is regarded as a foe worthy of his steel. Later plays use the shrew motive almost entirely for the purpose of amusement. Fletcher, in his sequel to Shakespeare's *Shrew*, *The Woman's Prize*, reverses the course of the action and builds a good farce comedy thereupon. Here Maria, by blockading herself indoors against her husband, who is a sottish, carnally minded brute, successfully acts the shrew and brings him to a respectful attitude towards her and a realization of his own shortcomings.[2] At bottom, this play is based on a serious idea, but since the action is developed by comic situation and characters, the basic theme can receive but little consideration as a serious issue. The remaining shrews of current

[1] An interesting contrast occurs between the two versions of Kate's last speech. In the earlier play, she harks back to Biblical authority for the subjection of woman; but Shakespeare's heroine finds her support in romantic traditions, whereby, since the husband suffers dangers and hardships abroad, the wife should be willing to follow and obey him at home.

[2] Mary in *Monsieur Thomas* plays similar tricks on her lover. Indeed, Fletcher's heroines in comedy are usually a bit shrewish, and like Kate in *The Shrew*, may indicate an increasing respect for woman's position and rights.

drama — for instance the hostile wives in Porter's *Two Angry Women of Abington*, Eyre's wife in Dekker's *Shoemakers' Holiday*, Candido's wife in Dekker and Middleton's *The Honest Whore*, Pt. 2, Lady Cressingham and Mrs. Chamlet in Middleton's *Anything for a Quiet Life* — play but small parts, present no new interests, and may be passed over with the remark that since the shrew motive by this time was used for comedy only, we cannot think that the situations based on it were aimed to give any more serious attention to such incompatibility of temper in the family than that of laughing the offender out of court.

The patient wife, though a frequent figure in the drama, presents but few cases of real interest.[1] She was used as early as 1538 by Radcliff in a non-extant play, but did not come into prominence as a type until the end of the century, when she appears as a victim in three situations: (1) as a deserted wife, remaining faithful to an absent husband (or lover); (2) as a "patient Grissel," loyal and loving in the face of her husband's cruelty; (3) in a triangle plot involving either her husband's pursuit of another woman or her own persecution by a would-be lover. In one way or another, most of the leading dramatists of the day used the patient wife motive, but it is difficult to say that it was employed in more than a few of these to present a definite moral idea. In *Othello*, for instance, Desdemona is entirely a lay figure, neither consciously furthering the action of the play nor awakening any particular interest on the part of the audience except as a pitiable victim of circumstance. The same may be said of most of the other women abused or deserted by husbands or lovers, such as Dorothea in Greene's *James IV*, Hero in Shakespeare's *Much Ado about Nothing*, Hermione in *The Winter's Tale*, Catherine in *Henry VIII*, Mrs. Arthur in *How a Man May Choose*, Bellafronte and Infaeliche in *The Honest Whore*, Luce in *The London Prodigal*, Isabella in

[1] This motive originated in the French moralities of the fourteenth century.

Webster's *White Devil*, and others. In some cases, the wife, though passive towards her husband's or lover's character, is active in rescuing him from trouble or in bringing his desertion to an end, as in *Patient Grissel*, by Dekker, Chettle, and Houghton, in Shakespeare's *All's Well that Ends Well*, and in Heywood's *Fair Maid of the West*, Pt. 2. In the first of these, she solves the situation by the mere stubbornness of her patience; in *All's Well*, she wins her husband back by deliberate plotting; and in *The Fair Maid*, she takes ship and goes in search of him. In a very few patient wife plots, notably *Patient Grissel*, the husband is confessedly "testing" his spouse — as God tested Job — and the play ends when he thinks she has had enough; in others, as *Henry VIII* and *The White Devil*, the wife drops out altogether, her case being hopeless; in two or three, *Othello* and *The Wonder of Women* for instance, the situation is allowed to run to its most logical conclusion and end in tragedy; and in others, most numerous of all, the author concludes a tiresome succession of sordid scenes by bringing husband and wife to a reconciliation, and having placed them in mutual embrace, leaves them to live happily together ever afterwards as a reward for never having been able to live happily together before.

It is evident to any one reading these plays that there must have existed in the minds of the dramatists some idea of setting forth patience as a wifely virtue, especially in such a play as *Patient Grissel;* but it is not safe to read more than this into the woman's end of the average plot. In the cases of Isabella and Catherine, one can hardly assert this much, as their careers cannot be taken as advertizing the desirable virtue except in so far as it fulfils specifications in being its own, and only, reward. In most of the plays, although the wife's patience surpasses the bounds of all reason, it really has little or no effect upon the plot except to provide a constant

Constance whenever the villainous husband is ready to reward her with an eleventh-hour reformation. In other words, the patient wife in such plays exists less as a model for womankind than as a convenient means to the dramatist for keeping one thread of his plot well in hand. Exception may be taken to the last two statements in the cases of *Patient Grissel*, *All's Well*, and Wilkins' *Miseries of Enforced Marriage*, since in these the wife puts herself in the wrong, to some degree at least, at the outset and may logically be expected to have to work out her own salvation. Grissel, like Margaret in Greene's *Friar Bacon and Friar Bungay*, consents to a marriage well above her own station of life and owes it to society to prove herself worthy of the alliance. Helena plays a far from gracious part at the opening of *All's Well* by forcing herself, with the help of the King, upon Bertram; and having thus usurped the authority over the man, must suffer in consequence. From the first, she is the protagonist; and as the abuse she receives from her husband is desertion only, which she fully deserved, she appears more as a woman fighting for what she believes to be her rights than as a patient wife waiting for them to be showered into her lap. Katherine, in *Miseries of Enforced Marriage*, is similar in some degree to Helena, since she allows herself to be party to a marriage forced upon Scarborow after he has been made to break his former contract with Clare; but like her sisters in *How a Man May Choose*, *The London Prodigal*, and other plays, her subsequent career amounts merely to watchful waiting for her husband to return to her arms after going to the devil in his own way. It seems clear in these three plays, as well as in a few others on the same motive which are noted below, that the dramatist was actually attacking the problem of the abused wife; but except in the case of Grissel, whose abuse was more apparent than real, he reached no conclusion.

Among the plays which we may classify as horrible examples of unfortunate marriages, we may cite two illustrating the evil of adultery and resultant viciousness, two dealing with forced marriage, and two whose titles suggest them to have been written with didactic intent. The first pair, the anonymous *Arden of Faversham* and *A Warning for Fair Women*, which are practically identical in plot, present a commonplace sequence of events leading from a triangle situation of husband, wife, and paramour. The greater part of both is taken up with the persistent attempts of the wife and her gallant to murder the husband, and both end with the villains in the hands of the law. As presenting the evil results of illicit love, these plays have a certain amount of crude force; but since the husband in each case offends only by existing, it would seem that the dramatist had aimed merely to exhibit the ugliness of sin and not to discuss the relations of husband and wife. Nevertheless, as attempts to deal with an existing domestic problem, these two plays are worthy of attention. The forced marriage situation occurs in *The London Prodigal* and *The Miseries of Enforced Marriage*, both of which fail to demonstrate convincingly the advertised lesson, since the unhappiness of each couple is due less to the forced marriage than to the simple fact that the husband is a rascal. This is apparent especially in *The London Prodigal*, where the man is anxious for the alliance but the girl is forced into it by her father. It should be said, however, that the forcing of the bride is not particularly emphasized, and perhaps the dramatist had no intention of making it a motivating element. But the title of the second play gives us distinctly to understand that the writer had in mind the presentation of a definite marriage problem, a forced marriage complicated by a broken contract.[1] This situation forecasts a very interesting

[1] It is worthy of note that *The Miseries of Enforced Marriage*, like *Arden of Faversham*, *A Warning for Fair Women*, and *The Yorkshire Tragedy*, deals with actual crimes recently committed.

play involving husband, former sweetheart, and wife; but none of the possibilities of the triangle are realized. The husband, angered at the marriage forced upon him, soon deserts his wife; but instead of returning to his sweetheart, he pursues the primrose path with evil companions until he is reduced to supporting himself by swindling and thievery. Just as he is preparing to add the murder of his wife and children to his other pleasant activities, he learns that his guardian, the original trouble-maker, is dead and that he is heir to a fortune. This solves every difficulty, brings order out of chaos, and unites husband and wife in marital bliss. Although, as may be seen, the miseries of the marriage are not convincingly shown to have resulted from its having been forced, the avowed attempt to present the problem is none the less important. The titles of the anonymous *A Warning for Fair Women* and of *How a Man May Choose a Good Wife from a Bad*, sometimes ascribed to Thomas Heywood, also tell of attempts at instruction on the subject of matrimony. The first, already noted, in a way fulfils its promise; the second does not get beyond the picturing of a patient wife — patient *ad infinitum* and *ad nauseam* — and of a villainous whore, her husband's mistress. Except in presenting models of a good wife and a bad woman, the secret of how the inexperienced are to tell the one from the other is not revealed. This play too, then, is a worthy effort but hardly an achievement of its apparent purpose. One criticism that must be passed on these unhappy-marriage plays, except the first two noted, is that at the end of each the author snatches the fat from the fire by reconciling all parties, and leaves the reader with the feeling that after all the marriage turns out successfully; so that much of the moral force present in the two murder plays is lost to the others. The fact that where the wife is the offender the plays result in tragedy, but where the husband performs equal and worse crimes they result in forgiveness and reconciliation, is no mere accident but in strict keeping with the domestic ideals of the day.

Plays involving the contention of children against parents in regard to marriage are worthy of consideration for a moment here only because of the attention given to this subject in the domestic books. In the drama, we find an interesting development in the use of the situation from the typical morality showing the evils of marriages made against the will of parents to the romantic comedy where the parents are made the dupes of the young people. The moralities *Juventus Pater Uxor* and *The Disobedient Child,* discussed above, illustrate the first use, and further comment upon them is unnecessary. Shakespeare evidently wished to emphasize the child-parent contention in *Romeo and Juliet,* since he altered the original story to make Juliet under the legal age for marriage and in addition shifted the contract made for her by her parents from the middle to the beginning of the play.[1] The emphasizing of the theme of crabbed age and youth certainly adds vastly to the original plot, but it may be pushing a point too far to consider this its chief motivation. The two plays in which a marriage is forced upon the young people, *The London Prodigal* and *Miseries of Enforced Marriage,* have already been commented upon. Up to this time, we may say that the dramatist evidently had some idea of driving home a moral, either for parents or children, in his use of the child *versus* parent motive; but in later plays, the situation becomes a typical starting point for comedy, although more serious use of it may occasionally be

[1] In the Bandello version of the story, Juliet is almost eighteen; in Broke's version, she is sixteen; in the play, she is just under fourteen, as is carefully brought to the audience's attention in act 1, sc. 3, and suggested as Lady Capulet's reason for wishing her contracted at once. The marriage with Paris is broached in the same scene, that is, before the meeting of Juliet with Romeo; thus in contracting herself to Romeo, Juliet consciously defies her parents' wishes.

found. Shakespeare himself used the motive for comedy in the Lorenzo-Jessica incident of *The Merchant of Venice.* In Houghton's *Englishmen for my Money,* three sisters outwit their father, who wishes to contract them to three foreigners, and marry their native lovers. In *The Shoemakers' Holiday,* Lacy, by means of a disguise, succeeds in carrying off Rose, though both families were opposed to the match. In *The Two Angry Women of Abington,* the mothers only oppose the union, but again it is successfully brought off. The cruel father in Drayton's *Merry Devil of Edmonton* puts his daughter in a nunnery in order to foil the persistent lover, but he, in the disguise of a priest, effects her escape and their subsequent marriage. Middleton's *Roaring Girl* presents a father who, having arranged a match for his son, tries to back out of the marriage settlement; but the son, by pretending to be in love with a supposed prostitute, succeeds in making his father carry out the original contract. In the subplot of *The Woman's Prize,* Livia outwits her father, who wishes to marry her to old Morosa, and with the help of a friend, weds the man of her choice. All of these plays are but superficially domestic; that is, the paternal and filial elements are very slight, and their place might be taken just as well by any other force standing in the way of the marriage. The most that can be said of this situation is that the parents furnish the dramatist with a convenient obstacle for the young people to overcome. The fact that the parents are made ridiculous in their attempt to carry out what was really their right, shows how far the drama had strayed from the use it originally made of the situation.

The triangle of husband, wife, and friend, which today is so often made the starting point of a domestic drama, was seldom developed in this way during the period under consideration. Although many plays may be found dealing with adultery, incest, and other crimes against marital society, such situations are used more as a means to introduce or complicate a plot of intrigue and adventure than to present the subtle and intimate relations of family life. Most of the triangle plays which do discuss or touch upon domestic problems have already been noted in other connections, for example, the two murder plays, several of the patient wife plays, and others. Of all the dramatists of the day, Thomas Heywood alone gives evidence of a realization of the great possibilities of the domestic drama, although others, Shakespeare especially, at moments rise to heights of unfulfilled promise in this field.[1]

Heywood drew his first picture of a noble husband and wife in *Edward IV.* Here Jane Shore is chosen for the "great promotion" of being the King's mistress. But amid the splendors of her new station, she remains true at heart to her husband; and he, realizing that she is powerless in the King's hands, is steadfast in his love and faith to her, and after she is cast out of court, he takes care of her at the peril of his life. Since opposition to the royal prerogative was impossible, Jane and Master Shore are able to contribute to the development of the play only a noble picture of husband and wife true to each other and to their marriage vows as far as they are able in the face of extreme persecution. The length to which this tableau is drawn out shows that the dramatist wished to emphasize the situation, although he was unable to use it as a motive force in the main plot. In *A Woman Killed with Kindness,* Heywood for the first time in English drama dealt tenderly with the erring wife. Here

[1] Heywood's interest in domestic literature has already been noted in connection with his books on women. (See above, p. 162.) It may be mentioned that the story of Geraldine occurs both in the *History of Woman,* Bk. IV, and in *A Woman Killed with Kindness.* Unfortunately only one tenth of Heywood's plays are extant, so that a complete or satisfactory study of his domestic ideas as shown in his dramatic work is impossible.

Mrs. Frankford, more out of sheer weakness than out of love for her tempter, falls a victim to his pursuit. At the discovery of her shame, Frankford conscientiously faces the problem thus brought before him and attempts to fit punishment to crime. Although his solution of the difficulty — that of shutting his wife up in solitary confinement — may leave a good deal to be desired, the fact that he acts without malice and forgives her in the end shows an entirely new attitude towards the fallen woman, who as a rule got but scant sympathy in either the drama or the life of the time. Mrs. Frankford, after her fall, plays a part almost equal to her husband's; for realizing her own guilt and his fineness of feeling towards her, she turns from her lover to her husband and at his forgiveness dies happy. In *The English Traveller*, Heywood again touched upon somewhat the same theme, this time basing it upon a January and May situation — a favorite problem of the day — and making the young wife intrigue with a false friend of her husband's. Most of the play is concerned with the pure love of another family friend (a theme in itself worthy of note), and the intrigue is not revealed until the last scene of the play. Again the erring wife casts off her lover and dies repentant and finally forgiven. Since all three of these plays are resolved by the very convenient death of the wife, it is evident that Heywood found no real solution of the domestic problem he attacked; but in his treatment of both husband and wife, he shows himself far ahead of his time and comes near to the modern attitude of malice towards none but charity for all.[1]

With this point of view in mind, the student will readily find touches in not a few plays which approach Heywood's attitude towards man and woman in their relations to each other. Othello's struggle between the faith of love and the

[1] Cf. also Master Generous and his attempt to redeem his wife in *The Late Lancashire Witches*.

evidence of circumstances is an obvious example, although this play is a study of the man only. One of the noblest couples in Elizabethan drama is Massinissa and Sophonisba in Marston's *The Wonder of Women,* where the husband preserves his faith in his wife despite slander, and the wife willingly gives her life in order to save her own honor and fulfil her husband's pledge. But it is unnecessary here to multiply examples.

As to the influence of the domestic and other conduct books on the drama or the drama's influence on the conduct books, we are forced to conclude that very little existed. On the whole, the most we can say is that in both we often find expression of the same attitudes and ideas, which in each case seem to have been the reflection of current thought rather than an influence from one field to the other. The drama, as well as the other forms of literature previously discussed, illustrates the attitudes of the time towards woman; and conversely, contemporary opinions regarding woman help to explain her position in the drama. It is noteworthy that in very few plays is she the protagonist. Her position of subservience in the family was probably the largest element in preventing the domestic relations of husband and wife from being by themselves the motivating force of a realistic play, except one of very light nature such as *The Shrew*. Elsewhere family relations are of secondary importance in the plot, which is motivated more by some influence from without than from within the home circle. Othello's tragedy, for instance, is brought about much more by Iago than by Desdemona or himself. The same situation occurs in the child *versus* parent play, the motive force being not the opposition of youth to age but the attraction of the child to the outside agent, here the lover. It is, of course, difficult to construct a play on domestic relations alone and uninfluenced strongly from without, but the modern and better way is to make the outside force contributary rather than fundamental.[1] To this ideal none of the Elizabethan playwrights reached; Heywood came the nearest, surpassing even Shakespeare, and in *Edward IV* and *A Woman Killed* constructed plays in which the outside influence ceases after bringing things to a climax, and the falling action, here more than usually important, is carried on by husband and wife alone. Despite the apparent lack of influence from the drama upon the conduct books, it is reasonable to believe that it had a distinct influence upon the thought of the day. Certainly the presentation of so many plays dealing with love, marriage, carnal sin, and so forth, whether romantic, historical, or domestic, must have had an effect upon the popular conception of family relations; and in the imaginative literature of the theatre, the idealization of woman and the recognition of woman's importance gained a public hearing which could not pass unnoticed.

[1] Cf., for instance, such a play as Ibsen's *Doll's House* or Brieux's *Blanchette*.

APPENDIX A

ENGLISH WRITING ON THE DIVORCE OF HENRY VIII AND CATHERINE

THE divorce of Henry VIII from his first wife, which occupied a large part of his attention from 1527 to 1534, was the subject of controversial writing in England, France, Germany, Italy, and Spain, and was of extreme importance politically in every country of Europe, affecting even Turkey. Every man of any prominence in England was involved in the agitation, either as a pamphleteer or as a political supporter of one side or the other. There were two main points in the controversy: (1) whether or not a man might marry his brother's widow; (2) whether the Pope had exceeded his authority in allowing Henry to marry Catherine, who had been the wife of his brother Arthur.[1] A third point, of less consequence, was the question as to whether the marriage of Arthur and Catherine had been consummated by bodily knowledge, and if so, or if not, what effect this had upon the case.[2] These three points were the entire subject matter of the debate.

[1] The King's supporters held, of course, that in no case might a man marry his brother's widow and that the Pope had had no proper authority to allow the marriage with Catherine in the beginning. The King's hypocrisy in the matter may be seen from the fact that a marriage with the sister of a mistress was as much against ecclesiastical law as one with the widow of a brother, since both were within the forbidden degrees of the Levitical law (see above, p. 10, nn. 1. 3). Anne Boleyn's sister Mary had been Henry's mistress (see statement by Pole, p. 222 below); thus the law he was trying to establish in order to invalidate the existing union with his wife, equally forbade the intended one with his sweetheart.

[2] The law of Deuteronomy (XXV, 5) enjoining the marriage of a man with his brother's widow in case she was childless, if proved to supersede that of Leviticus (XVIII, 16, and XX, 21), which men-

In the *Letters and State Papers of Henry VIII*, there are listed some sixty or seventy documents, preserved at the London Record Office and elsewhere, dealing with this controversy, which range from manuscripts of a few pages to printed books of considerable length.[1] Almost all of them are in Latin, and only a few ever appeared in printed form. In addition to these, there are several better known works on the subject. No account of this controversy as a whole has ever been given, but a few of the books involved have been mentioned, usually with mistakes as to date, in works on the Reformation.

Difficulties as to date, authorship, etc., arise at the very outset of our investigation and grow more complicated the further we go in it. The first mention of any controversial writing, according to the present chronological arrangement of state documents, is in two letters to the King, one by Richard Pace and the other by Robert Wakefield. Neither of the original manuscripts bears a date, but both are included in the *State Papers* under the year 1527.[2] The reason for thus placing them is that they occur in printed form at the end of a book by Wakefield, *Kotser Codicis R. Wakefeldi*, where they are dated 1527. It is clear from internal evidence that Wakefield's letter was written a day or two after Pace's; thus we may consider them together. The information supplied by them is: (1) from Pace, that he had prepared a treatise "not without the Councell of Maister Wakfeld" in behalf of the King; (2) from Wakefield, "I have and will . . . answer the bishop of Rochester's[3] book." These letters and their supposed date have been made the starting point of a good deal of

tioned no exceptions to its forbidden degrees, would render Henry's cause without Biblical support. To obviate this, in any case, his supporters interpreted the word childless to mean virginal. Thus the point as to whether there had been *carnalis copula* between Arthur and Catherine, was of some importance.

[1] Most of these are listed at the beginning of Vol. V, but others are mentioned both before and after this.

[2] *State Papers*, IV, 3233 and 3234. They are here summarized only. They are given in full form in Knight, *Erasmus*, App. VIII and IX.

[3] John Fisher was Bishop of Rochester.

history and biography. I am now able to demonstrate that they were antedated (probably by Berthelet, the printer, who is often in error as to dates) and were in fact not written until 1529, as follows: (1) The *Kotser Codicis,* in which they are first given a date, could not possibly have been printed before December, 1530, as is shown below.[1] (2) In 1527, the divorce was still a secret matter and was not discussed outside of a very narrow circle. (3) Wakefield says in his letter that he shifted from the Queen's side to the King's because of the claim, which he believed true, that she had been carnally known by Arthur. This point was first officially advanced on June 28, 1529. (4) All evidence (except Wakefield's letter) points to the fact that Fisher's first writing on the subject was the "little book" presented at the Queen's trial on June 28, 1529 (Wakefield could not have undertaken to answer Fisher's book before it was written). (5) Pace in his letter speaks of an "Alphabete in Hebrewe Tunge" and asks the King "to delyver the saide Alphabete to Maister Foxe your selfe." This reference is, of course, to Edward Foxe, who in 1527 had never been heard of by the court. His admission as prebendary of Osbaldwicke on Nov. 8, 1527, was his first step out of obscurity. But in 1528, he gained prominence through being sent by Gardiner to Rome, and after his return, was in attendance upon the King at Waltham during August, 1529. The letters then, are definitely settled to have been written during that month, and the history and biography based on the earlier date must be revised.

The writings mentioned by Pace and Wakefield being out of the way for the present, we find that the King himself was the first in the field of written controversy. Whether he entered upon his own initiative and wrote according to his own knowledge and skill, or whether, in the whole course, he acted upon the suggestion and with the assistance of his ecclesiastical advisers, we cannot say. In 1528, he writes to Anne Boleyn that he has a book in progress, to which he had devoted four hours' work that very day.[2] Later, in 1532, Chapuys, in writing to Charles V of Foxe's

[1] See below, p. 221.

[2] *State Papers,* IV, 4597. This letter is not dated, but it is recorded under the year 1528.

journey to France, says that he carried "many books touching the divorce most of them written by the King." [1] Other references occur in letters of the time to "the King's book"; but it is impossible to tell whether these are to the work mentioned by the King and, if so, what it was, or whether the phrase means a book of the King's authorship or merely one in his cause. At any rate, no extant book is now attributed to him, except the *Glasse of the Truthe*, whose slight claim to royal authorship is discussed below.[2]

John Fisher, then, is the first man to whom we can definitely assign a book on this subject which is now extant and correctly attributed to him. During the course of the divorce, he was the author of seven or eight books on the Queen's side of the dispute, most of which were never printed. Fisher's biographers have overlooked these almost entirely.[3] On June 28, 1529, Fisher was called upon to appear before the Pope's legates, and there he both defended the Queen's cause and presented a "little book" on the subject of the divorce. The title of this work is given in the *State Papers* as *Licitum fuisse matrimonium Henr. VIII cum Catherina relicta fratris sui Arthuri.*[4] The book was never printed, but a manuscript copy still exists in the Cambridge University Library, No. 1315 (12). It is but forty-four leaves in all. Tanner mentions this book also, giving it the title *Defensorum matrimonii*

[1] *State Papers*, V, 251.

[2] See below, p. 219 ff.

[3] Bridgett, *Blessed John Fisher*, p. 162 ff. and notes, is the only biographer to give any account of Fisher's writings on the divorce (even the *Camb. Hist. Eng. Lit.* is deficient here), and his remarks are both inadequate and inaccurate. He says that some were printed in Spain, which is true, but goes on to mention three, which investigation proves to be all the same one, the *De Causa*, inaccurately described in different ways. He says further: "MS. copies of these treatises are in the Record Office, the British Museum, and the Cambridge University Library. The library of St. John's College, Cambridge, possesses one of his printed books." This printed book, however, is not on the divorce; and I have been able to find no manuscript treatise of it in the British Museum. The other documents I mention below.

[4] *State Papers*, IV, 5728.

regis cum Catherina, lib. 1,[1] but describes it as beginning with the same words as does the Cambridge manuscript. He says further, "*Saepissime citatur a Nic. Harpsfeld in Hist. divortii.*" He is wrong here; the book discussed by Harpsfield is not this one.[2] The King replied to Fisher in a declaration to the judges, in which "the Latin vocabulary is ransacked for the choicest epithets of vituperation." [3] On Feb. 6, 1530, Chapuys, writing to Charles V, says, "Since my last the bishop of Rochester has finished revising the book he lately wrote. . . . Since then he was written another." [4] The last previously recorded letter from Chapuys to Charles is dated Oct. 25, 1529. The new book by Fisher is probably the *De Causa Matrimonii*, described in the *State Papers* as "Fisher's Second Book on the Divorce." [5] This book was published at Compluti, Spain, in August, 1530. It consists of forty-one folios of weighty scholasticism, discussing the disputed passages of Leviticus and Deuteronomy, especially the latter, and giving opinions and examples on the subject from the time of the early fathers down. Chapuys refers to the publication of Fisher's books in Spain in a letter to the Emperor dated Nov. 27, 1530, and further says that he has commissioned May to have two of them printed for distribution in Parliament.[6] On Dec. 4, he writes again, "The bishop of Rochester has finished a book in favour of the Queen." [7] It would seem that this was a later book, but further identification is impossible.

About this time, Thomas Abel, the Queen's chaplain, appears to have busied himself in her cause. Wood says that in 1529 or 1530 "he shewed himself a zealous advocate against the divorce of the said queen. . . . At which time he wrote, *Tract. de non dissolvendo Henrici & Catherinae matrimonio.*" [8] Tanner mentions

[1] Tanner, *Bibliotheca Britannica-Hibernica*, p. 281.

[2] See below, p. 217 ff.

[3] *State Papers*, IV, p. ccccixxix.

[4] *Ibid.*, 6199.

[5] *Ibid.*, IV., 6596. Although quite accessible, this book is not even mentioned in the *D.N.B.* account of Fisher.

[6] *Ibid.*, IV, 6738.

[7] *Ibid.*, IV, 6757.

[8] Wood, *Athenae Oxonienses*, I, 119.

another book by Abel on the subject, *Invicta Veritas: An Answer that by no manner of law it may be lawful for the King to be divorced from the Queen's Grace, etc.*[1] This seems to have been in English. It is mentioned by Wakefield in his *Kotser Codicis*, and, as Tanner says, "*citat et repugnat.*" Both of Abel's books are apparently non-extant. The *State Papers*, under the year 1531, cite three treatises in reply to Abel,[2] one of which is entitled, *A confutation of that answer which Master John Abell, priest, lately made against the Book of Determinations of the Universities in the King's cause.*"[3] This seems to refer to Abel's second treatise. The determinations of the universities were not rendered until 1530; the date of the book containing them — another problem — is discussed below.[4] Chapuys, writing in 1532, speaks of a book by a chaplain of the Queen (doubtless Abel) as being in print but prohibited by the King.[5]

Wakefield fulfilled his promise to reply to the Bishop of Rochester's book by writing the *Kotser Codicis R. Wakefeldi quo praeter ecclesiae . . . decretum, probatur conjugium cum fratria carnaliter cognita, illicitum . . . interdictumque esse, etc.*[6] Pocock has overthrown the date originally set for this book (1528),[7] but has come to no definite conclusion himself as to the correct date of either its writing or its publication. The matter is so involved with the date of Wakefield's other book on the subject that it seems best to postpone the problem for the moment.[8] Suffice it to say here that my conclusion is that it was written immediately after Fisher's first book — that is in the summer of 1529 — and that it was not

[1] Tanner, p. 1.

[2] *State Papers*, V, 1.

[3] There is still a question as to whether "John Abell, priest," may be taken to refer to the Queen's chaplain, whose first name was Thomas. The index to the volume cites the two names separately, but I can find no other reference to any John Abell.

[4] See below, p. 214 ff.

[5] *State Papers*, V, 1256.

[6] Wood correctly describes this book as the one mentioned by Bale and Pitts under the title of *De non ducenda Fratria.*

[7] Pocock, in notes to his edition of Harpsfield's *Pretended Divorce*, p. 309.

[8] See below, p. 221.

published until 1536. The *Kotser Codicis* is aimed to be a thorough refutation of Fisher's argument; but despite the author's conceited remark that he intended to so humble his opponent that he would "be ashamed to wade or meddle any further in the matter," [1] the book seems to have passed entirely unnoticed by the leaders on both sides of the controversy.

In the summer of 1529, Cranmer was presented to the King by Foxe, and shortly afterwards suggested an argument in favor of the divorce in which Henry declared that he "had the right sow by the ear." The book which resulted, at the King's order, from this conversation, has had a strange history at the hands of biographers and bibliophiles. A reference to it in a letter from Gardiner to the King, dated February, 1530, fixes its date pretty accurately.[2] Harpsfield, who in his *Pretended Divorce between Henry VIII and Catherine* (written in Mary's reign) attempted to refute all important works on the King's side, does not even mention this book. Strype seems to be the only historian to have seen it, but it is impossible to tell from his account whether it was in print or in manuscript only.[3] Pocock, in his *Records of the Reformation*, prints chapter headings under the caption of "Cranmer's book in favour of the divorce." [4] Jenkyns reports the book as lost and repudiates the articles printed by Pocock.[5] The latter is clearly wrong in printing these headings as coming from Cranmer's book, for, as Jenkyns points out, the Archbishop's name on the first leaf of the manuscript copy (now in the British Museum) denotes his ownership only. Furthermore, the articles therein do not agree with Strype's description of the work in question. The book, so far as I can find, is non-extant; but Jenkyns goes wrong in attempting to describe it, for not having seen it himself, he has no right to attribute to it points not mentioned by Strype; nor has

[1] Wakefield, letter to Henry, *State Papers*, IV, 3234.

[2] *State Papers*, IV, 6247.

[3] Strype, *Memorials of Cranmer*, I, 7. Todd, in his *Life of Cranmer*, I, 21, also gives an account of the book but furnishes no evidence of having seen it himself.

[4] Pocock, *op. cit.*, I, 334. An annotator in Burnet's *Reformation*, I, 146, makes a similar mistake.

[5] Jenkyns, *Remains of Cranmer*, I, viii and notes.

he any authority for saying that its arguments were summarized in a book "published . . . by . . . Berthelet, with the judgments of the Universities prefixed," by which he evidently refers to the *Censurae*.[1] Although the two are similar in some respects, they differ in others. Strype describes Cranmer's treatise as showing that "no man, *jure divino*, could or ought to marry his brother's widow" and that "the Bishop of Rome ought by no means to dispence to the contrary."[2] The King was much pleased with the book when it appeared, and its influence in winning the English universities over to his side is well attested. Cranmer was despatched in the same year to spread its gospel throughout France, Germany, and Italy, and even went to Rome to defend its principles in public debate before the Pope, but an opportunity was not granted him.[3]

In 1530, seven continental universities returned their decisions on the divorce question in favor of the King. These resulted in a weighty book, dated in the colophon April, 1530, entitled *Gravissimae atque exactissimae illustrissimarum totius Italiae, et Galliae Academiarum Censurae . . . de veritate illius propositionis, Videlicet que ducere relictam fratris mortui sine liberis ita sit de iure divino et naturali prohibitum: ut nullus Pontifex super huiusmodi matrimoniis contractis, siue contrahendis dispensare possit.*[4] Although this book may have been undertaken by April, this date is out of the question for its publication, as only one of the university decisions, which are printed in the first part of the volume, was rendered by that time.[5] Pocock says that these pages were "certainly printed

[1] An annotator in Burnet's *Reformation*, I, 148, goes wrong in describing the *Censurae* in a note regarding Cranmer's book, as if he either confused the two or took them to be identical.

[2] Strype, *Cranmer*, I, 13.

[3] From the circulation of the book, it would seem as if it must have been in print; but if so, it is difficult to account for its subsequent disappearance.

[4] Herein referred to, for short, as the *Censurae*.

[5] The dates of these decisions are: Orleans, Apr. 5, 1529; Paris (*facultas decretorum*), May 23, 1530; Angers, May 7, 1530; Paris (*facultas theologicum*), July 2, 1530; Bourges, June 10, 1530; Bologna, n. d.; Padua, July 1, 1530; Toulouse, Oct. 1, 1530.

after the rest of the book."[1] I fail to see any evidence for such a statement, as the decisions of the universities are referred to occasionally throughout the work.[2] It seems much more likely that the book was misdated by Berthelet and that April, 1531, is the correct date. Further evidence on this point is: (1) There are no references to it in 1530. (2) It seems not to have been translated until 1531. (3) Fisher's reply was not undertaken until the summer of 1531. (4) Vives' reply was not published until 1532. (5) Strype says that the decisions of the universities were presented to the House of Commons in January, 1531, "and afterwards, being made into a book, were printed, entitled *Gravissimae, etc.*" (giving the title in full).[3] (6) Three contemporary references, which seem to be to this book, all point toward 1531 as its date of publication. On Nov. 27, 1530, Chapuys writes to Charles V, "The Dean of the Chapel, in the King's behalf, has presented eight instruments to the Archbishop of Canterbury, respecting the divorce; two from Paris, the others from Toulouse, Orleans, Bruges, Bologna, Padua, and Pavia. They are likely to publish these documents, as they have more influence than any book."[4] In a later letter to Charles, June 6, 1531, he speaks of a book in the King's behalf as "lately printed."[5] Ortiz, writing to Charles, June 24, 1531, mentions a "book in favour of the King."[6] The date of the *Censurae*, then, being settled, we may attack the problem of its authorship. Harpsfield says that the authors were "the two archbishops of the realm besides divers bishops and many notable lawyers and divines."[7] Strype agrees with this in substance, saying that "an abundance of learned men had now employed their pens in this argument to the number of above an hundred, whereof Dr. Cran-

[1] See Harpsfield's *Pretended Divorce*, p. 309.

[2] On fols. A3, A4, C4, I4, Q4.

[3] Strype, *Ecclesiastical Memorials*, I, 216.

[4] *State Papers*, IV, 6738. In the same letter, Chapuys states that a book is "being printed" in favor of the King. I cannot identify this work.

[5] *Ibid.*, V, 278.

[6] *Ibid.*, V, 309.

[7] Harpsfield, p. 172.

mer was one."[1] Burnet says that "some learned men were appointed," who compiled the book from all that had been previously written.[2] Two writers in the *Dictionary of National Biography* have complicated matters further by identifying this book (without giving any evidence for so doing) with the one mentioned by Stokesley in a letter to Cromwell dated 1535.[3] Speaking of his opinion of the divorce, Stokesley says that it was expressed "in the King's book that Mr. 'Ampner' [Foxe], Dr Nicolas, and I made before going over sea in embassy and was afterwards translated into English, with additions and changes, by my lord of Canterbury."[4] Since this journey over sea was undertaken towards the end of 1529, it is not possible that the book mentioned in this letter is the *Censurae*, although it may readily have been one of those worked over by the authors of the later volume. My own conclusion is that it was composed, as the older biographers say, by many hands, and was probably of gradual growth; that it may possibly have been set up tentatively as early as April, 1530, the references to the universities being introduced later, but that it certainly did not appear in print until April, 1531. The title is very misleading, for except for the few references *en passant* already mentioned, the universities and their views are totally ignored. However, the argument thrashes over the three points of the controversy, especially the Levitical law, in every conceivable aspect, and gives at length the opinions of councils, popes, saints, schoolmasters, and others. The *Censurae* was translated in November, 1531,[5] under the title *Determinations of the moste famous and moste excellent universities of all Fraunce and Italy, etc.* The translation amplifies the original slightly.[6] The sentence, "The King has

[1] Strype, *Ecc. Mem.*, I, 217.

[2] Burnet, *Reformation*, I, 166.

[3] See article on Stokesley by A. F. Pollard and on Nicholas de Burgo by A. G. Little.

[4] *State Papers*, VIII, 1054.

[5] Ames, *Typog. Antiq.*, I, 418, gives Nov. 7, 1530. The year given is conjecture only, as it does not appear in the title or colophon. One of the British Museum copies is identical with that described by Ames, but the other has the addition of the year 1531 in the colophon.

[6] The slight amplifications do not meet the expression "additions

printed his book in English and scattered it all over the kingdom," in a letter of Nov. 25, 1531, from Chapuys to Charles,[1] refers doubtless to this book. Again, in a letter of Jan. 22, 1532, Chapuys speaks of "the King's book" and mentions Sir Thomas Elyot as one of the translators.[2]

As soon as the *Censurae* appeared, Fisher seems to have set about to answer it. Agrippa writes to Chapuys on July 21, 1531, "Fisher's book is good." [3] This refers probably to the first part of the reply. On Aug. 22, 1531, Ortiz writes to Charles, "May has ordered me to read the bishop of Rochester's apology which has just been sent me from England, in which he answers two chapters of the book composed in favour of the King." [4] On Oct. 24, he writes to Chapuys for "the rest of Fisher's apology." [5] Chapuys writes to Charles on Oct. 1, 1531, "The bishop of Rochester has finished his answer to the book printed by the King." [6] Following this letter in the *State Papers*, is inserted a notice of manuscript in the Record Office, under the caption "Bishop Fisher, His book on the Divorce, replying to the arguments of those who sought to prove the invalidity of the King's marriage." Although I must confess to not having read through the 198 folio pages of crabbedly written Latin which compose this manuscript, I am con-

and changes" in Stokesley's letter, above referred to, thus giving further evidence that the writers in the *D.N.B.* have made a mistake.

[1] *State Papers*, V, 546.

[2] *Ibid.*, V, 737. Not a little confusion has arisen among bibliophiles through a failure to realize that there were several such sets of articles, similar in content, but actually quite distinct. The one Pocock fell foul of is the Latin MS. Vesp. B5 (Brit. Mus.), entitled *Articuli duodecim, quibus plane admodum demonstrabat, divortium . . . necessario esse faciendum,* which consists of twelve propositions, each fully worked out. Another set, which got into print, is bound with one of the British Museum copies of the *Glasse of the Truthe,* and bears the title, *Articles devised by the consent of the King's council, etc.* This is composed of eight short articles in English.

[3] *Ibid.*, V, app. 13.

[4] *Ibid.*, V, 378.

[5] *Ibid.*, V, 492.

[6] *Ibid.*, V, 460.

fident that it is not the book in question.[1] Harpsfield, in his *Pretended Divorce*, gives the substance of Fisher's reply to the *Censurae* (which I have nowhere found dignified with a title), compiled from the author's original Latin.[2] It is not possible to tell whether or not Harpsfield abbreviated Fisher's original in translating it; as given, it occupies almost 100 quarto pages. Harpsfield states that he has never seen a printed copy of this book and doubts if it was ever published. In the form given it in the translation, it is a close and detailed refutation, point by point, of the *Censurae*, written in a straightforward and common-sense manner that is much more convincing than the ponderous scholasticism of its opponent.

The cause for the Queen was further strengthened at this point by a book from Reginald Pole, which is said to have so affected the King that he almost gave up further effort for the divorce. Strype says that it "was penned about the year 1530." [3] He is mistaken here. The book was the result of a conference which Pole had with the King in the late spring of 1531. Moreover, Cranmer's letter to the Earl of Wiltshire describing the book is dated June 13, 1531. Tanner gives its title as *De non dissolvendo connubio regis Henr. VIII et Catherinae.*[4] Strype says, "the book, though the argument of it chiefly depended on divinity, proceeded more on political principles than divine." [5] Cranmer, in the letter just mentioned, says that "it was writ with that eloquence that if it were set forth and knowne to the commen people, I suppose yt were not possible to persuade them to the contrary." [6] The book was in manuscript

[1] This MS. is in two handwritings. The first runs to thirty folios. The second writer wrote only in a narrow column down one side of the page, so that his part would not make more than thirty-five full folios. The MS. is imperfect, lacking both beginning and ending. I do not know why it is ascribed to Fisher.

[2] Harpsfield, *op. cit.*, Part I.

[3] Strype, *Cranmer*, I, 9.

[4] Tanner, p. 603.

[5] Strype, *ibid.*

[6] Strype, *ibid.*, II, No. 1; also *State Papers*, V, app. 10. This letter gives a pretty full account of the contents of the book.

only, probably in Latin, and was evidently shown only to a very few. Pole wrote the King's council in 1537 that he had not yet had it printed, on account of his love for his Majesty,[1] and doubtless it never was, although the substance of it was more than likely incorporated in his *Pro Ecclesiasticae Unitatis Defensione*.[2]

Almost simultaneously with Pole's treatise, there was published in English a book entitled *A Glasse of the Truthe*, in the form of a dialogue, the only work of a popular nature in the whole controversy. Most of the bibliophiles who have noticed this book are inclined to date it 1532 — Pocock says "as early as September, 1532"[3] — because it is mentioned in a letter of Sept. 17, 1532, and because, according to Pocock, it was answered by a Latin work published at Luneburg in 1533. All are wrong here. The correct date is 1531, as the book is mentioned as "lately printed" in a letter from Chapuys to Charles, dated June 24, 1531. "The English," he says, "have lately printed a little dialogue . . . a thing so feeble and cold that it is a disgrace to them."[4] Pocock is also wrong on two points in regard to Vives' book, to which his vague reference evidently applies. It was in fact an answer to the *Censurae* and was published at Luneburg in 1532. The authorship of the *Glasse* is still a matter of doubt, but in all probability it was written by the King's advisers, perhaps with his help. Latin and French translations were made at his command in 1532, and a German one was projected but seems to have failed. Nicholas Hawkins was appointed to push the distribution of the book on the continent, and Sir Richard Croke performed a similar mission at home. A pretense was maintained that the King was the author, but I doubt very much if he had more than a hand in it, at the most. Croke, writing from Oxford on Sept. 23, 1532, says that he has not had much success in persuading the people of the royal authorship but that the book itself had done more than all previous ones in winning them over to the King's side.[5] Hawkins, in

[1] *State Papers*, XII, 444.
[2] See below, p. 222–223.
[3] Pocock, *Records*, I, xxi.
[4] *State Papers*, V, 308.
[5] *Ibid.*, V, 1338.

a letter to Henry, calls the book "your Highness dialogue," but in speaking of certain quotations which had been omitted from the translation, he refers the King to "Master Cranmer or Master Gudric [Goodrich] to write them in, word for word, as they be in the originals." [1]

This work is entirely different from any other in the controversy, since it not only is written for the man in the street rather than for the scholar or the court, but also makes a show of some literary pretentions. The preface describes it as a "clere glasse wherein the whiche ye shall see . . . the playne truthe of our mooste noble and lovinge princes cause, which by unmete and unkynde handlynge hath hytherto had so overlonge a staye"; but the intelligent reader will be more likely to agree with Chapuys that it is a sorry affair. The argument, if it may be so called, is entirely on the side of the King; and for this reason, the dialogue can hardly be said to be spirited, since each of the disputants speaks only to have his ideas confirmed by the listener, who plays the part of Greek chorus with fervor and despatch. Harpsfield judges the book pretty fairly in saying, "You shall find them [the arguments] none other in substance but such as he took out of the book that the Bishop of Rochester hath already confuted.[2] . . . And all this is conveyed in a dialogue between a sorry doting divine and a sorry lewd lawyer, framing out of their own heads new divinity and new laws ecclesiastical." [3] Still, one can readily understand how the ignorant public might have been influenced by the book, as Croke says they were.

Vives' reply to the *Censurae*, entitled *Non esse . . . prohibitum, quin Summus Pontifex dispensare possit, ut frater siue liberis fratris uxorem ligitimo matrimonio sibi possit adiungere, etc.*, and published at Luneburg in September, 1532, presents no difficulties. Some vague references in letters of 1531 [4] inform us that Vives had expressed himself before that year on the subject, but these treatises were evidently not printed and were probably very brief.

[1] *State Papers*, V, 1660.
[2] That is, those of the *Censurae*.
[3] Harpsfield, p. 170.
[4] *State Papers*, V, 46 and app. 13 and 14.

There is slight evidence that Vives committed some of his ideas to paper as early as 1527.[1] The *Non esse prohibitum* consists of 162 pages of the usual scholastic *a priori* argument. The date is given on the title page.

This book seems to be the last that appeared in print before the actual divorce took place. Wakefield, however, presented another book on the subject, the dating of which is the most difficult problem we have yet encountered. It is necessary to consider first the date of his earlier *Kotser Codicis*. I have already said that Pocock has overthrown the date first set for it, but he offers none of his own except in showing that its publication must have been later than Dec. 8, 1529.[2] In a letter printed with the *Kotser* from Wakefield to Fisher, Stokesley is spoken of as "*Londoninensis iam episcopus*." As Stokesley was not made Bishop of London until Nov. 27, 1530, we are able to shove the date of publication along one year more. The reference on the first page of the treatise itself to "a book thought to be by Vives or Agrippa" must apply to Vives' book above mentioned, which did not bear any name on its title page. As this book was not published until September, 1532, the *Kotser* cannot be dated earlier than this.[3] Wakefield's second book, *Syntagma de Hebraeorum codicum incorruptione, etc.*, complicates matters still more. This book was printed by Wynkyn de Worde and therefore before 1535, since Worde's will was proved on January 19 of that year. The sentence on the verso of the first leaf, *Primum tamen quaestionem per Johannem Fissherium . . . propositam atque responsionem quam illi codici meo adhibui annos antehac fere septem in medium his asseram*, gives us the information that the *Kotser* was written seven years previously. I have already demonstrated that the *Kotser* could not possibly have been published before 1530, and probably not before 1532 (unless, of course, the extant copies are not first editions,

[1] See article on Vives in *D.N.B.*

[2] See above, p. 212.

[3] The British Museum catalogue gives "1532?". Ames, *Typog. Antiq.*, I, 417, gives 1530, but this is evidently conjecture only. The references in the *Kotser* to Abel's book (see above, p. 212) might be useful if we could get more definite information about Abel.

which is very unlikely).[1] Furthermore, in the undated letter from Wakefield to Fisher, Wakefield says that Foxe came to consult him "*nomine Regis*" some seven years earlier about the marriage of a man with his brother's widow. Seven years previous to either 1530 or 1532 would be before Henry had thought of a divorce and before Foxe was connected with the court. The only way out of this difficulty is to suppose that the *Kotser* was written in the summer of 1529 (being the book referred to by Wakefield in his letter of that date [2]), but was not published until seven years later, when the references to Vives and Abel and the letters mentioned were added, and that the reference in the *Syntagma* is to it in its manuscript and not its printed form. The *Syntagma* itself, written "*annos fere septem*" later than the *Kotser*, would thus seem to have been published in 1536 also. But Worde, the printer, was dead by that time. The only possible solution of this second difficulty is to suppose that Wakefield spoke inaccurately in saying "*annos fere septem,*" for it is out of the question to think the *Kotser* written before 1529, as I have already shown. The *Syntagma* is a small Latin pamphlet of only fifty-six pages. It was projected in 1524 as a part of the author's earlier work, *Oratio de laudibus et vtilitate tuum linguarum Arabicae, Chaldicae et Hebraeicae, etc.*, but the controversy over the royal divorce altered altogether the nature of its intended content.[3] Harpsfield gives an outline of it in his *Pretended Divorce,* where he attempts to refute its arguments.

When Henry repudiated the Pope as head of the church, he appealed to Pole, then in Italy, for his opinion on the whole situation. In the book with which Pole replied, *Reginaldi Poli . . . ad Henricū octavum . . . pro ecclesiasticae unitatis defensione libri quatuor,* he re-expressed his opinion upon the King's divorce, among other things pointing out that by marrying Anne he was

[1] There is no record of there having been a second edition, nor is there any reason for supposing that a book of so little importance would have appeared more than once.

[2] See above, p. 208.

[3] See Maitland, *Early Printed Books in the Lambeth Library,* Nos. 509 and 510, and Note GG.

violating the very law which he had established in order to divorce Catherine.[1] Tanner dates the book 1536; the catalogue of the British Museum dates its copy "[1538]," which may be a second edition.[2] Wood describes the book as one "wherein he answers many things that Samson had wrote to please the king; presseth the king earnestly to return to the obedience of Rome; exciteth the emperor to revenge the injury done unto his aunt, (the divorced queen) and many other things." [3] On the question of the divorce, the writer certainly does not spare his sovereign. [4]

Besides the books discussed above, Wood mentions John Holyman's *Defensio Matrimonii Reginae Catherinae Cum Rege Henrico Octavo* and Bishop Tunstall's *Treatise in Defense of the Marriage of Queen Katherine with Henry 8;* but on these books I am unable to find any information whatever.

A very few books were put out on the subject of the divorce after the immediate excitement had died down. The only one of these worth mentioning here is Harpsfield's *Pretended Divorce between Henry VIII and Queen Catherine*, which has been referred to many times already. It was written in Mary's reign, but more accurate dating seems impossible.[5] It existed in manuscripts only, four of which are still extant, until Pocock printed it in 1878. This is the longest and most comprehensive work of all on the subject. Harpsfield explains that his purpose in writing it was to justify Sir Thomas More for refusing to take the oath ratifying the whole

[1] See above, p. 207, n. 1. This part of Pole's treatise is translated by Bridgett, *Blessed John Fisher*, p. 148, n.

[2] It seems more likely, however, that Tanner is mistaken and that the two books are identical, 1538 being the correct date. The work was finished by May, 1536 (according to *D.N.B.*), but in 1537 Pole wrote the King's council that his love for Henry had caused him to withhold his first book on the divorce from publication. This does not seem compatible with the sentiments expressed in the *Pro Ecclesiasticae* nor with the fact that immediately upon the appearance of the latter, the King divested Pole of all his dignities in England.

[3] Wood, I, 285.

[4] The divorce is discussed in Lib. III, especially f. Lxxv ff.

[5] Pocock makes no apparent attempt to date accurately the writing of the book.

course of the King's actions; and this he does by showing that Henry had been in the wrong throughout. The treatise is divided into three parts, as follows: (1) reasons to justify the marriage of Henry and Catherine, in the form of a reproduction of Fisher's reply to the *Censurae*; (2) refutation of four other important books on the subject (that of Egidius Bellamera, long before this time; that of Marcus Mantua, a contemporary lawyer of Padua; the *Syntagma* of Wakefield; and the *Glasse of the Truthe*), together with a history of the divorce; (3) a discussion of the parliamentary acts after the divorce and an account of Henry's later political and matrimonial difficulties. This book is of extreme value for the light it throws on the history of the divorce, on the books which it reviews, and on conditions of matrimony and divorce at the time of writing.

APPENDIX B

THE DATE AND OCCASION OF MILTON'S FIRST DIVORCE TRACT

Edward Philips, Milton's nephew, is responsible for the statement that *The Doctrine and Discipline of Divorce* was conceived about Michelmas (Sept. 29), 1643. This approximate date was accepted until Masson pointed out that Thomason, the collector of manuscripts at the British Museum, had added *Aug. 1* to the year 1643 on the title page of the Museum copy. Thomason was in the habit of affixing dates to the pamphlets he acquired; and as these seem clearly to refer to his acquisition of the pamphlets rather than to their publication, we may take them as the latest possible times for the appearance of tracts otherwise undated. A comparison of Thomason's dates for the year of 1643 and thereabouts with those in the *Stationers' Register*, shows that the former vary from one day to several months later than those of registration. This being the case, if we accept Thomason's date at all, we may say that Milton's tract appeared certainly as early as some time in July.

Against the acceptance of this date, stands the statement of Philips that Milton turned his thoughts to the subject of divorce because the delay of his wife in returning from her visit to her parents "so incensed our author that he thought it would be dishonourable ever to receive her again after such a repulse, so he forthwith prepared to fortify himself with arguments for such a resolution, and accordingly wrote two treatises, by which he undertook to maintain that it was against reason and the enjoinment of it not provable by Scripture for any married couple disagreeable in humour and temper or having an aversion to each [other] to be forced to be yoked together all their lives." Philips continues, "The first was his *Doctrine and Discipline of Divorce,* of which there was printed a second edition with some additions. The other in prosecution of the first was called *Tetrachordon.* Then better to confirm his own opinion by the attestation of others, he set out a piece called *The Judgment of Martin Bucer.* . . . Lastly he wrote an answer to a pragmatical clerk . . . his *Colasteron.*" [1]

Before Masson pointed out that Philips was probably wrong in stating that the first tract was not started until Sept. 29, biographers, in attempting to explain its cause, imagined that Milton must have become disgusted with his young wife and have written the tract as a result of domestic unhappiness. Since Masson's discovery, they have been unable to repudiate Thomason's date and yet unwilling to give up their ingeniously built theories on the subject. The result in biographies of Milton, including Masson's own, has been that the writer has presented both conflicting accounts, either saying naively, as Masson does, that he doesn't know what on earth to do about it, or else, like Pattison, supposing some offense on Mary's part of sufficient magnitude to start her husband writing tracts during his honeymoon.[2]

In attempting to overthrow the whole structure of this specimen of scholarly architecture, I shall start with the top story first, that is, the contribution of the late biographers. This obviously rests

[1] Philips, *Life of Milton,* in Godwin's *Lives of E. and J. Philips,* p. 365 ff. Godwin has not helped matters by putting the wrong years in the margin of his reprint. These are not present in the original.

[2] Masson suggests timidly as a possible way out that Philips' date of Milton's marriage may be considerably too late, but hastily shies off from the results of such a supposition. Pattison, in casting about for some offense to saddle upon Mary, suggests that perhaps she refused Milton the marriage right. Both seem to overlook the fact that Philips' statement is that the tract was first conceived as a result of Mary's protracted visit at Michelmastide, so that neither explanation clears up the case at all. To consider Philips wrong in the matter of the tract's date in order to consider him right in the matter of its cause, or vice versa, is no solution of the problem, especially as the critics cannot agree on which to throw overboard. Pattison's suggestion simply shows his ignorance of existing divorce practices, for the condition of affairs he suggests would have rendered a divorce even more readily obtainable by Milton than it already was.

on two things, the evidence of the tract itself, as a foundation, and Philips' statement as an intervening story.

It must be admitted that Mary's apparent desertion of her husband suggests that there was some trouble between them, although her delay in returning from her visit might have originally been caused by the entreaties of her friends and relatives alone; but if there was any such dissatisfaction or contrariety of mind, the facts involved show that it was felt by her rather than by him, since he made repeated efforts to hasten her return. Moreover, the muck-rakers who in later controversies with him attempted to assail his character, and even dug up his college career to support their assertions, were unable to find a single fact of his domestic life that might be interpreted to his disadvantage. It should be carefully noted also that not a word appears in the early biographies — those of Philips, Toland, Aubrey, and Wood — to the effect that he had any criticism to make upon his wife's character or fitness of disposition. This is all later invention. Furthermore, it must be pretty clear from my discussion of the agitation and writing on the subject of divorce that there is no need of looking into a man's private life in order to explain why he should have turned his thoughts to this problem, especially when he expresses other reasons for his action, as Milton does. Thus the *Doctrine and Discipline* needs no personal justification from the author's own life. Furthermore, Milton's ideas on the subject remained the same after he was happily reunited with his wife.

The above facts remove both the supposed evidence of the first tract in favor of the traditional cause of its writing and also the argument drawn from it for the acceptance of Philips' date. Let us now consider the statement of Philips himself, the second story of our scholarly structure. As to the cause of the tract, Philips' theory — for it certainly was theory — that it was written in order to establish grounds whereby Milton might obtain a divorce, in the light of my discussion of divorce legislation and practice at the time, is ridiculous on the face of it. Milton had ample cause for divorce, according to the teaching and practice of his own church, on the ground of desertion, in case his wife failed to return. We have incontrovertible evidence, also, that he was well aware of the fact, as I have already shown.[1] A further proof of this, if we can believe Philips at all, lies in the fact that a marriage between Milton and a daughter of Dr. Davis was "more than probably thought to be in agitation" at the time of Mary's delayed return.[2]

To summarize, my position stands thus: (1) there was ample cause for Milton to write a tract on divorce whatever his own married life may have been; (2) by the existing practices of the Puritan churches, Milton had recognized grounds for divorce, and knew it, if his wife failed to return to him; (3) the only reasons for Philips' belief that the tract was planned about Michelmas and for our acceptance of his statement to that effect, are thus removed; (4) the evidence, then, naturally favors Thomason's testimony, given in 1643, as against Philips', given in 1694. The points in the argument against me represent at best a case of "together we stand, divided we fall." I think I have shaken all of them pretty severely; and if I can overthrow one completely the others must go by the board in consequence. The most important one, without which the others become absolutely unsupported, is the date given by Philips for the conception of the tract. On this point, I submit the following evidence in addition to that given by Thomason:

(1) Philips is absolutely untrustworthy. He seldom makes a definite statement, but in several places where he does, he is considerably out of the way, for example, in the dates of Milton's birth, death, his entrance in Cambridge, the publication of *Paradise Lost*, and some minor events.[3] That he was very uncertain

[1] See above, p. 86.

[2] The fact, if it be a fact, that Milton contemplated a second marriage at this time, has appeared to some to argue that his first was unhappy. This reasoning is ingenious but hardly convincing. A man deserted by his wife would be much more likely to seek another if his first venture at the altar had been happy; nor, if it had been unhappy, would he rush quite so precipitously into marriage again as Philips asserts Milton was ready to do.

[3] These he gives as occurring in 1606, in 1673, at the age of fifteen, and in 1666, respectively. The correct facts are: Milton was born Dec.

of the facts connected with the divorce tracts, is shown by his saying that the *Doctrine and Discipline* and the *Tetrachordon* were planned together as the result of his wife's behavior and were followed by the *Judgement of Martin Bucer*, whereas we know that the *Tetrachordon* resulted from the criticisms on the first tract,[1] that it did not appear until 1645, and that it was preceded by the *Martin Bucer* tract.

(2) The second edition of the *Doctrine and Discipline* is dated by Thomason, Feb. 2, 1643–4. As shown above, this date is probably some time later than the tract's actual appearance, but let us accept it nevertheless as the day of publication. The second edition was an entire reworking of the first, increasing it more than one-third of its original length, and introducing new authorities, whose works required considerable study. It hardly seems possible that the tract could have been originally conceived, planned, written, and published, the subject reinvestigated, and the first edition reworked and published in its new form, all in the space of four months (Sept. 29 – Feb. 2).

(3) Milton, in his *Colasteron* says, "Whenas the *Doctrine and Discipline* had now a whole year been published a second time . . . this idle pamphlet comes reeling forth against the first edition only." [2] The *Answer*, to which Milton refers here, is recorded in the *Stationers' Register*, on Oct. 31, 1644, and was dated by Thomason Nov. 19, 1644. If Milton is speaking accurately in saying "a whole year," it is evident that Thomason's date for the second edition is considerably later than that of its publication, as many of his dates are. The effect of this evidence is either to shorten down the time between the original conception of the tract and its second publication (already too short, if we accept Philips' date) or else to show that it was started before Philips says.

9, 1608; died Nov. 8, 1674; entered college at the age of sixteen; and published *Paradise Lost* in 1667. In the light of such glaring errors, it seems hardly worth while to consider Philips' statements as to minor dates worth anything at all.

[1] So Milton says himself, *Prose Works*, II, 115–116.

[2] Milton, II, 243.

(4) Milton, in his *Second Defense*, says clearly: "When the bishops could no longer resist the multitude of their assailants, I had leisure to turn my thoughts to other subjects; to the promotion of real and substantial liberty. . . . When, therefore, I perceived that there were three species of liberty which are essential to the happiness of social life; religious, domestic, and civil; and as I had already written concerning the first, and the magistrates were strenuously active concerning the third, I determined to turn my attention to the second, or domestic species."[1] The overthrow of the bishops, both in their controversy with the Smectymuuns and in their opposition in the House of Lords to the new church government, took place in 1642,[2] before Milton was married.

The obvious conclusions from the whole of the above discussion are: (1) Philips, who was but fifteen years old at the time of the publication of the tract, and who was not at all in sympathy with his uncle's principles, was simply conjecturing as to the date and occasion of it when he wrote his biography of Milton fifty-one years later, and that he was mistaken, as in other places, on both points. (2) The *Doctrine and Discipline* was planned in 1642, as Milton clearly states, was published on or before Aug. 1, 1643, and had no connection whatever with his own domestic life. (3) The theories as to Milton's disgust with his young wife and his disgruntled attitude towards the marriage state (he who was thrice married), the scenes depicted as resulting therefrom (including, alas, such triumphs of the imagination as Masson's picture of the parting of husband and wife and his account of the excitement caused in the lobby of the House of Commons by the scandal), and finally the calumnies cast upon this unromantic and rather humdrum couple, might well be omitted from future biographies.[3]

[1] Milton, VI, 405.

[2] See above, p. 85.

[3] To save some one else unnecessary labor, it may be worth while to state that I have carefully run down the following clues without gaining any further information: (1) Palmer's sermon, *The Glasse of God's Providence*, Aug. 13, 1644, referred to by Milton, *Prose Works*, II, 113; (2) Grotius' *Annotationes in Libros Evangeliorvm*, 1641, mentioned by Milton, *ibid.*, I, 345; (3) Prynne's *Queries*, referred to by

Milton, *ibid.*, II, 240; (4) Featley's *Dippers dipt*, 1644–5, mentioned by Milton, *ibid.*, II, 116 (John Featley is mistaken in implying, in his *Dr. D. Featley revived*, pp. 64 and 70, that this tract preceded *The Gentle Lash*, pub. Jan. 2, 1643–4); (5) Howell's letter, mentioned by Masson, *Life of Milton*, III, 62; (6) the possible reference to Milton's divorce ideas in the *Annotations of the Books of the Old and New Testament* (see above, pp. 93–94 and n. 1).

APPENDIX C

DIRECTIONS FOR MATRIMONY FROM HARRINGTON'S BOOK[1]

HOWE MATRYMONY IS MADE WITH THE CYRCUMSTAŨCE AND SOLEMPNYTE AS APPERTAYNETH THERTO

As touchynge the seconde partye / it is to be knowen that man and woman dothe entre this holy ordre and sacramente of matrymony by expresse and free consente of bothe partyes/ that is to say: when both the man and the woman dothe consente bothe in one tyme to be husbonde and wyfe/ and that consente doo shewe eyther to other by expresse wordes of the tyme presente/ as by these wordes or other lyke/ I take the to my wyfe/ or I frome this tyme forwarde wyll haue the to my wyfe. And yf the woman also incontynentely expresse the same or other lyke wordes. then there is contracte matrymony betwyxte them. . . . But and they vse wordes of the tyme to come As yf the man saye thus/ I shall take the to my wyfe. And the woman saye/ I shall take the to my husbonde or other lyke wordes of tyme to come/ then it is noo matrymony. But promyse to make matrymony. . . . This consent whiche maketh matrymony ought to be in bothe theyr soules by true loue so yt ether shuld consent to loue other aboue all ye creaturs of the worlde. It shulde also be in theyr bodyes by true observaũce and kepynge . . . theyr bodyes to other clene and pure from all other creatures. It shulde also be in theyr temporall gooddes by a due cōmunyon so that eyther of them shuld consent that suche goodes as they haue or shall haue shall be cōmune betwyxte them.

Moreouer this consent whiche doth make matrymony ought to be groũded of a good cause and intent/ yt is to saye those yt wyll entre in to this holy ordre . . . must doo it pryncypally for one of thre causes/ that is to saye/ other to the entente for to brynge forth chyldren to be norysshed in the lawes & seruyce of god and

[1] Harrington, *Cōmendacions of Matrymony*, f. Aii *b* ff.

that is ye moost pryncypall cause . . . or els secondarly for remedy ayenst synne/ as suche as ben inclyned naturally to the synne of ye flesshe and wyll not endeuer them selfe to lyue chaste may make matrymony for that cause to avoyde the synne of fornycacyon. . . . Or elles thyrdely for solace and helpe whiche eyther may have of other without the acte of flesshely medlynge. . . . Secondarely there be other causes whiche mouen rather to take one ꝑson than another/ as ryches/ beaute/ refourmynge of peace or suche other. . . . But suche as dothe not marry pryncypally for one of the thre causes afore sayde but rather pryncypally for ryches beaute or frends or such other do not marry godly nor gracyously/ but they synne deedly/ and the deuyll hath grete power of them. . . . Moreouer this consent which doth make matrymony ought to be expressed & shewed in open and in honest places afore & in the p̄sence of honest & laufull wytnesses called specyally therefore. ii. at ye leest/ for & it be otherwyse . . . yt is called matrymony clādestinat whiche for many causes is forboden by the lawe. . . .

And when matrymony is thus laufully made/ yet the man maye not possesse the woman as his wyfe/ nor the woman the man as her husbonde . . . afore suche tyme as that matrymony be approued and solempnysed by oure mother holy chyrche/ and yf they do in dede they synne deedly. And to that solempnyte are many thynges requyred by the lawe. Fyrste is that the banes must be asked iii sondayes or other festyuall dayes. . . . And euery man and woman whiche dothe knowe ony impedymente or haue ony lykely coniecture of ony impedymente are bounde for to come and at the leest denounce and shewe the same to the curate. . . . The curate also him selfe is bounden for to make dylygente serche and inquisycyon for to knowe yf ony impedymente be or ony lykelyhode of impedymente to let the matrymony. . . .

More ouer it is to understonde that he sayde solēnysation of matrimony which is required to be made in the face of the chirche may not be made euery tyme of the yere. . . .

And this solempynsacyon oughte to be made in the face of the chyrche in the clere daye after the sonne be rysen and with honoure and reuerence.

APPENDIX D

CONTENTS OF TYPICAL DOMESTIC BOOKS

I. Chapter Headings from Perkins' *Christian Oeconomie*

Chaps.		Pages
1.	Of Christian Oeconomie, and of the Familie	1
2.	Of the Household seruice of God	7
3.	Of Maried folkes	8
4.	Of the Contract [i.e. spousals *de praesenti*]	6
5.	Of the choice of persons fit for Marriage	44
6.	Of consent in the Contract	8
7.	Of Reiection or Refusall of the Contract	7
8.	Of Mariage [i.e. the solemnization]	14
9.	Of the duties of married persons	12
10.	Of the Communion of married folkes, and of due beneuolence	12
11.	Of the Husband	6
12.	Of the Wife	4
13.	Of the Parent	12
14.	Of the Sonne	6
15.	Of the Master	4
16.	Of the Seruant	7
17.	Of the Master of the familie or goodman of the house	9
18.	Of the Mistresse of the familie or goodwife of the house	3

II. Outline of Gouge's *Domestical Duties* [1]

I Treatise.

An exposition of those parts of the Scriptures upon which the book is based: 133 topics, referred to Scriptural texts; 103 pages in all.

[1] This summary is made from the table of contents of the book. Many minor topics cannot be classified; such are omitted.

II Treatise.

Part I. Concerning the Marriage Contract, 28 topics, 20 pages.

1. What persons are fit to marry, 8 topics.
2. Suitable matches, 5 topics.
3. The contract [i.e. spousals *de praesenti*], 10 topics.
4. The religious ceremony, 1 topic.
5. The purpose of marriage, etc., 5 topics.

Part II. Mutual Duties of Husband and Wife, 45 topics, 32 pages.

1. Unity and chastity, 8 topics.
2. Love, peace, etc., 6 topics.
3. Of absence from one another, 3 topics.
4. Of prayers, 4 topics.
5. Mutual care and help, 9 topics.
6. Of keeping up family respect and credit, 9 topics.
7. Joint government of the family, 2 topics.
8. Hospitality, 2 topics.
9. Charity, 2 topics.

III Treatise. The Wife's Duties, 74 topics, 44 pages.

1. Wife's inferiority and subjection to husband, mildness, obeisance, modesty in apparel, meekness of speech, etc., 17 topics.
2. The necessity of the husband's consent in family matters, in the management of the house, and in the disposition of property, 5 topics.
3. Various kinds of subjection on the part of the wife to the husband, 11 topics.
4. The wife's obedience, meekness, forebearance, humility, cheerfulness, etc. (also the opposite qualities) in various matters, 26 topics.
5. Husband and wife in general, the former resembling Christ, and the latter the church, 5 topics.

IV Treatise. The Husband's Duties, 76 topics, 40 pages. A detailed but poorly organized account of the husband's authority and superiority over the wife and of how these should be used to the best advantage, under such captions as:

Of husbands wise maintaining his authority.

Of husbands courteous accepting their wives reuerend carriage.

Of an husbands manner in teaching his wife.

Of undue reproofe.

Of husbands beating their wives.

Of an husband prouiding for his wife.

Of husbands constancy in loue.

V Treatise. Children's Duties, 64 topics, 36 pages.

1. Love, fear, and obedience to parents, 11 topics.
2. Of children's entrance into business or profession, 3 topics.
3. Of Parents' consent in the marriage of children, 7 topics.
4. Obedience and submission of children to parents under various conditions, 20 topics.
5. Care of parents in sickness, age, and death, 8 topics.
6. Obedience to others over them, 3 topics.

VI Treatise. Duties of Parents to Children, 79 topics, 48 pages.

1. General care and love of children, 8 topics.
2. Birth and nourishment of a child, 8 topics.
3. Baptism, 6 topics.
4. Nurture, 5 topics.
5. Instruction in manners and profession, 6 topics.
6. Instruction in piety, 3 topics.
7. General points in the nurture, instruction, and correction of children, 13 topics.
8. Providing them with calling or profession, 4 topics.
9. Providing for them in marriage, 4 topics.
10. Duties of parent upon death of child, 8 topics.
11. Duties of foster parents, guardians, and others, 9 topics.

VII Treatise. Servants' Duties, 43 topics, 30 pages.

1. Fear and reverence of masters, 6 topics.
2. Obedience, etc., to masters, 10 topics.

3. Different manners of serving (with diligence, quickness, etc.), 5 topics.
4. Of servants' faithfulness in various offices, 11 topics.
5. Motives for good service, 4 topics.

VIII Treatise. Masters' Duties to servants,[1] 49 topics, 26 pages.

1. Choice of servants, 2 topics.
2. The master's authority and charge over servants, 16 topics.
3. Management of servants' affairs and duties, 26 topics.

III. Griffith's *Bethel*

Reprint of Table of Contents

A Plat-forme of the whole Building

[1] The relations of the servants to the household, according to Gouge, are entirely the concern of the master. In his treatise of the wife's duties, he gives her charge of the household only in case her husband is "very blockish and stupid," or unfit to manage his affairs on account of "some distemper, wound, or sickness." Most writers allow the wife more authority in household affairs.

Fifthly p. 12.

May not then an house bee govern'd by policy?

It may; so the worke of the braine hinder not the worke of the conscience.

Sixthly p. 18.

How may I bee sure that my House is built by God?

When it is God's {
Timber.
Framing.
Setting up.
Finishing.
Furnishing.
}

Seventhly p. 19.

What is Gods Timber?

Single persons: (who if they cannot abstaine, they must marrie) and they are { Old / Young } Men, or Women.

Eighthly p. 30.

How must Old men be framed?

They must be {
Sober.
Honest.
Discreet.
Sound in { Faith. / Love. / Patience. }
}

Ninethly p. 114.

How must Old Women be framed?

They must {
Be of such behaviour as becommeth holinesse.
Not be false-accusers.
Not given to much Wine.
Be teachers of honest things to younger Women.
}

10. p. 141.

How must young { Men / Women } be framed?

They must {
Remember their Creatour in the dayes of their youth.
Be sober-minded, and flye the lusts of youth.
Honour the person of the Aged.
Feare the Lord.
}

11. p. 223.

Seeing that a familie built by God, stands upon a foundation, and that foundation is mariage in the Lord: tell me what mariage is?

It is a convenant of God, whereby all sorts of people may, of two, bee made one flesh; for

The { Multiplying of an holy seed.
Avoiding of fornication.
Mutuall comforting of each other.

12. p. 244.

The our mariage may bee in the Lord, what should wee chiefely doe before we marrie?

We may do well to see that wee make { A right choyce.
An holy contract.

13. p. 245.

What should we looke into in our choyce?

That we { Choose not within the degrees forbidden.
Take more care for inward goodnesse, than outward goods

14. p. 255.

How may we so choose that (probablie) we may have vertuous Wives?

By { Report.
Lookes.
Talke, and silence.
Apparell.
Company.
Education.

15. p. 269.

What is an holy contract?

A marriage-desiring promise between two persons: with consent

Of { Parents.
Parties.

16. p. 273.

That our marriage may bee in the Lord, what things especially should accompanie it?

The { Gift of the Parent.
Blessing of the Priest.
Mutuall rejoycing of Friends.

17. p. 280.

What must follow a godlie marriage?

{ Cohabitation.
Communion.

18. p. 287.

The foundation of a godlie familie being thus laid; and the upper building standing in relations betweene Man, and Wife; Parents, and children; Maisters, and servants, say first, what are the common duties of the Husband, and his Wife?

To { Love. . . .
Be faithfull to } each other.

19. p. 316.

What is the particular dutie of the Husband?

He must { Dwell with his Wife like a man of Knowledge.
Give her honour
Leave Father, and Mother and cleave unto her.

20. p. 332.

What is the particular dutie of the Wife?
She must be subject to her Husband.

21. p. 334.

What are the duties of parents to their Children?

They must { Bring them up { Naturally.
Civilly.
Religiously.
Dispose of them to { Some calling.
Marriage.

22. p. 366.

What are the duties of Children?

They are:
- Reverence. } to their parents.
- Obedience. } to their parents.
- Thankefulnesse. } to their parents.
- Love to each other.

23. p. 379.

What are the duties of Maisters?

They must:
- Choose their servants by the feare of God.
- Enjoyne them labour but not above { Measure. / Strength.
- Recompense their diligence by given them sufficient { Meate. / Drinke. / Cloathing.

24. p. 383.

What are the duties of Servants?

They must:
- Be subject.
- Please their Maisters in all things.
- Not answer againe.
- Be faithfull.

25. p. 391.

How must Gods building be finished?

By an orderly government under the { Father / Mother } of the familie.

26. p. 393.

What are the duties of the Father of the familie?

Hee must:
- Be carefull that his house-hold serve God { Every day. / On the Sabbath.
- Provide for it.
- Exercise discipline in it.

27. p. 412.

What are the duties of the Mother, or Mistris of the familie?

Shee must { Keepe at home. / Governe the house in her place. / Give the portion of food in her house-hold. }

28. p. 418.

Gods building being thus framed, and finish'd; how may we procure Gods furniture for our houses?

By { Getting our goods by honest labour. / Doing, as wee would bee done unto, in . . . { Buying. / Selling. / Letting. / Borrowing. / Lending. } }

29. p. 429.

Gods building being finish'd, and furnish'd; what must every member of the same doe as the summe of their dutie?

They must { Feare { God. / the King. } / Not meddle with them that be seditious. }

30. p. 453.

You have hitherto taught us how to serve God in life; now say (in one word) how may we serve him even in death?

You must die in the Lord: and this you then only doe, when you prepare for death, by a { Godlie Life. / Penitent end. }

BIBLIOGRAPHIES

I. Early Books of Domestic Relations, etc.
II. Books on Henry VIII's Divorce
III. Later Books of Reference

These bibliographies contain by no means all the books that have been examined for this work, among which are many whose titles are sueggstive but whose contents are worthless for our purpose. Well-known books to which no page reference has been made are also omitted. In the first two lists, the dates given for publication are those of first editions except where noted. In all cases, the edition first named is that here used. Books marked with a star have not been available.

I. Early Books of Domestic Relations etc.

A., O., *The Uncasing of Heresie*, [Louvain?] 623 [1623].

Agrippa, H. C., *Commendation of Matrimony* (tr. David Clapham), London, 1545. [40pp. 8°]

——, * *De Nobilitate & Praecellentia Foeminei Sexus, etc.* (tr. David Clapham), 1542.

Alday, John, see Bouaistuau, P.

Anonymous, Anonymous books are listed under their titles.

Answer to a Book, Intituled, The Doctrine and Discipline of Divorce, An, London, 1644.

Apologie or Defense of svch trve Christians as are commonly (but vniustly) called Brovvnists, An, [Amsterdam?], 1604. (By Barrow and others. 1st ed. Dort., 1590.)

Asylum Veneris, or a Sanctuary for Ladies, etc. London, 1616.

Averell, William, *A dyall for dainty darlings, rockt in the cradle of securitie. A glasse for all disobedient sounes to look in. A myrrour for vertuous maydes*, London, 1584.

Aylmer, John, *An Harborwe for faithfull and trewe Subjectes against the late bloune Blaste, etc.*, Strassburg, 1559.

Ayrault, Pierre, A *Discovrse for Parents Honour and Authoritie* (tr. John Budden), London, 1614.

B., J., see Viret, P.

B., R., see Brathwait, R.

B., T., see Primaudaye, P. de la.

Baillie, Robert, *A Dissvasive from the Errours of the time*, London, 1645.

Bansley, Charles, *Pryde and abuse of women*, [1540–1550].

Barckley, Richard, *A Discovrse of the Felicitie of Man. Or his Summum bonum*, London, 1603.

Barclay, A., see Mancinus, D.

Barrow, Henry, *A Brief Discovery of the False Churches, etc.*, London, 1707 (1st ed. Dort, 1590).

Batty, Bartholomaeus, *The Christian man's Closet, etc.* (tr. Wm. Lowth), London, 1581.

Becon, Thomas, *Homily against Whoredom*, in *Early Works of Becon* (Parker So.), Cambridge, 1843.

——, *Worckes* (containing *The Boke of Matrimony* [115pp. fol.], and the *Catechism*), London, 1564–60–63.

Bercher, William, *Nobylytie off Wymen*, 1559. (Roxb. Club, London, 1904–5.)

Bèze, Théodore de, *Tractatio de repudiis et divortiis, etc.*, Geneva, 1569.

Biblia, dat is De gantsche Heylighe Schrift, etc., Delft, 1582, and Leyden, 1589.

Bishops' Book, see *Institutions of a Christian Man.*

Blandy, W., see Osorio, J.

Blount, Ed., see Ducci, L.

Bodenham, John, *Politeuphuia; Wits Commonwealth*, London, 1597.

Boke of Mayd Emlyn, The, John Scot, [n.d.].

Bouaistuau, Pierre, *Theatrum Mundi* (tr. J. Alday), London, [1566?].

——, See also Chelidonius, T.

Bradshaw, William, *English Puritanisme*, [Amsterdam?], 1605.

Brathwait, Richard [Philogenes Panedonius, *pseudonym*], *Ar't asleepe Husband? A boulster lecture*, London, 1640.

——, *The English Gentleman*, London, 1630.

——, *The English Gentlewoman*, London, 1631.

——, *The Good Wife*, [R. B.], London, 1619.

BRINSLEY, JOHN, *A Looking-Glasse for Good Women, etc.*, London, 1645.

BROWN, ROBERT, *A Booke which sheweth the life and manners of all true Christians, etc.*, Middelburg, 1582.

BRYSKETT, LUDOWICK, *A Discovrse of Civill Life*, London, 1606.

BUCER, MARTIN, *De Regno Christi*, Basel, 1557.

BUDDEN, J., see Ayrault, P.

BUGENHAGEN, JOHANN, *De Conjunctio episcopum*, Wittenberg, 1525.

BULLINGER, HENRY, *The Christen state of Matrimonye* (tr. Coverdale), London, 1541. [156pp. 8°]

BUNNY, EDMUND, *Of Divorce for Adulterie and Marrying againe, etc.*, Oxford, 1610.

BURROUGHES, JEREMIAH, *An Exposition of the Prophesie of Hosea*, [London], 1643.

C., R. [Robert Cleaver?], *A Godly Form of Hovseholde Gouernement, etc.*, London, 1598. [392pp. 8°].

C., R., Gent., *The Happy Mind*, [London], 1640.

CARTER, THOMAS, *Carters Christian Commonwealth*, London, 1627. [275pp. 8°]

CARTWRIGHT, THOMAS, *A Directory of Church-government. Anciently contended for, and as farre as the Times would suffer, practiced by the first Non-conformists in the daies of Queen Elizabeth* (tr. from Travers' Latin), London, 1644. (First printed in 1584 but suppressed.)

——, *A full and plaine declaration of Ecclesiasticall discipline owt of the word of God, etc.* (tr. from Travers' Latin), Middelburg, 1574.

Catechisme of the Christian Religion with the Confession of the Faith, A. As revised by the Synod of Dordrecht (tr. M. C. Coorne), Middelburg, 1721.

CAXTON, see Le Grand.

CHELIDONIUS, TIGURINUS, *A most excellent Hystorie of . . . Christian Princes* (tr. from Latin into French by Bouaistuau and from French into English by James Chillester), London, 1571.

CHILLESTER, J., see Chelidonius, T.

CLAPHAM, D., see Agrippa, H. C.

COKE, EDWARD, *The Second Part of the Institutes of the Laws of England*, London, 1669.

Commyssion unto all those whose wyves be thayr masters, A, Lacy, [1564–5].

Complaynt of them that be to soone maryed, A, Wynkyn de Worde, 1535.

Confession of faith of certayne English people, living in exile in the low countreys, The, contained in the *Apologie or Defense of . . . Brovvnists.*

Confessions of Faith, Catechisms, Directories, Form of Church-Government, Discipline, &c. . . . of the Church of Scotland, The, Edinburgh, 1725. (Reprints of earlier documents.)

Confession de Foy des Eglises Reformées du Païs Bas, etc., La, Rotterdam, 1726. (1st ed., Leyden, 1669.)

COVERDALE, M., see Bullinger, H.

Curtaine Lecture, A, (Dedication signed T. H. [editor?], probably Thos. Heywood), London, 1637.

DEKIN, H., see Herman V.

DEKKER, THOMAS, *The Bachelars Banquet*, London, 1603.

Directory of Public Worship, London, 1645.

Discovrse of the Married and Single Life, A; London, 1621.

Display of Duty, A., London, 1589.

DONNE, JOHN, *Works*, London, 1829.

DOVE, JOHN, * *Doctoris Pyi impium dogma*, [1604?].

——, *Of Divorcement*, London, 1601.

DUCCI, LORENZO, *Ars Avlica or The Courtiers Arte* (tr. Ed. Blount), London, 1607.

DYKE, WILLIAM, * *A Discourse on Matrimony*, London, 1642.

E., T. [Thomas Edwards?], *The Lawes Resolvtions of Womens Rights*, London, 1632.

EDWARDS, THOMAS, *Antapologia: or, A Full Answer to the Apologeticall Narration, etc.*, London, 1644.

ELYOT, THOMAS, *The defense of good women*, London, 1545.

ERASMUS, DESIDERIUS, *Annotationes in Novum Testamentum*, Basel, 1519.

——, *Matrimonii Christiani Institutio*, Basel, 1526. [442pp. 8°]

——, *Matrimonii Encomium* (tr. Richard Taverner under the title *A ryght frutefull Epystle . . . in laude and prayse of Matrymony*, London, [1536?]).

Faret, N., *The Honest Man: or, The Art to please in Court* (tr. Ed. Grimstone), London, 1632.

Featley, Daniel, *Καταβαπτισται καταπτυστοι. The Dippers dipt. or The Anabaptists Dvck't and Plvng'd Over Head and Eares*, London, 1645.

Fenner, Dudley, *The Artes of Logike and Rethorike* (containing *The Order of Household*), [Middelburg], 1584.

Ferne, John, *The Blazon of Gentrie*, London, 1586.

Fiore, *The boke of wisdome otherwise called the Flower of Vertue* (tr. J. Larke), London, [1565].

Fit John, John, *A Diamonde Most precious*, London, 1577. [75pp. 4°]

Forme of Prayers and administration of the Sacraments, &c. Vsed by the English Congregation at Geneva: and approved by . . . John Calvin, The, London, 1643. (Reprinted from first edition of 1558.)

Fox, John, *Acts and Monuments*, London, 1843–49. (Written in 1554.)

——, See also *Reformatio Legum*.

Fuller, Thomas, *A Sermon on Reformation*, London, 1643.

Gibbon, Charles, *A Work worth the Reading*, London, 1591.

——, * *Compendius Form of Domestical Duties*, 1589.

Gibson, Anthony, *A Womans Woorth*, London, 1599.

Godolphin, John, *Repertorium Canonicum*, London, 1678.

Gosson, Stephen, *Pleasant Quippes for Upstart Newfangled Gentlewomen*, London, 1595.

Gosynhyll, Edward, *Prayse of all women*, 1541.

Gouge, William, *Domestical Duties*, London, 1626. (2nd ed.) [386pp. fol.]

Griffith, Matthew, *Bethel: or, Forme for Families*, London, 1633. [528pp. 4°]

Grimstone, E., see Faret, N.

H., T., see *Curtaine Lecture, A.*

Haec-Vir: or, The Womanish-Man: Being an Answere to a late Booke intitulit Hic-Mulier, London, [1620?].

Hall, Joseph, *Salomons Divine Arts*, London, 1609. [32pp. 8°]

Hannay, Patric, *A Happy Husband*, London, 1618.

Harrington, William, *In this boke are conteyned the cōmendacions of matrymony/ the maner & fourme of contractyng solempnsy-ynge and lyuyng in the same, etc.*, London, 1528. [42pp. 4°]

HEMMINGIUS, NICOLAS, *Libellus de Coniugio, Repudio, & Divortio*, Leipsig, 1572.

HERMAN V, *A briefe and plaine declaration of the duety of maried folkes, etc.* (tr. Hans Dekin), London, [1588?]. [33pp. 8°]

HERVET, G., see Xenophon.

HEYWOOD, JOHN, *A Dialogue . . . in a matter concerninge two maner of mariages*, London, 1561.

HEYWOOD THOMAS, *The Exemplary Lives and Memorable Acts of Nine the Most Worthy Women of the World*, London, 1640.

——, *Γυναῖκειον: or, Nine Bookes of Various History concerninge Women*, London, 1624.

——, See also *Curtaine Lecture, A.*

Hic-Mvlier: or, The Man-Woman; Being a Medicine to cure the Coltish Disease of the Staggers in the Masculine-Feminines of our Times, [London, 1620?].

HOOPER, JOHN, *Early Writings* (Parker So.), Cambridge, 1843.

HOWSON, JOHN, *Uxore dismissa propter Fornicationem aliam non licet superinducere*, Oxford, 1606. (1st ed. 1602.)

Hundreth poyntes of evell huswrifrye, An, Alde, 1565–6.

HYRDE, R., see Vives, J. L.

Institutions of a Christian Man, London, 1537.

K., T., see Tasso, T.

King's Book, see *Necessary Doctrine, etc.*

KINGSMILL, ANDREW, *A Viewe of mans estate . . . where unto is annexed a goodlie advise . . . touching mariage*, London, 1574. (Written in 1560.)

KNOX, JOHN, *The first Blast of the Trumpet against the Monstrous Regiment of Women*, [Geneva], 1558.

——, *The History of the Reformation in Scotland*, Glascow, 1761. (Written in 1567; apparently first printed in 1586.)

KYD, T., see Tasso, T.

Late Assembly of Divines Confession of Faith, The, London, 1651.

LARKE, J., see Fiore.

LECHFIELD, THOMAS, *Plaine-dealing: or, Newes from New England*, London, 1642.

LE GRAND, *Boke of Good Manners* (tr. Caxton), London, 1487. [118pp. fol.]
Little Nonsuch, London, 1646.
LOWTH, W., see Batty, B.
MANCINUS, DOMINICUS, *A Myrrour of Good Manners* (tr. Alex. Barclay), London, 1523.
MARKHAM, FRANCIS, *The Booke of Honour*, London, 1625.
MILTON, JOHN, *The Doctrine and Discipline of Divorce, etc.*, London, 1643.
——, *Prose Works* (ed. C. Symmons), London, 1806.
Muld Sacke: or The Apologie of Hic-Mulier: To the late Declamation against her, etc., London, 1620.
MUNDA, CONSTANTIA, [pseudonym] *The Worming of a mad Dogge: or, a Soppe for Cerberus the Iaylor of Hell*, London, 1617.
N., A. [Anthony Nixon], *The Dignitie of Man*, London, 1612.
Necessary Doctrine for any Christian Man, The, London, 1543.
NICCHOLES, ALEXANDER, *A Discovrse of Marriage and Wiving, etc.*, London, 1620.
NIXON, ANTHONY, see N., A.
NORDEN, JOHN, *The Labyrinth of Mans Life*, London, 1614.
* *Order of Household Instruction*, London, 1596.
OSORIO DA FONSECA, JERONIMO, *The five Bookes of . . . H. Osorius . . . of Civill and Christian Nobilitie* (tr. Wm. Blandy), London, 1576.
OVERBURY, THOMAS, *A Wife*, London, 1614.
PAGE, THOMAS, * *A Demonstration of Family Duties*, London, 1643.
PAGET, EPHRIAM, *Heresiography: or, A description of the Heretickes, etc.*, London, 1645.
PAGET, JOHN, *An Arrow against the Separation of the Brownists*, Amsterdam, 1618.
PALMER, HERBERT, *The Glasse of Gods Providence*, [London], 1644.
PANEDONIUS, P., see Brathwait, R.
Payne and sorowe of ewytl Maryage, The, Wynkyn de Worde, [n.d.].
PAYNELL, T., see Vives, J. L.
PEACHAM, HENRY, *The Compleat Gentleman*, London, 1622.
PERKINS, WILLIAM, *Christian Oeconomie* (tr. Thos. Pickering), London, 1609. (Written in 1590.) [175pp. 8°]

Perkins, William, *The Golden Chain*, London, 1591.
Philotus, Ane verie excellent and delectabill Treatise intitulit Philotus, Edinburgh, 1603.
Pickering, T., see Perkins, W.
Primaudaye, Pierre de la, *The French Academie* (tr. T. B.), London, 1586.
Proude Wyves Paternoster, The, Kynge, 1560.
Pye, Thomas, * *Epistola ad Jo. Howsonum contra novum ejus Dogma de Divortiis Judaeorum*, London, 1603.
R., T. [Thomas Rogers], *The Anatomie of the minde*, London, 1576.
Rainolds, John, *A Defence of the Ivdgment of the Reformed Churches, etc.*, [London], 1609.
Raleigh, Walter, *Remains of Sir Walter Raleigh*, London, 1675.
Reformatio Legum Ecclesiasticarum (ed. John Fox), London, 1571.
Rich, Barnaby, *The Excellency of good women*, London, 1613.
——, *My Ladies Looking Glasse*, London, 1616.
Ridley, Thomas, *A Viewe of Civile and Ecclesiasticall Law*, Oxford, 1676. (1st ed., 1607.)
Robinson, John, *A iust and necessarie Apologie of certain Christians no lesse contumeliously than commonly called Brownists or Barrowists*, [Leyden?], 1625. (1st. ed., Latin, 1619).
Robson, S., *The Covrt of ciuill Courtesie*, London, 1591.
Rogers, Daniel, *Matrimoniall Honovr*, London, 1642. [387pp. 4°]
Rogers, T., see R., T.
Rous, Francis, *The Art of Happiness*, London, 1619.
S., S., * *Brief Instructions for Families*, 1583.
Schole-howse of women, The, Wyer, [n.d.].
Segar, William, *Honor Military and Ciuill*, London, 1602.
Selden, John, *De Jure naturali et Gentium juxta Disciplinam Hebraeorum libri septem*, London, 1640.
Shrewde and Curste Wyfe lapped in Morrelles skin, A, Jackson, [n.d.].
Smith, Henry, *A Preparative to Mariage*, London, 1591. [96pp. 8°]
Snawsel, Robert, *A Looking Glasse for maried Folkes*, London, 1610.
Sowernam, Ester, [pseudonym] *Ester hath hang'd Haman, etc.*, [London, 1617].

SPEGHT, RACHEL, *A Mouzell for Melastomus, the Cynicall Bayter of, and foule mouthed Barker against Evahs sex*, London, 1617.
STAFFORD, ANTHONY, *The Gvide to Honovr*, London, 1634.
STOCKWOOD, JOHN, *A Bartholmew Fairing for Parentes*, London, 1589.
SWETNAM, JOSEPH, see Teltruth, T.
Swetnam the Woman-hater, arraigned by women, London, 1620.
SWINBURNE, HENRY, *A Treatise of Spousals*, London, 1686. (Written c. 1600.)
T., R., see Tasso, H. and T.
TASSO, HERCULES and TORQUATO, *Of Mariage and Wiuing* (tr. R. T.), London, 1599.
TASSO, TORQUATO, *The Housholders Philosophie* (tr. T. K. [Thomas Kyd]), London, 1588.
TAVERNER, R., see Erasmus, D.
TELTRUTH, THOMAS (*i.e.* Joseph Swetnam), *The Araignment of Lewde, idle, froward, and vnconstant women*, London, 1615.
Testimony to the Truth of Jesus Christ, A, London, 1647.
TILNEY, EDMUND, *The Flower of Friendship, etc.*, London, 1568.
TINDALE, JOHN, * *Matrimonium.* (But see p. 114, n. 1, above.)
TOPSELL, EDWARD, *The House-holder; or, Perfect Man*, [London], 1610.
TORSHELL, SAMUEL, *The Womans Glorie*, London, 1645.
TOUTEVILLE, DANIEL, * *Saint Paul's Threefold Cord*, London, 1635.
Tractatus modestas et Christianus, contra reprehensiones T. Pyi (Published with Howson's *Uxore dismissa*), Oxford, 1606.
TRAVERS, WALTER, *Ecclesiasticae Disciplinae, et Anglicanae Ecclesiae ab illa aberrationis, plane è verbo Dei, & dilucida explicatio*, La Rochelle, 1574.
——, See also Cartwright, T.
Twelve mery gestys of one called Edyth, Rastell, 1525.
VAUGHAN, WILLIAM, *The Golden Grove, moralized in three Bookes*, London, 1608 (1st ed., 1599). [59pp. 8°]
VIRET, PIERRE, *The Schoole of Beastes, intituled, the good Householder, etc.* (tr. J. B.), London, 1585.
VIVES, J. L., *Instruction of a Christian Woman* (tr. Rich. Hyrde), London, [1540?]. [310pp. 4°]. (Original, *De Institutione Foeminae Christianae*, 1523.)

Vives, J. L., *The Office and duetie of an Husband* (tr. Thos. Paynell), London, [1553]. [410pp. 8°]
W., R., * *Order of Matrimony*, London, 1580.
Wedlocke, Walter, *A lyttle treatyse called the Image of Idlenesse, conteynynge certeyne matters moued betwene Walter Wedlocke and Bawdin Bacheler, London,* [1550?].
Whately, William, *A Bride-bush*, London, 1619. [220pp. 4°]
Whitford, Richard, *A werke for housholders/ or for them yt haue the gydynge or gouernaunce of any company*, London, 1533. [43pp. 8°] (1sr ed., 1531.)
Whitgift, John, *Works* (Parker So.), Cambridge, 1851–53.
Wiclif, John, *Of Weddid Men and Wifis and of Here Children also*, in *Select English Works of John Wyclif* (ed. Arnold), Oxford, 1871.
Willoby, Henry, *Willobie his Avisa: or, the true picture of a modest Maide, and of a chaste and constant wife*, London, 1594.
Wright, Leonard, *A Display of dutie, dict with sage sayings, pythie sentences, and proper similies*, London, 1589.
Xenophon, *Treatise of an Houshold* (tr. G. Hervet), London, 1532. [105pp. 8°]

II. Books on Henry VIII's Divorce

Disputed points as to date, authorship, etc., are discussed in Appendix A, above.

Abel, Thomas, * *Invicta Veritas: An Answer that by no manner of law it may be lawful for the King to be divorced from the Queen's Grace, etc.*, MS. c. 1530. (London Record Office.)
——, * *Tract. de non dissolvendo Henrici & Catherinae matrimonio*, MS. c. 1530. (Record Office.)
Articles devised by the consent of the King's council, etc., pub. with *A Glasse of the Truthe*, London, [1531].
Articuli duodecim, quibus plane admodum demonstrabat, divortium . . . necessario esse faciendum. MS. c. 1530. (British Museum.) Printed in Pocock's *Records of the Reformation*, I, 334.
Censurae, see *Gravissimae, etc.*

* *Confutation of that answer which Master John Abell, priest, lately made against the Book of Determinations of the Universities in the King's cause, A*, MS. c. 1530. (Record Office.)

CRANMER, THOMAS, * His book in favor of the King (apparently non-extant). MS.? 1530.

Determinations of the moste famous and moste excellent universities of Italy and Fraunce, that it is so unlefull for a man to marie his brothers wyfe, that the pope hath no power to despence therwith, The, [London, 1531]. [308pp. 8°]

FISHER, JOHN, *De Causa matrimonii Regis Angliae liber*, [M. de Eguia, Compluti, Spain], 1530. (Also published by Alcala de Henares, 1530.)

——, * *Defensorum matrimonii regis cum Catherina, etc.* Begin: "*Licitum fuisse matrimonium Henr. VIII.*" MS. 1529. (Cambridge Univ. Lib.)

——, His reply to the *Censurae*, trans. in Harpsfield, *Pretended Divorce*, Pt. I.

——, MS. in Record Office. (See above, p. 217.)

Glasse of the Truthe, A, London, [1531].

Gravissimae atque exactissimae illustrissimarum totius Italiae, et Galliae Academiarum Censurae . . . de veritate illius propositionis, Videlicet que ducere relictam fratris mortui sine liberis ita sit de iure divino et naturali prohibitum: ut nullus Pontifex super huiusmodi matrimoniis contractis, siue contrahendis dispensare possit, London, 1530, [*i.e.* 1531]. [142pp. 4°]

HARPSFIELD, NICHOLAS, *Treatise on the Pretended Divorce between Henry VIII and Catherine of Aragon*, London, 1878. (Written in Queen Mary's reign.)

HOLYMAN, JOHN, * *Defensio Matrimonii Reginae Catherinae Cum Rege Henrico Octavo.*

POLE, REGINALD, * *De non dissolvendo connubio regis Henr. VIII et Catherinae*, MS.? 1531.

——, *Reginaldi Poli . . . ad Henricū octavum . . . pro ecclesiasticae unitatis defensione libri quatuor*, [1538].

TUNSTALL, CUTHBERT, * *Treatise in Defense of the Marriage of Queen Katherine with Henry 8.*

VIVES, *Non esse, neque diuino neque naturae iure prohibitum, quin*

Summus Pontifex dispensare possit, ut frater siue liberis fratris uxorem ligitimo matrimonio sibi possit adiungere, adversus aliquot Academiarum censuras tumulturia ac perbreuis Apologia siue confutatio, Luneburg, 1532.

WAKEFIELD, ROBERT, *Kotser Codicis R. Wakefeldi quo praeter ecclesiae . . . decretum, probatur conjugium cum fratria carnaliter cognita, illicitum . . . interdictumque esse, etc.*, London, [1536?]. (Written in 1529.)

——, *Syntagma de Hebraeorum codicum incorruptione*, [London, 1535?].

III. LATER BOOKS OF REFERENCE

AMES, JOSEPH, *Typographical Antiquities* (ed. Herbert), London, 1785.

BACON, LEONARD, *The Genesis of the New England Churches*, New York, 1874.

Biographia Britannica (ed. Kippis), London, 1778.

BISHOP, J. P., *New Commentaries on Marriage, Divorce, and Separation*, Chicago, 1891.

BLUNT, J. H., *The Doctrine of the Church of England*, London, 1868.

BRADFORD, WILLIAM, *History of Plymouth Plantation, 1620–1647*, Boston, 1912.

BREWER, J. S., and GAIRDNER, JAMES, *Letters and State Papers of the Reign of Henry VIII*, London, 1862, etc.

BRIDGETT, THOMAS E., *Life of Blessed John Fisher*, London, 1888.

BROOK, BENJAMIN, *The Lives of the Puritans*, London, 1813.

BRYDGES, SAMUEL E., *Censura Literaria*, London, 1805–9.

BURN, RICHARD, *Ecclesiastical Law*, London, 1842.

BURNET, GILBERT, *The History of the Reformation* (ed. Pocock), Oxford, 1865.

Cambridge History of English Literature, The (ed. A. R. Waller and A. W. Ward), New York, 1908, etc.

Child Marriages, etc., see Furnivall.

COUDERT, F. R., *Marriage and Divorce Laws in Europe*, New York, 1893.

EINSTEIN, LEWIS, *The Italian Renaissance in England*, New York, 1902.

ESMEIN, A., *Le Mariage en droit canonique*, Paris, 1891.

FEATLEY, JOHN, *Featlaei Παλιν γενεσια: or Dr. D. Featley revived, etc.*, London, 1660.

FRIEDBERG, EMIL, *Das Recht der Eheschliessung*, Leipsig, 1865.

FURNIVALL, F. J., *Child Marriages, Divorces, and Ratifications, . . . A.D. 1561–6*, London, 1897.

GAGE, MATILDA J., *Women, Church and State*, Chicago, 1893.

HANBURY, BENJAMIN, *Historical Memorials relating to the Independents*, London, 1839.

HEYLYN, PETER, *Aerius redivivus: or The History of the Presbyterians*, Oxford, 1670.

HILL, GEORGIANA, *Women in English Life*, London, 1896.

HOWARD, GEORGE E., *A History of Matrimonial Institutions*, Chicago, 1904.

INDERWICK, F. W., *The Interregnum*, London, 1891.

JEAFFRESON, J. C., *Brides and Bridals*, London, 1872.

JENKYNS, HENRY, *The Remains of Cranmer*, Oxford, 1833.

KITCHIN, S. B., *A History of Divorce*, London, 1912.

KNIGHT, SAMUEL, *The Life of Erasmus*, Cambridge, 1726.

LINGARD, JOHN, *The History of England*, London, 1849.

MAITLAND, F. W., *Roman Canon Law in the Church of England*, London, 1898.

MAITLAND, G. R., *Early Printed Books in the Lambeth Library*, London, 1843.

MASSON, DAVID, *Life of John Milton*, Cambridge, 1859–1894.

NEAL, DANIEL, *The History of the Puritans*, London, 1822.

PHILIPS, EDWARD, *The Life of Milton* (written in 1694, published with Wm. Godwin's *Lives of Edward and John Philips*), London, 1815.

PHILLIMORE, G. G., *Ecclesiastical Law of the Church of England*, London, 1895.

POCOCK, NICHOLAS, *Records of the Reformation*, Oxford, 1870.

POLLOCK, F., and MAITLAND, F. W., *The History of English Law*, Cambridge, 1895.

RENTON, A. W., and PHILLIMORE, G. G., *The Comparative Law of Marriage and Divorce*, London, 1910.

RUSHWORTH, JOHN, *Historical Collections, 1618–1648*, London, 1659–1701.

RYE, WILLIAM, *England as seen by Foreigners in the days of Elizabeth and James the First*, London, 1865.

SCOBELL, HENRY, *A Collection of Acts and Ordinances of Parliament, 1640–1656*, London, 1658.

SMITH, MUNROE, *Marriage in Universal Cyclopedia.*

SPARROW, J. SHAW, *The English House*, London, 1908.

State Papers, see Brewer and Gairdner.

Statutes of the Realm, The, London, 1817.

STEVENSON, R. L., *Familiar Studies of Men and Books*, London, 1882.

STRYPE, JOHN, *Ecclesiastical Memorials*, Oxford, 1822.

——, *Memorials of Thomas Cranmer*, Oxford, 1812.

TANNER, THOMAS, *Bibliotheca Britannica-Hibernica*, London, 1748.

THWING, C. F. and C. F. B., *The Family*, Boston, 1887.

TODD, H. J., *The Life of Archbishop Cranmer*, London, 1831.

WATT, ROBERT, *Bibliotheca Britannica*, Edinburgh, 1824.

WHITMORE, W. H., *Colonial Laws of Massachusetts*, Boston, 1887.

WILKINS, D., *Concilia Magnae Britanniae et Hiberniae*, London, 1737.

WILKINS, H. J., *The History of Divorce and Remarriage*, London, 1910.

WINTHROP, JOHN, *The History of New England from 1630–1649* (ed. Savage), Boston, 1853.

WOOD, ANTHONY À, *Athenae Oxonienses* (ed. Bliss), London, 1813–1820.

WOOLSEY, THEODORE D., *Divorce and Divorce Legislation*, New York, 1882.

INDEX

Titles of books are here given in abbreviated form; for exact titles see bibliographies.

REPRINTS OF LEGAL CLASSICS PUBLISHED BY THE LAWBOOK EXCHANGE, LTD.

A'Beckett, Gilbert Abbott. *The Comic Blackstone* **[bound with] [Anstey, John].** *The Pleader's Guide, A Didactic Poem by John Surrebutter; American edition by James L. High.* With illustrations by George Cruikshank. Chicago: Callaghan & Cockcroft, 1870. xii, 376, 57, 65 pp. Reprint available February 2001 by The Lawbook Exchange, Ltd. ISBN 1-58477-104-6. Cloth. $95.

Anderson, William C. *A Dictionary of Law, Consisting of Judicial Definitions and Explanations of Words, Phrases, and Maxims, and an Exposition of the Principles of Law Comprising a Dictionary and Compendium of American and English Jurisprudence.* Chicago: T.H. Flood and Company, 1889. viii, 1140pp. Reprinted 1996 by The Lawbook Exchange, Ltd. LCCN 96-35844. ISBN 1-886363-23-4. Cloth. $125.

Ashburner, Walter. *The Rhodian Sea-Laws. Edited from the Manuscripts.* Oxford: Clarendon Press, 1909. ccxvi, 132 pp. Reprint available May 2001 by The Lawbook Exchange, Ltd. ISBN 1-58477-173-9. Cloth. $75.

Austin, John. [1790-1859]. *The Province of Jurisprudence Determined.* London: John Murray, 1832. xx, 392, lxxvi pp. Reprinted 2000 by The Lawbook Exchange, Ltd. LCCN 99-33457. ISBN 1-58477-023-6. Cloth. $75.

Baldwin, Henry. *A General View of the Origin and Nature of the Constitution and Government of the United States, Deduced from the Political History and Condition of the Colonies and States, from 1774 until 1788. And the Decisions of the Supreme Court of the United States. Together with Opinions in the Cases Decided at January Term, 1837, Arising on the Restraints on the Powers of the States.* Philadelphia, Printed by J. C. Clark, 1837. v, [1], 197 p. Reprinted 2000 by The Lawbook Exchange, Ltd. LCCN 00-026728. ISBN 1-58477-098-8. Cloth. $60.

Bancroft, George. *History of the Formation of the Constitution of the United States of America. Second Edition.* New York: D. Appleton and Company, 1882. Two volumes. xxiv, 520; xiv,501 pp. Reprinted 2000 by The Lawbook Exchange, Ltd. LCCN 99-23946. ISBN 1-58477-002-3. Cloth. $175.

Bar, Carl Ludwig von. *A History of Continental Criminal Law.* Boston: Little, Brown, and Company, 1916. lvi, 561 pp. Reprinted 1999 by The Lawbook Exchange, Ltd. LCCN 99-32341. ISBN 1-58477-013-9. Cloth. $90.

Barton, Dunbar Plunket. *Shakespeare and the Law.* With a foreword by James M. Beck. Boston: Houghton Mifflin Company, 1929. xl, 167 pp. Reprinted 1999 by The Lawbook Exchange, Ltd. LCCN 99-26602. ISBN 1-58477-000-7. Cloth. $60.

Bauer, Elizabeth Kelley. *Commentaries on the Constitution 1790-1860.* New York: Columbia University Press, 1952. 400 pp. Reprinted 1999 by The Lawbook Exchange, Ltd. LCCN 98-45409. ISBN 1-886363-66-8. Cloth. $75.

Beard, Charles Austin. *The Office of the Justice of the Peace in England, in its Origin and Development.* New York: Columbia University Press, 1904. 184, [1] pp. Reprint available February 2001 by The Lawbook Exchange, Ltd. ISBN 1-58477-102-X. Cloth. $60.

Beard, Charles. *An Economic Interpretation of the Constitution of the United States.* New York: The Macmillan Company, 1952. xxi, 330 pp. Reprint available March 2001 by The Lawbook Exchange, Ltd. LCCN 00-036834. ISBN 1-58477-111-9. Cloth. $80.

Beard, Charles A. *The Supreme Court and the Constitution.* New York: The Macmillan Company, 1912. vii, 127 pp. Reprinted 1999 by The Lawbook Exchange, Ltd. LCCN 98-50368. ISBN 1-886363-78-1. Cloth. $45.

Beck, Theodric Romeyn. *Elements of Medical Jurisprudence.* Albany: Websters and Skinners, 1823. Two volumes. xxxiv, 418; viii, [9]-471 pp. Reprinted 1997 by The Lawbook Exchange, Ltd. LCCN 96-35845. ISBN 1-886363-24-2. Cloth. $125.

Benedict, Russell. *Acts and Laws of the Thirteen Original Colonies and States: Constituting the extraordinary collection of Hon. Russell Benedict.* New York: American Art Association, 1922. [272]pp. Reprinted 1998 The Lawbook Exchange, Ltd. LC 98-20196 ISBN 1-886363-56-0. Cloth. $85.

Bentham, Jeremy. [1748-1832]. *A Fragment on Government. Edited with an Introduction by F. C. Montague.* Oxford: The Clarendon Press, 1891. xii, 241 pp. Reprint available May 2001 by The Lawbook Exchange, Ltd. ISBN 1-58477-166-6. Cloth. $65.

Bentham, Jeremy. *Plan of Parliamentary Reform, in the Form of a Catechism, with Reasons for each Article. With an Introduction, Shewing the Necessity of Radical, and the Inadequacy of Moderate, Reform.* London: T.J. Wooler, 1818. 156 pp. Reprint available January 2001 by The Lawbook Exchange, Ltd. LCCN 00-058816.

ISBN 1-58477-121-6. Cloth. $65.

Black, Henry Campbell. *A Dictionary of Law Containing Definitions of the Terms and Phrases of American and English Jurisprudence, Ancient and Modern. Including the Principal Terms of International, Constitutional, and Commercial Law; with a Collection of Legal Maxims and Numerous Select Titles from the Civil Law and Other Foreign Systems.* St. Paul, Minn.: West Publishing, 1891. x, 1253 pp. Reprinted 1991 by the Lawbook Exchange, Ltd. LCCN 91-62383. ISBN 0-9630106-0-3. $125.

Black, Henry Campbell. *A Law Dictionary. Containing Definitions of the Terms and Phrases of American and English Jurisprudence, Ancient and Modern. And Including the Principal Terms of International, Constitutional, Ecclesiastical and Commercial Law, and Medical Jurisprudence, with a Collection of Legal Maxims, Numerous Select Titles from the Roman, Modern Civil, Scotch, French, Spanish, and Mexican Law, and Other Foreign Systems, and a Table of Abbreviations.* St. Paul, Minn.: West Publishing, 1910. 1314 pp. Reprinted 1995 by the Lawbook Exchange, Ltd. LCCN 97-10320. ISBN 1-886363-10-2. Cloth. $150.

[Blackstone, William]. Eller, Catherine Spicer. *The William Blackstone Collection in the Yale Law Library. A Bibliographical Catalogue.* New Haven: Yale University Press, 1938. xvii, 113 pp. Reprinted 1993 by The Lawbook Exchange, Ltd. LCCN 99-38826. ISBN 0-9630106-5-4. Cloth. $50.

Bondy, William. *Separation of Governmental Powers in History, in Theory, and in the Constitutions.* New York: Columbia College, 1896. Reprinted 1999 by The Lawbook Exchange, Ltd. vi,[7]-185,[1] pp. LCCN 98-44994. ISBN 1-886363-65-X. Cloth. $65.

Bonner, Robert J. and Gertrude Smith. *The Administration of Justice from Homer to Aristotle.* Chicago: The University of Chicago Press, [1930]. Two volumes. ix, 390; vii,[320] pp. Reprint available October 2001 by The Lawbook Exchange, Ltd. ISBN 1-58477-117-8. Cloth. $160.

Botsford, George Willis. *The Roman Assemblies from their Origin to the End of the Republic.* New York: The Macmillan Company, 1909. x, 521 pp. Reprint available May 2001 by The Lawbook Exchange, Ltd. ISBN 1-58477-165-8. Cloth. $85.

Bouvier, John. [1787-1851]. *Institutes of American Law. New Edition by Daniel A. Gleason. In Two Volumes.* Boston: Little, Brown, & Company, 1880. lxviii, 651; iv, 798pp. Reprinted 1999 by The Lawbook Exchange, Ltd. LCCN 98-54288. ISBN 1-886363-80-3. Cloth. $250.

Bouvier, John. *A Law Dictionary Adapted to the Constitution and Laws of the United States of America, and of the Several States of the American Union; with References to the Civil and Other Systems of Foreign Law.* Philadelphia: T. & J.W. Johnson, 1839. Two volumes. 559; 628 pp. Reprinted 1993 by The Lawbook Exchange, Ltd. LCCN 99-047231. ISBN 0-9630106-7-0. Cloth. $130.

Brackenridge, Hugh. *Law Miscellanies: Containing an Introduction to the Study of Law; notes on Blackstone's Commentaries, Shewing the Variations of the Law of Pennsylvania from the Law of England, and what Acts of Assembly Might Require to be Repealed or Modifies; Observations on Smith's Edition of the Laws of Pennsylvania; Strictures on Decisions of the Supreme Court of the United States, and on Certain Acts of Congress, with Some Law Cases, and a Variety of Other Matters, Chiefly Original.* Philadelphia: P. Byrne, 1814. 588 pp. Reprint available October 2001 by The Lawbook Exchange, Ltd. LCCN 00-059548. ISBN 1-58477-161-5. Cloth. $100.

[Brandeis, Louis D.]. [1856-1941]. *Brandeis on Zionism. A Collection of Addresses and Statements by Louis D. Brandeis with a Foreword by Mr. Justice Felix Frankfurter.* Washington, D.C.: Zionist Organization of America, [1942]. viii, 156 pp. Reprinted 1999 by The Lawbook Exchange, Ltd. LCCN 98-49331. ISBN 1-886363-60-9. Cloth. $65.

Broom, Herbert. *A Selection of Legal Maxims, Classified and Illustrated. Eighth American, from the Fifth London Edition, with References to American Cases.* Philadelphia: T. & J.W. Johnson & Co., 1882. lxxviii, 993 [i.e. 779] pp. Reprinted 2000 by The Lawbook Exchange, Ltd. LCCN 99-049329. ISBN 1-58477-052-X. Cloth. $125.

Brown, Basil. [1860-1928]. *Law Sports at Gray's Inn (1594) Including Shakespeare's connection with the Inns of Court, the origin of the Capias Utlegatum re Coke and Bacon, Francis Bacon's connection with Warwickshire, together with a reprint of the Gesta Grayorum.* New York: [Privately Printed by the Author], 1921. xciv, 188, 88, [9] pp. LCCN 99-049829. ISBN 1-58477-056-2. Reprint available March 2001 by The Lawbook Exchange, Ltd. Cloth. $85.

Brown, Everett S. *The Constitutional History of the Louisiana Purchase 1803-1812.* Berkeley: University of California Press, 1920. xi, 248 pp. Reprint available January 2001 by The Lawbook Exchange, Ltd. ISBN 1-58477-151-8. Cloth. $75.

Browne, Arthur. *A Compendious View of the Civil Law and of the Law of the Admiralty: being the substance of a course of lectures read in the University of Dublin.* New York: Halstead and Voorhies, 1840. Two volumes. xvi, 536; xi, 567 pp. Reprinted 2000 by The Lawbook Exchange, Ltd. LCCN 99-18284. ISBN 1-886363-88-9. Cloth. $175.

Buckland, W.W. *The Roman Law of Slavery: The Condition of the Slave in Private Law from Augustus to Justinian.* Cambridge: Cambridge University Press, 1908. xii, [2], 735 pp. Reprint available January 2001 by The Lawbook Exchange, Ltd. LCCN 99-056922. ISBN 1-58477-068-6. Cloth. $175.

Burrill, Alexander M. *A New Law Dictionary and Glossary: Containing Full Definitions of the Principal Terms of the Common and Civil Law; Together with Translations and Explanations of the Various Technical Phrases in Different Languages, Occurring in the Ancient and Modern Reports, and Standard Treatises; Embracing Also All the Principal Common and Civil Law Maxims. Compiled on the Basis of Spelman's Glossary, and Adapted to the Jurisprudence of the United States; with Copious Illustrations, Critical and Historical.* New York: John S. Voorhies, 1850. Two volumes. xviii, 1099 pp. Reprinted 1998 by The Lawbook Exchange, Ltd. LCCN 97-38481. ISBN 1-886363-32-3. Cloth. $175.

Bussell, F.W. *The Roman Empire. Essays on the Constitutional History from the Accession of Domitian (81 A.D.) to the Retirement of Nicephorus III. (1081 A.D.)* London: Longmans, Green, and Co., 1910. Two volumes. xiv, 402; xxiii, 521 pp. Reprinted 2000 by The Lawbook Exchange, Ltd. LCCN 99-087026. ISBN 1-58477-082-1. Cloth. $175.

Calabresi, Guido. *A Common Law for the Age of Statutes.* Cambridge: Harvard University Press, 1982. xi, 319 pp. Reprinted 2000 by The Lawbook Exchange, Ltd. LCCN 99-44889. ISBN 1-58477-040-6. Cloth. $85.

Calhoun, George M. *The Growth of Criminal Law in Ancient Greece.* Berkeley: University of California Press, 1927. x, 149 pp. LCCN 99-43192. ISBN 1-58477-037-6. Reprinted 2000 by The Lawbook Exchange, Ltd. Cloth. New. $50.

Campbell, John, Baron. [1779-1861]. *Shakespeare's Legal Acquirements Considered.* London: John Murray, 1859. vi, 117 pp. Reprint available October 2001 by The Lawbook Exchange, Ltd. ISBN 1-58477-126-7. Cloth. $60.

[Cardozo, Benjamin]. *Law is Justice. Notable Opinions of Mr. Justice Cardozo.* Foreword by Robert F. Wagner. Edited by A.L. Sainer. New York: Ad Press

Ltd., [1938]. xvii, 441 pp. Frontis. Reprinted 1999 by The Lawbook Exchange, Ltd. LCCN 99-34154. ISBN 1-58477-010-4. Cloth. $75.

Cardozo, Benjamin. *The Paradoxes of Legal Science.* New York: Columbia University Press, 1928. v, 142 pp. Reprinted 2000 by The Lawbook Exchange, Ltd. LCCN 00-024469. ISBN 1-58477-097-X. Cloth. $75.

Chafee, Zechariah. *Free Speech in the United States.* Cambridge, Massachusetts: Harvard University Press, 1967. xviii, 634 pp. Reprint available January 2001 by The Lawbook Exchange, Ltd. LCCN 99-087317. ISBN 1-58477-085-6. Cloth. $125.

[Cherokee Laws]. *Compiled Laws of the Cherokee Nation.* Tahlequah, I.T.: National Advocate Print, 1881. 370pp. Reprinted September 1998 by The Lawbook Exchange, Ltd. With a new introduction by Michael Weber. LCCN 98-12741. ISBN 1-886363-42-0. Cloth. $60.

Cherry, Richard R. *Lectures on the Growth of Criminal Law in Ancient Communities.* London: Macmillan and Co., 1890. xi, 123 pp. Reprint available September 2001 by The Lawbook Exchange, Ltd. LCCN 00-067010. ISBN 1-58477-167-4. Cloth. $65.

Chipman, Nathaniel. *Principles of Government. A Treatise on Free Institutions Including the Constitution of the United States.* Burlington: Edward Smith, 1833. viii, 144, 145a-188a, [145]-330 pp. Reprint available January 2001 by The Lawbook Exchange, Ltd. LCCN 99-048863. ISBN 1-58477-046-5. Cloth. $80.

Chitwood, Oliver Perry. *Justice in Colonial Virginia.* Baltimore: Johns Hopkins Press, 1905. 123, [1] pp. Reprint available February 2001 by The Lawbook Exchange, Ltd. ISBN 1-58477-114-3. Cloth. $65.

Clark, H.B. *Biblical Law: Being a text of the statutes, ordinances, and judgments established in the Holy Bible-with many allusions to secular laws-ancient, medieval, and modern-documented to the Scriptures, judicial decisions, and legal literature.* Portland, Ore.: Binfords & Mort, [1943]. xxiv, 304 pp. Reprinted 2000 by The Lawbook Exchange, Ltd. LCCN 99-053316. ISBN 1-58477-062-7. Cloth. $75.

Cohn, Morris M. *An Introduction to the Study of the Constitution; A Study showing the Play of Physical and Social Factors in the Creation of Institutional Law.* Baltimore: The Johns Hopkins Press, 1892. xi, 235 pp. Reprinted 2000 by The Lawbook Exchange, Ltd. LCCN 99-38730. ISBN 1-58477-032-5. Cloth. $50.

Coke, Edward Sir. *The First Part of the Institute of the Laws of England, or, A commentary upon Littleton. Not the name of the Author only, but of the Law Itself. Revised and Corrected With Additions of Notes, References, and Proper Tables, by Francis Hargrave and Charles Butler, Esqrs. Of Lincoln's Inn, Including also The Notes of Lord Chief Justice Hale and Lord Chancellor Nottingham; and An Analysis of Littleton, written by an unknown Hand in 1658-9.* By Charles Butler, Esq. The Eighteenth Edition, Corrected. London, J. & W.T. Clarke, 1823. Two volumes. ccxvi,[606]; iv, [772] pp. Reprinted 2000 by The Lawbook Exchange, Ltd. LCCN 99-41675. ISBN 1-58477-033-3. Cloth. $195.

[Continental Legal History]. *A General Survey of Events, Sources, Persons & Movements in Continental Legal History. By Various European Authors.* With an introduction by Albert Kocourek. Boston: Little, Brown, 1912. liii, 754pp. Reprinted 1998 by The Lawbook Exchange, Ltd. LCCN 98-11159. ISBN 1-886363-47-1. Cloth. $110.

Cooley, Thomas M. [1824-98]. *A Treatise on the Constitutional Limitations which Rest Upon the Legislative Power of the States of the American Union. Fifth edition.* Boston: Little, Brown, and Co., 1883. lxxxi, 886pp. Reprinted 1998 by The Lawbook Exchange, Ltd. LCCN 98-12730. ISBN 1-886363-53-6. Cloth. $120.

Cooley, Thomas M. *The General Principles of Constitutional Law in the United States* of America. Boston: Little, Brown, and Company, 1880. xxxix, 376 pp. Reprint available February 2001 by The Lawbook Exchange, Ltd. LCCN 00-056301. ISBN 1-58477-120-8. Cloth. $85.

Cooley, Thomas McIntyre. [1824-1898]. *A Treatise on the Constitutional Limitations Which Rest Upon the Legislative Power of the States of the American Union. [1st edition].* Boston: Little, Brown, and Co., 1868. xlvii, 720pp. Reprinted 1999 by The Lawbook Exchange, Ltd. LCCN 99-20589. ISBN 1-886363-92-7. Cloth. $95.

Corwin, Edward. *The Doctrine of Judicial Review: Its Legal and Historical Basis and Other Essays.* Princeton: Princeton University Press, 1914. ix, 178 pp. Reprinted 2000 by The Lawbook Exchange, Ltd. LCCN 99-32362. ISBN 1-58477-011-2. Cloth. $60.

Curtis, George Ticknor [1812-1894] and Joseph Culbertson Clayton. *Constitutional History of the United States from their Declaration of Independence to the Close of the Civil War.* New York: Harper & Brothers, 1889, 1896. Two volumes. xiii, 774; x, 780 pp. Reprint available September 2001 by The Lawbook Exchange, Ltd. LCCN 00-065554. ISBN 1-58477-129-1. Cloth. $250.

Darrow, Clarence and William J. Bryan. *The World's Most Famous Court Trial. Tennessee Evolution Case. A Complete Stenographic Report of the Famous Court Test of the Anti-Evolution Act, at Dayton July 10 to 21, 1925, Including Speeches and Arguments of*

Whitney, 1925. Three volumes. 1216; 1280; 1264 pp. Reprinted 1993 by The Lawbook Exchange, Ltd. LCCN 99-047228. ISBN 0-9630106-6-2. Cloth. $295.

Friedberg, Emil Albert [1837-1910]. Richter, Aemilius Ludwig [1808-1864]. *Corpus iuris canonici.-Editio Lipsiensis secunda / post Aemilii Ludouici Richteri curas ad librorum manu scriptorum et editionis Romanae fidem recognouit et adnotatione critica instruxit Aemilius Friedberg.* Liepzig : Tauchnitz, 1879-1881. Two volumes. civ, 1472 columns (736 pp.); lxxxii, 1340 columns (670 pp.) LCCN 99-088231. Reprinted 2000 by The Lawbook Exchange, Ltd. LCCN 99-088231. ISBN 1-58477-088-0. Cloth. $300.

Friend, Willam L. *Anglo-American Legal Bibliographies. An Annotated Guide.* Washington, D.C.: United States Government Printing Office, 1944. xii, 166 pp. Reprinted 1996 by The Lawbook Exchange, Ltd. LCCN 96-11002. ISBN 1-886363-21-8. Cloth. $65.

Fuller, Lon L. *The Law in Quest of Itself.* Boston: Beacon Press, 1966. [vi], 150 pp. Reprinted 1999 by The Lawbook Exchange, Ltd. LCCN 99-32863. ISBN 1-58477-016-3. Cloth. $45.

Futrell, William H. *The History of American Customs Jurisprudence.* New York: Published privately, 1941. 314pp. Reprinted 1998 by The Lawbook Exchange, Ltd. LCCN 98-11342. ISBN 1-886363-51-X. Cloth. $60.

Gest, John Marshall. *The Lawyer in Literature.* London: Sweet & Maxwell, Limited, 1913. xii, 249 pp. Reprinted 1999 by The Lawbook Exchange, Ltd. LCCN 99-18365. ISBN 1-886363-90-0. Cloth. $60.

Giesecke, Albert Anthony. *American Commercial Legislation before 1789* agents, 1910. 167 pp. Reprint available November 2001 by The Lawbook Exchange, Ltd. LCCN 00-058813. ISBN 1-58477-153-4. Cloth. $65.

Gilmore, Grant. *Security Interests in Personal Property.* Boston: Little, Brown & Company, 1965. Two volumes. xxxiv, 651; xiii, 653-1508 pp. Reprinted 1999 by The Lawbook Exchange, Ltd. LCCN 99-10258. ISBN 1-886363-81-1. Cloth. $195.

Girard, Paul F. *A Short History of Roman Law Being the First Part of his Manuel Elementaire De Droit Romain. Translated by Augustus Henry Frazer and John Home Cameron.* Toronto: Canada Law Book Company, 1906, v, 220 pp. Reprinted 2000 by The Lawbook Exchange, Ltd. LCCN 99-087383. ISBN 1-58477-078-3. Cloth. $55.

Goodenough, Edwin R. *The Jurisprudence of the Jewish Courts in Egypt: Legal Administration by the Jews under the Early Roman Empire as Described by Philo Judaeus.* New Haven: Yale University Press, 1929. vii, 268 pp. Reprint available January 2001 by The Lawbook Exchange, Ltd. ISBN 1-58477-152-6. Cloth. $75.

Goodhart, Arthur L. *Five Jewish Lawyers of the Common Law.* London: Oxford University Press, 1949. [4], 74 pp. Reprinted 2000 by The Lawbook Exchange, Ltd. LCCN 99-049934. ISBN 1-58477-045-7. Cloth. $60.

Gould, James. *A Treatise on the Principles of Pleading in Civil Action.* Boston: Lilly and Wait, 1832. x, 536 pp. Reprint available December 2000 by The Lawbook Exchange, Ltd. LCCN 00-059549. ISBN 1-58477-158-5. Cloth. $95.

Greenidge, A.H.J. *The Legal Procedure of Cicero's Time.* Oxford: The Clarendon Press, 1901. xiii, 599 pp. Reprinted 2000 by The Lawbook Exchange, Ltd. LCCN 99-26771. ISBN 1-886363-99-4. Cloth. $85.

Greenleaf, Simon. *The Testimony of the Evangelists Examined by the Rules of Evidence Administered in Courts of Justice with an Appendix Containing a History of the Most Ancient Manuscript Copies of the New Testament, and a Comparison of their Text with that of the King James' Bible by Constantine Tischendorff. Also a Review of the Trial of Jesus.* New York: James Cockcroft & Company, 1874. Reprint available March 2001 by The Lawbook Exchange, Ltd. xxiii, 613 pp. LCCN 00-021510. ISBN 1-58477-020-1. Cloth. $95.

Greenleaf, Simon. *A Treatise on the Law of Evidence.* Boston: Little, Brown, and Company, 1899. Three volumes. Reprint available March 2001 by The Lawbook Exchange, Ltd. LCCN 00-065554. ISBN 1-58477-116-X. Cloth. $350.

Haines, Charles Grove. *The Conflict over Judicial Powers in the United States to 1870.* New York: Columbia University Press, 1909. 180 pp. Reprint available June 2001 by The Lawbook Exchange, Ltd. LCCN 99-088241. ISBN 1-58477-080-5. Cloth. $60.

Hale, Matthew. *The History and Analysis of the Common Law of England.* Stafford: J. Nutt, 1713. [x], 264, [28], 176 pp. Reprinted 2000 by The Lawbook Exchange, Ltd. LCCN 99-33739. ISBN 1-58477-024-4. Cloth. $85.

Harper, Robert Francis. *The Code of Hammurabi King of Babylon. About 2250 B.C. Autographed Text transliteration..* Chicago: The University of Chicago

Press, 1904. xxviii, 194, ciii (plates) pp. Illus. Reprinted 2000 The Lawbook Exchange, Ltd. LCCN 99-23953. ISBN 1-58477-003-1. Cloth. $75.

Harris, Virgil M. *Ancient, Curious, and Famous Wills*. Boston: Little, Brown, and Company, 1911. xiv, 472 pp. Reprinted 1999 by The Lawbook Exchange, Ltd. LCCN 99-20588. ISBN 1-886363-93-5. Cloth. $75.

Hearn, William Edward. *The Aryan Household Its Structure and its Development. An Introduction to Comparative Jurisprudence.* London and New York: Longmans, Green, and Co., 1891. viii, 494 pp. Reprint available January 2001 by The Lawbook Exchange, Ltd. ISBN 1-58477-124-0. Cloth. $90.

Henderson, Gerard Carl. *The Position of Foreign Corporations in American Constitutional Law. A Contribution to the History and Theory of Juristic Persons in Anglo-American Law.* Cambridge: Harvard University Press, 1918. xix, 199 pp. Reprinted 1999 by The Lawbook Exchange, Ltd. LCCN 99-18233. ISBN 1-886363-89-7. Cloth. $50.

Hicks, Frederick. *Men and Books Famous in the Law. With an introduction by Harlan F. Stone.* Rochester, New York: Lawyers Co-operative Publishing, 1921. 259 pp. Reprinted 1992 by The Lawbook Exchange, Ltd. LCCN 92-070809. ISBN 0-9630106-2-X. Cloth. $50.

Hohfeld, Wesley. *Fundamental Legal Conceptions as Applied in Judicial Reasoning.* Edited by Walter Wheeler Cook, with a New Foreword by Arthur L. Corbin. New Haven: Yale University Press, 1964. xv, 114 pp. Reprinted 2000 by The Lawbook Exchange, Ltd. LCCN 00-064108. ISBN 1-58477-162-3. Cloth. $55.

Holdsworth, William S. *Charles Dickens as a Legal Historian.* New Haven: Yale University Press, 1929. 157 pp. Reprinted 1995 by The Lawbook Exchange, Ltd. LCCN 96-46579. ISBN 1-886363-06-4. Cloth. $40.

Holdsworth, William S. *Essays in Law and History.* Edited by A.L. Goodhart and H.G. Hanbury. Oxford: At the Clarendon Press, 1946. xv, 302 pp. Reprinted 1995 by The Lawbook Exchange, Ltd. LCCN 99-047234. ISBN 1-886363-13-7. Cloth. $65.

Holdsworth, W.S. *The Historians of Anglo-American Law.* New York: Columbia University Press, 1928. 175 pp. Reprinted 1994 by The Lawbook Exchange, Ltd. ISBN 0-9630106-9-7. Cloth. $50.

Holt, W. Stull. *Treaties Defeated by the Senate. A Study of the Struggle Between President and Senate Over the Conduct of Foreign Relations.* Baltimore: The Johns Hopkins Press, 1933. vi, [1],328 pp. Reprinted 2000 by The Lawbook Exchange, Ltd. LCCN 99-39606. ISBN 1-58477-029-5. Cloth. $65.

Holthouse, Henry James. *A New Law Dictionary, Containing Explanations of Such Technical Terms and Phrases As Defined in the Works of Legal Authors, in the Practice of the Courts, and in the Parliamentary Proceedings of the Houses of Lords and Commons, To Which Is Added An Outline of An Action at Law and of A Suit in Equity. Edited, from the Second and Enlarged London Edition, With Numerous Additions, by Henry Penington.* Philadelphia: Lea and Blanchard, 1847. viii, [17]-495 pp. Reprinted 1999 by The Lawbook Exchange, Ltd. LCCN 98-49350. ISBN 1-886363-67-6. Cloth. $75.

Horton, John Theodore. *James Kent: A Study in Conservatism, 1763-1847.* New York: D. Appleton-Century Co., [1939]. xi, 354 pp. Reprinted 2000 by The Lawbook Exchange, Ltd. LCCN 99-056927. ISBN 1-58477-069-4. Cloth. $80.

Huebner, Rudolf. *A History of Germanic Private Law.* Translated by Francis S. Philbrick; with an editorial preface by Ernest G. Lorenzen and introductions by Paul Vinogradoff and by William E. Walz. Boston: Little, Brown and Company, 1818. lix, 788 pp. Reprinted 2000 by The Lawbook Exchange, Ltd. LCCN 99-055138. ISBN 1-58477-065-1. Cloth. $120.

Hurst, James Willard. *Law and Social Order in the United States.* Ithaca: Cornell University Press, 1977. 318 pp. Reprinted 2000 by The Lawbook Exchange, Ltd. ISBN 1-58477-113-5. Cloth. $85.

Ilbert, Courtenay. *The Mechanics of Law Making.* New York: Columbia University Press, 1914. viii, 209 pp. Reprint available February 2001 by The Lawbook Exchange, Ltd. LCCN 99-047156. ISBN 1-58477-044-9. Cloth. $70.

Jackson, E. Hilton. *Latin for Lawyers. Containing I: A Course in Latin, with Legal Maxims and Phrases As a Basis of Instruction. II. A Collection of Over One Thousand Latin Maxims, with English Translations, Explanatory Notes, and Cross-References. III. A Vocabulary of Latin Words.* London: Sweet & Maxwell, 1915. viii, 300 pp. Reprinted 1992 by The Lawbook Exchange, Ltd. LCCN 92-074408. ISBN 0-9630106-4-6. Cloth. $50.

Jacob, Giles. [1686-1744]. *The Law Dictionary: Explaining the Rise, Progress, and Present State of the English Law; Defining and Interpreting the Terms or Words* *of Art; and Comprising Copious Information on the Subjects of Law, Trade, and Government. Corrected and Greatly Enlarged by T[homas] E[dlyne] Tomlins.* New York: Printed for, and Published by I. Riley, 1811. Six volumes. viii, 531; [2], 543; [2],618; [2], 472; [2], 553; [2], 471pp. Reprinted 2000 by The Lawbook Exchange, Ltd. LCCN 98-49349. ISBN 1-886363-68-4. Cloth. $495.

Jaques, E.T. *Charles Dickens in Chancery: Being an Account of his Proceedings in Respect of the "Christmas Carol" with Some Gossip in Relation to the Old Law Courts at Westminster.* London: Longmans, Green & Company, 1914. 95 pp. Reprint available March 2001 by The Lawbook Exchange, Ltd. ISBN 1-58477-106-2. Cloth. $60.

Jhering, Rudolf Von. *Law as a Means to an End.* Translated from the German by Isaac Husik with an Editorial Preface by Joseph H. Drake and with Introductions by Henry Lamm and W.M. Geldart. Boston: The Boston Book Company, 1913. lxi, 483 pp. Reprinted 1999 by The Lawbook Exchange, Ltd. LCCN 99-23754. ISBN 1-58477-009-0. Cloth. $80.

Jhering, Rudolph von. *The Struggle for Law Translated from the Fifth German Edition by John J. Lalor. Second Edition, with an Introduction by Albert Kocourek.* Chicago: Callaghan and Company, 1915. lii, 138 pp. Reprinted 1997 by The Lawbook Exchange, Ltd. LCCN 97-6826. ISBN 1-886363-25-0. Cloth. $60.

Johns, C.H.W. *Babylonian and Assyrian Laws, Contracts and Letters.* Edinburgh: T. & T. Clark, 1904. xxii, 424 pp. Reprinted 2000 by The Lawbook Exchange, Ltd. LCCN 99-32862. ISBN 1-58477-022-8. Cloth. $75.

Johns, C.H.W., translator. *The Oldest Code of Laws in the World: The Code of Laws Promulgated by Hammurabi, King of Babylon, B.C. 2285-2242.* Edinburgh: T. & T. Clark, 1926. xii, 88 pp. Reprinted 2000 by The Lawbook Exchange, Ltd. LCCN 99-053070. ISBN 1-58477-061-9. Cloth. $60.

Kames, Henry Home, Lord. [1696-1782]. *Historical Law Tracts. The Second Edition.* Edinburgh: A. Kincaid, 1761. xv, 463 pp. LCCN 99-43133. ISBN 1-58477-038-4. Reprinted 2000 by The Lawbook Exchange, Ltd. Cloth. $95.

Keller, Morton. *Affairs of State: Public Life in Late Nineteenth Century America.* Cambridge: Harvard University Press, 1977. ix, 631 pp. Reprinted 2000 by The Lawbook Exchange, Ltd. LCCN 99-087921. ISBN 1-58477-086-4. Cloth. $95.

Kelsen, Hans. [1881-1973]. *General Theory of Law and State.* Translated by Anders Wedberg. Cambridge: Harvard University Press, 1945. xxxiii, 516pp. Reprinted 1999 by The Lawbook Exchange, Ltd. LCCN 98-32334. ISBN 1-886363-74-9. Cloth. $75.

Kelsen, Hans. *The Law of the United Nations. A Critical Analysis of Its Fundamental Problems.* New York: Frederick A. Praeger, [1964]. xvii, 994 pp. Reprinted 2000 by The Lawbook Exchange, Ltd. ISBN 1-58477-077-5. Cloth. $125.

Kelsen, Hans. *Peace Through Law* Chapel Hill: The University of North Carolina Press, 1944. xii, 155 pp. Reprint available February 2001 by The Lawbook Exchange, Ltd. ISBN 1-58477-103-8. Cloth. $60.

Kelsen, Hans. *Society and Nature: A Sociological Inquiry.* London: K. Kegan Paul, Trench, Trubner & Co., Ltd., [1946]. viii, 391 pp. Reprinted 2000 by The Lawbook Exchange, Ltd. LCCN 99-054869. ISBN 1-58477-064-3. Cloth. $85.

Kelsen, Hans. *What is Justice? Justice, Law and Politics in the Mirror of Science.* Berkeley: University of California Press, 1957. [vi], 397 pp. Reprinted 2000 by The Lawbook Exchange, Ltd. ISBN 1-58477-101-1. Cloth. $95.

Kent, William. *Memoirs and Letters of James Kent, L.L.D.* Boston: Little, Brown, and Company, 1898. x, 341 pp. Reprint available July 2001 by The Lawbook Exchange, Ltd. ISBN 1-58477-100-3. Cloth. $75.

Kovalevsky, Maxime. *Modern Customs and Ancient Laws of Russia. Being the Ilchester Lectures for 1889-90.* London: David Nutt, 1891. x, 260 pp. Reprinted 2000 by The Lawbook Exchange, Ltd. LCCN 99-16487. ISBN 1-58477-017-1. Cloth. $65.

Kulsrud, Carl J. *Maritime Neutrality to 1780. A History of the Main Principles Governing Neutrality and Belligerency to 1780.* Boston: Little, Brown, and Company, 1936. x, 351 pp. Reprinted 2000 by The Lawbook Exchange, Ltd. LCCN 99-38825. ISBN 1-58477-027-9. Cloth. $65.

Langdell, C.C. [1826-1906]. *A Selection of Cases on the Law of Contracts. With References and Citations. Prepared for Use as a Text-book in Harvard Law School.* Boston: Little, Brown & Co., 1871. xvi, 1022 pp. Reprinted 1999 by The Lawbook Exchange, Ltd. LCCN 99-28293. ISBN 1-58477-001-5. Cloth. $120.

Lauterpacht, H[ersch]. *The Function of Law in the International Community.* Oxford: Clarendon Press, 1933. xxvi, 470 pp. Reprinted 2000 by The Lawbook Exchange, Ltd. LCCN 00-022124. ISBN 1-58477-090-2. Cloth. $90.

[Legal History]. *Select Essays in Anglo-American Legal History. By Maitland, Pollock, Holmes, Beale, Holdsworth and Others.* Boston: Little, Brown, and Company, 1907. Three volumes. 847; 823; 862 pp. Reprinted 1992 by The Lawbook Exchange, Ltd. LCCN 91-77977. ISBN 0-9630106-1-1. Cloth. $195.

Lieber, Francis. *On Civil Liberty and Self-government. Enlarged edition in one volume.* Philadelphia: J.B. Lippincott & Co.. 1859. xix, [15]-629 pp. Reprint available July 2001 by The Lawbook Exchange, Ltd. LCCN 99-056928. ISBN 1-58477-070-8. Cloth. $100.

Livingston, Edward. *A System of Penal Law, for the State of Louisiana: Consisting of A Code of Crimes and Punishments, A Code of Procedure, A Code of Evidence, A Code of Reform and Prison Discipline, A Book of Definitions. Prepared Under the Authority of a Law of the Said State. To Which are Prefixed a Preliminary Report on the Plan of a Penal Code, and Introductory Reports to the Several Codes Embraced in the System of Penal Law.* Philadelphia: James Kay, Jun. & Brother, 1833. v, 745 pp. Reprinted 1999 by The Lawbook Exchange, Ltd. LCCN 99-11403. ISBN 1-886363-83-8. Cloth. $95.

Llewellyn, Karl N. *Jurisprudence. Realism in Theory and Practice.* [Chicago]: The University of Chicago Press, 1962. viii, 531 pp. Reprinted 2000 by The Lawbook Exchange, Ltd. LCCN 99-056923. ISBN 1-58477-067-8. Cloth. $95.

[Macaulay, Thomas Babington]. *A Penal Code Prepared by the Indian Law Commissioners, and published by Command of the Governor General of India in Council.* London: Pelham Richardson, Cornhill, 1838. viii, 138 pp. Reprint available April 2001 by The Lawbook Exchange, Ltd. LCCN 99-16486. ISBN 1-58477-018-X. Cloth. $65.

[MacDonell, Sir John and Edward Manson]. *Great Jurists of the World.* Edited by Sir John MacDonell and Edward Manson. With an Introduction by Van Vechten Veeder. Boston: Little, Brown, and Company, 1914. Illustrated. xxxii, 607 pp. Reprinted 1997 by The Lawbook Exchange, Ltd. LCCN 97-8298. ISBN 1-886363-28-5. Cloth. $95.

[Madison, James]. Hunt, Gaillard, Scott, James Brown. *The Debates in The Federal Convention of 1787 Which Framed the Constitution of the United States of America.* New York: Oxford University Press, 1920. xcvii, [1], 731 pp. Reprinted 1999 by The Lawbook Exchange, Ltd. LCCN 98-51911. ISBN 1-886363-77-3. Cloth. $110.

Maitland, Frederic William. *Roman Canon Law in the Church of England: Six Essays.* London: Methuen & Co., 1898. vii, 184 pp. Reprinted 1998 by The Lawbook Exchange, Ltd. LCCN 98-22357. ISBN 1-886363-57-9. Cloth. $65.

Maitland, Frederick W., Montague, Francis C., *A Sketch of English Legal History.* Edited with Notes and Appendices by James F. Colby. New York: G.P. Putnam's Sons, 1915. x, 234pp. Reprinted 1998 by The Lawbook Exchange, Ltd. LCCN 98-11337. ISBN 1-886363-50-1. Cloth. $50.

Maitland, Frederick William. *English Law and the Renaissance (The Rede Lecture for 1901) with Some Notes.* Cambridge: at the University Press, 1901. 98 pp. Reprinted 2000 by The Lawbook Exchange, Ltd. LCCN 99-41654. ISBN 1-58477-034-1. Cloth. $60.

Maitland, F.W. *The Constitutional History of England. A Course of Lectures Delivered.* Cambridge: Cambridge University Press, 1908. xxviii, 547 pp. Reprint available July 2001 by The Lawbook Exchange, Ltd. LCCN 00-068895. ISBN 1-58477-148-8. Cloth. $95.

Mangum, Charles. *The Legal Status of the Negro.* New York: D. Appleton-Century Co., [1939]. xi, 354 pp. Reprinted 2000 by The Lawbook Exchange, Ltd. LCCN 99-056927. ISBN 1-58477-081-3. Cloth. $80.

Marke, Julius J., editor. *A Catalogue of the Law Collection at New York University With Selected Annotations.* New York: The Law Center of New York University, 1953. xxxi, 1372 pp. Reprinted 1999 by The Lawbook Exchange, Ltd. LCCN 99-19939. ISBN 1-886363-91-9. Cloth. $185.

Marsden. R.[eginald]. G.[odfrey], ed. *Documents Relating to Law and Custom of the Sea.* [n.p.]: The Navy Record Society, 1915-6. Two volumes. xxxiii, 561; xl, 457, [5] pp. Reprinted 1999 by The Lawbook Exchange, Ltd. LCCN 99-24138. ISBN 1-886363-96-X. Cloth. $175.

Marshall, John. *The Constitutional Decisions of John Marshall*, Edited, with an introductory essay by Joseph P. Cotton, Jr. New York: G.P. Putnam, 1905. Two volumes. viii, 144, 145a-188a, [145]-330 pp. Reprint available February 2001 by The Lawbook Exchange, Ltd. LCCN 99-048862. ISBN 1-58477-050-3. Cloth. $175.

[Marshall, John]. Servies, James Albert. *A Bibliography of John Marshall.* Washington: United States Commission for the Celebration of the Two Hundredth Anniversary of the Birth of John Marshall, 1956. xix, 182 pp. Reprinted 2000 by The Lawbook Exchange, Ltd. LCCN 99-088239. ISBN 1-58477-083-X. Cloth. $65.

Mathews, John. *Legislative and Judicial History of the Fifteenth Amendment.* Originally published Baltimore: The Johns Hopkins Press, 1909. x, 11-126 pp. Reprint available July 2001 by The Lawbook Exchange, Ltd. ISBN 1-58477-176-3. Cloth. $60.

Maxwell, W. Harold and C.R. Brown. *A Complete List of British and Colonial Law Reports and Legal Periodicals. Arranged in Alphabetical and in Chronological Order with Bibliographical Notes.* **[With]:** *Check List of Canadian and Newfoundland Statutes.*[Third Edition]. Toronto: The Carswell Company, Limited, 1937. viii, 141, 49 pp. Reprinted 1995 by The Lawbook Exchange, Ltd. LCCN 96-14504. ISBN 1-886363-11-0. Cloth. $70.

McCulloch, J.R. *The Works of David Ricardo, Esq., M.P. with a Notice of the Life and Writings of the Author.* London: John Murray, 1846. xxxiii, 584 pp. Reprinted 2000 by The Lawbook Exchange, Ltd. LCCN 99-39612. ISBN 1-58477-028-7. Cloth. $90.

McKechnie, William Sharp. *Magna Carta. A Commentary on the Great Charter of King John. With an Historical Introduction. Second Edition, Revised and in part Re-written.* Glasgow: James Maclehose and Sons, 1914. xvii, 530, [2] pp. Reprinted 2000 by The Lawbook Exchange, Ltd. LCCN 99-38731. ISBN 1-58477-031-7. Cloth. $95.

McLaughlin, Andrew C. *The Courts, The Constitution and Parties. Studies in Constitutional History and Politics.* Chicago: University of Chicago Press, 1912. vii, 299 pp. Reprint available August 2001 by The Lawbook Exchange, Ltd. LCCN 00-058812. ISBN 1-58477-155-0. Cloth. $80.

McNamara, M. Frances. *Ragbag of Legal Quotations*. Albany: Matthew Bender & Company, 1960. xi, 334 pp. Reprinted 1992 by The Lawbook Exchange, Ltd. LCCN 92-074141. ISBN 0-9630106-3-8. Cloth. $50.

Meiklejohn, Alexander. *Free Speech and Its Relation to Self Government.* New York: Harper Brothers Publishers, [1948]. xiv, 107pp. Reprint available July 2001 by The Lawbook Exchange, Ltd. LCCN 99-87204. ISBN 1-58477-087-2. Cloth. $80.

Mendelsohn, S. *The Criminal Jurisprudence of the Ancient Hebrews. Compiled from the Talmud and other Rabbinical Writings, and Compared with Roman and English Penal Jurisprudence.* Baltimore: M. Curlander, 1891. 270 pp. Reprint available October 2001 by The Lawbook Exchange, Ltd. ISBN 1-58477-150-X. Cloth. $80.

Merriam, C.E., Jr. *History of the Theory of Sovereignty Since Rousseau.* New York: Columbia University Press, [1900]. x, [11]-233 pp. Reprinted 1999 by The Lawbook Exchange, Ltd. LCCN 98-32385. ISBN 1-886363-76-5. Cloth. $65.

Minor, Raleigh C. *Notes on the Science of Government and the Relations of the States to the United States*. [Charlottesville]: University of Virginia, 1913. x, 171 pp. Reprinted 1995 by The Lawbook Exchange, Ltd. LCCN 99-047233. ISBN 1-886363-09-9. Cloth. $40.

Moore, Blaine Free. *The Supreme Court and Unconstitutional Legislation.* New York: Columbia University Press, 1913. 158 pp. Reprint available March 2001 by The Lawbook Exchange, Ltd. ISBN 1-58477-099-6. Cloth. $60.

Morris, Robert C. *International Arbitration and Procedure.* New Haven: Yale University Press, 1911. x, 238 pp. Reprint available February 2001 by The Lawbook Exchange, Ltd. LCCN 00-059547. ISBN 1-58477-160-7. Cloth. $70.

Morris, Thomas D. *Free Men All: The Personal Liberty Laws of the North 1780-1861.* Baltimore: The Johns Hopkins University Press, 1974. xii, 253 pp. Reprint available April 2001 by The Lawbook Exchange, Ltd. ISBN 1-58477-107-0. Cloth. $75.

Neely, Robert D. *The Lawyers of Dickens and Their Clerks.* Boston: The Christopher Publishing House, [1936]. 67pp. Reprint available November

2001 by The Lawbook Exchange, Ltd. LCCN 00-021520. ISBN 1-58477-091-0. Cloth. $60.

Neilson, George. *Trial by Combat.* Glasgow: William Hodge & Co., 1890. xiv, 348 pp. Reprinted 2000 by The Lawbook Exchange, Ltd. LCCN 99-059101. ISBN 1-58477-075-9. Cloth. $75.

[Nichols, J.]. *A Collection of all the Wills, Now Known to Be Extant, of the Kings and Queens of England, Princes and Princesses of Wales, and every Branch of the Blood Royal, from the Reign of William the Conqueror, to that of Henry the Seventh Exclusive: With Explanatory Notes and a Glossary.* London: J. Nichols, 1780. x, 434 pp. Reprinted 1999 by The Lawbook Exchange, Ltd. LCCN 99-17114. ISBN 1-886363-87-0. Cloth. $75.

Ogle, Arthur. *The Canon Law in Mediaeval England. An Examination of William Lyndwood's "Provinciale," in Reply to the Late Professor F. W. Maitland.* London: John Murray, 1912. xv, 220 pp. Reprinted 2000 by The Lawbook Exchange, Ltd. LCCN 99-33827. ISBN 1-58477-026-0. Cloth. $65.

Oldroyd, Osborn H. *The Assassination of Abraham Lincoln. The Flight, Pursuit, Capture and Punishment of the Conspirators.* Washington, D.C.: O.H. Oldroyd, 1901. xviii, 305pp. Illustrated. Reprint available September 2001 by The Lawbook Exchange, Ltd. ISBN 1-58477-125-9. Cloth. $75.

[Parker, James]. [Legal Manual]. *Conductor Generalis, or The Office, Duty and Authority of Justices of the Peace, High Sheriffs, Under-Sheriffs, Goalers, Coroners, Constables, Jury Men, Over-seers of the Poor, and also The Office of Clerks of Assiza And of the Peace &c. Collected out of all the Books hitherto written on those Subjects, whether of Common or Statute Law. To which is added, A Collection out of Sir Matthew Hales concerning The Descent of Lands. The Whole Alphabetically Digested Under the Several Titles, With a Table Directing to the Ready finding out Proper Matter under those Titles.* Philadelphia: Printed and Sold by Andrew Bradford, 1722. [8], xii, 232pp. **[with]** *The Office, Duty and Authority of Sheriffs, How and in what Manner to execute the same, according to the Common and Statute Laws of Great-Britain, which are now in Force and Use. Likewise, Of Under-Sheriffs and their Deputies; and where the High-Sheriff shall be answerable for their Defaults, and where not, &.* Philadelphia: Andrew Bradford, 1721. [233]-299, [1] pp. Reprint available October 2001 by The Lawbook Exchange, Ltd. LCCN 00-058810. ISBN 1-58477-123-2. Cloth. $80.

Perry, Ross R. *Common-law Pleading: Its History and Principles. Including Dicey's Rules Concerning Parties to Action and Stephen's Rules of Pleading.*

Boston, Little, Brown and Company, 1897. xxvi, 494 pp. Reprint available February 2001 by The Lawbook Exchange, Ltd. ISBN 1-58477-105-4. Cloth. $95.

Phillimore, John George [1808-1865]. *Principles and Maxims of Jurisprudence.* Originally published London: John W. Parker and Son, 1856. xxiv, 408 pp. Reprint available August 2001 by The Lawbook Exchange, Ltd. ISBN 1-58477-177-1. Cloth. $85.

Pollock, Frederick and Frederic William Maitland. *The History of English Law before the Time of Edward I.* Cambridge: Cambridge University Press, 1898. Two volumes. xxxviii, 688; xiv, 691 pp. Reprinted 1996 by The Lawbook Exchange, Ltd. LCCN 96-16003. ISBN 1-886363-22-6. Cloth. $165.

Pollock, Sir Frederick. *The Expansion of the Common Law* London: Stevens and Sons, Limited, 1904. vii, 164pp. Reprint available September 2001 by The Lawbook Exchange, Ltd. LCCN 00-067015. ISBN 1-58477-169-0. Cloth. $65.

Pollock, Sir Frederick. *The Genius of the Common Law.* New York: The Columbia University Press, 1912. vii, 141 pp. Reprinted 2000 by The Lawbook Exchange, Ltd. LCCN 99-047160. ISBN 1-58477-043-0-1. Cloth. $55.

Pomeroy, John N. *A Treatise on Equity Jurisprudence As Administered in the United States of America. Adapted for All the States and to the Union of Legal and Equitable Remedies under the Reformed Procedure.* San Francisco and New York: Bancroft-Whitney and Lawyers Cooperative, 1941. Five volumes. 914; 1134; 1063; 1104; 716 pp. Reprinted 1995 by The Lawbook Exchange, Ltd. ISBN 1-886363-05-6. Cloth. $450.

Pothier, R.J. (1699-1772)]. *Treatise on the Contract of Sale.* Translated from the French by L.S. Cushing. Boston: Charles C. Little and James Brown, 1839. xvi, 406 pp. Reprinted 2000 by The Lawbook Exchange, Ltd. LCCN 99-10260. ISBN 1-886363-82-X. Cloth. $70.

Pothier, Robert Joseph [1699-1772]. *A Treatise on the Law of Obligations, or Contracts. Translated from the French, with an Introduction, Appendix, and Notes, Illustrative of the English Law on the Subject. By William David Evans.* London: A. Strahan, 1802. Two volumes. [1], 578, [1]; iv, 715, [1]pp. Reprinted 2000 by The Lawbook Exchange, Ltd. LCCN 99-26397. ISBN 1-886363-98-6. Cloth. $195.

Pothier, Robert Joseph [1699-1772]. *A Treatise on Obligations, Considered in a Moral and Legal View Translated from the French of Pothier. Translated by Francois-Xavier Martin.* Newburn, N.C.: Martin & Ogden, 1802. 2 vols. in 1 book. Reprinted 2000 by The Lawbook Exchange, Ltd. With a new introduction by Warren M. Billings. LCCN 98-38360. ISBN 1-886363-62-5. Cloth. $75.

Pound, Roscoe. *Jurisprudence.* St. Paul, Minn.: West Publishing Co., 1959. Five volumes. Reprinted 2000 by The Lawbook Exchange, Ltd. ISBN 1-58477-119-4. Cloth. $495.

Powell, Chilton Latham. *English Domestic Relations 1487-1653. A Study of Matrimony and Family Life in Theory and Practice as Revealed by the Literature, Law, and History of the Period.* New York: Columbia University Press, 1917. xii, 274 pp. Reprint available March 2001 by The Lawbook Exchange, Ltd. ISBN 1-58477-096-1. Cloth. $75.

Radin, Max. *Law as Logic and Experience.* New Haven: Yale University Press, 1940. ix, [1], 171 pp. Reprinted 2000 by The Lawbook Exchange, Ltd. LCCN 99-30670. ISBN 1-58477-008-2. Cloth. $55.

Rapalje, Stewart and Lawrence, Robert L. *A Dictionary of American and English Law with Definitions of the Technical Terms of the Canon and Civil Laws. Also, Containing a Full Collection of Latin Maxims, and Citations of Upwards of Forty Thousand Reported Cases, in which Words and Phrases Have Been Judicially Defined or Construed.* Jersey City: Frederick C. Linn & Co., 1888. Two volumes. xxxviii, 1380 pp. Reprinted 1997 by The Lawbook Exchange, Ltd. LCCN 97-38484. ISBN 1-886363-33-1. Cloth. $195.

Reeve, Tapping. [1744-1823]. *The Law of Baron and Femme, of Parent and Child, Guardian and Ward, Master and Servant, and of the Powers of the Courts of Chancery; with an Essay on the Terms Heir, Heirs, Heirs of the Body. Third Edition, With Notes and References to English and American Cases by Amasa J. Parker and Charles E. Baldwin, Counselors-At-Law.* Albany: William Gould, 1862. xlvi, 677pp. Reprinted 1998 by The Lawbook Exchange, Ltd. LCCN 98-36057. ISBN 1-886363-58-7. Cloth. $75.

Richards, John T. *Abraham Lincoln The Lawyer-Statesman.* Boston: Houghton Mifflin, 1916. Frontis. Illustrated. xii, 260 pp. Reprinted 1999 by The Lawbook Exchange, Ltd. LCCN 99-20587. ISBN 1-886363-94-3. Cloth. $60.

Roby, Henry John. *An Introduction to the Study of Justinian's Digest Containing an Account of its Composition and of the Jurists Used or Referred to Therein.* Cambridge: At the University Press, 1886. cclxxix pp. Reprinted 2000 by The Lawbook Exchange, Ltd. ISBN 1-58477-073-2. Cloth. $65.

Roby, Henry John. *Roman Private Law in the Times of Cicero and of the Antonines.* Cambridge: At the University Press, 1902. Two volumes. xxxii, 543; xiii, [1], 560 pp. Reprinted 2000 by The Lawbook Exchange, Ltd. ISBN 1-58477-074-0. Cloth. $180.

Sandys, Sir John Edwin. *Aristotle's Constitution of Athens. A Revised Text with an Introduction Critical and Explanatory Notes Testimonia and Indices. Second edition, Revised and Enlarged.* London: Macmillan & Co., Limited, 1902. xcii, 331 pp. Frontis. Illus. Reprinted 2000 by The Lawbook Exchange, Ltd. LCCN 99-23952. ISBN 1-58477-004-X. Cloth. $75.

Schechter, Frank I. *The Historical Foundations of the Law Relating to Trade-Marks.* New York: Columbia University Press, 1925. xxviii, 211 pp. Reprinted 2000 by The Lawbook Exchange, Ltd. LCCN 99-41673. ISBN 1-58477-035-X. Cloth. $60.

Schroeder, Theodore. *Constitutional Free Speech Defined and Defended in an Unfinished Argument in a Case of Blasphemy.* New York: Free Speech League, 1919. 456 pp. Reprint available April 2001 by The Lawbook Exchange, Ltd. LCCN 99-049361. ISBN 1-58477-053-8. Cloth. $90.

Schroeder, Theodore. *Free Speech Bibliography Including Every Discovered Attitude Toward the Problem Covering Every Method of Transmitting Ideas and Abridging Their Promulgation upon Every Subject-Matter.* New York: The H.W. Wilson Company, 1922. 456 pp. Reprint available July 2001 by The Lawbook Exchange, Ltd. LCCN 99-049361. ISBN 1-58477-053-8. Cloth. $85.

Schroeder, Theodore. *"Obscene" Literature and Constitutional Law A Forensic Defense of Freedom of the Press.* New York: Privately Printed for Forensic Uses, 1911. 439 pp. Reprint available April 2001 by The Lawbook Exchange, Ltd. LCCN 00-58815. ISBN 1-58477-154-2. Cloth. $85.

Schulte, Joh. Friedrich von. *Die Geschichte der Quellen und Literatur der canonischen Rechts.* Stuttgart: Verlag von Ferdinand Enke, 1875. Two volumes. Reprinted 2000 by The Lawbook Exchange, Ltd. LCCN 99-087494. ISBN 1-58477-089-9. Cloth. $225.

Schwartz, Bernard, editor. *The Code Napoleon and the Common-Law World. The Sesquicentennial Lectures Delivered at The Law Center of New York University December 13-15, 1954.* New York: New York University Press, 1956. x, 438pp. Reprinted 1998 by The Lawbook Exchange, Ltd. LCCN 98-34100. ISBN 1-886363-59-5. Cloth. $65.

Schwarz, Philip J. *Twice Condemned: Slaves and the Criminal Laws of Virginia, 1705-1865.* [Baton Rouge: Louisiana State University Press]. [1988]. xvi, 354pp. Reprinted 1998 by The Lawbook Exchange, Ltd. LCCN 98-4424 ISBN 1-886363-54-4. Cloth. $75.

Scott, Henry W. *The Courts of the State of New York: Their History, Development and Jurisdiction: Embracing a complete history of all the Courts and Tribunals of Justice, both Colonial and State, established from the first settlement of Manhattan Island and including the status and jurisdiction of all the Courts of the State as now constituted.* New York: Wilson Publishing Co., 1909. Reprint available August 2001 by The Lawbook Exchange, Ltd. LCCN 99-10259. ISBN 1-886363-84-6. Cloth. $95.

Scott, James Brown. *James Madison's Notes of Debates in the Federal Convention Convention of 1787 and their Relation to a More Perfect Society of Nations.* New York: Oxford University Press, 1918. xviii, 149pp. Reprint available September 2001 by The Lawbook Exchange, Ltd. ISBN 1-58477-164-X. Cloth. $65.

Scott, James Brown. *The Spanish Origin of International Law. Francisco De Vitoria and His Law of Nations.* London: Humphrey Milford, 1934. 19a, 288, clviii pp. Frontispiece and portrait. Reprinted 2000 by The Lawbook Exchange, Ltd. LCCN 00-036835. ISBN 1-58477-110-0. Cloth. $90.

Scott, S.P. *The Civil Law Including the Twelve Tables, The Institutes of Gaius, The Rules of Ulpian, the Opinions of Paulus, The Enactments of Justinian, and the Constitutions of Leo: Translated from the original Latin, edited, and compared with all accessible systems of jurisprudence ancient and modern. In Seventeen Volumes. In seven books.* Cincinnati: The Central Trust Company, 1932. Reprint available May 2001 by The Lawbook Exchange, Ltd. ISBN 1-58477-130-5. Cloth. $750.

Sears, John H. *Trust Estates as Business Companies.* [*Second Edition*]. Kansas City, Mo.: Vernon Law Book Company, 1921. xx, 782 pp. [1921]. Reprinted 1998 by The Lawbook Exchange, Ltd. LCCN 97-32423 ISBN 1-886363-41-2. Cloth. $95.

Shumaker, Walter A. *The Cyclopedic Law Dictionary Comprising the Terms and Phrases of American Jurisprudence, Including Ancient and Modern Common Law, International Law, and Numerous Select Titles from the Civil Law, the French and the Spanish Law, etc., etc. with an Exhaustive Collection of Legal Maxims. Second Edition by James C. Cahill.* Chicago: Callaghan and Company, 1922. xii, 545 pp. Reprint available February 2001 by The Lawbook Exchange, Ltd. LCCN 99-11404. ISBN 1-886363-85-4. Cloth. $150.

Spooner, Lysander. *An Essay on the Trial by Jury.* Boston: Bela Marsh, 1852. 224 pp. Reprint available April 2001 by The Lawbook Exchange, Ltd. LCCN 00-058811. ISBN 1-58477-156-9. Cloth. $70.

[St. Germain, Christopher]. [1460-1540]. *The Doctor and Student or Dialogues Between a Doctor of Divinity and a Student in the Laws of England Containing the Grounds of Those Laws Together with Questions and Cases Concerning the Equity Thereof Revised and Corrected by William Muchall, Gent. to which are added two pieces concerning Suits in Chancery by Subpoena.* Cincinnati: Robert Clarke & Co., 1874. xiv, 401pp. Reprinted 1998 by The Lawbook Exchange, Ltd. LCCN 98-11338. ISBN 1-886363-49-8. Cloth. $65.

Stammler, Rudolph. *The Theory of Justice.* Translated by Isaak Husik. New York: The Macmillan Company, 1925. xli, 591 pp. Reprinted 2000 by The Lawbook Exchange, Ltd. LCCN 99-054019. ISBN 1-58477-066-X. Cloth. $95.

Stammler, Rudolph. *The Theory of Justice.* Translated by Isaak Husik. New York: The Macmillan Company, 1925. xli, 591 pp. Reprinted 2000 by The Lawbook Exchange, Ltd. LCCN 99-054019. ISBN 1-58477-066-X. Cloth. $95.

Stimson, Frederic Jesup. *Glossary of Technical Terms, Phrases, and Maxims of the Common Law.* Boston: Little, Brown, and Company, 1881. iv, 305pp. Reprinted 1999 by The Lawbook Exchange, Ltd. LCCN 98-50813. ISBN 1-886363-70-6. Cloth. $60.

Stimson, Frederic Jesup. *Popular Law-Making. A Study of the Origin, History, and Present Tendencies of Law-Making by Statute.* New York: Charles Scribner's Sons, 1910. xii, 545 pp. Reprint available April 2001 by The Lawbook Exchange, Ltd. LCCN 00-022513. ISBN 1-58477-094-5. Cloth. $85.

Stokes, I.N. Phelps. *The Iconography of Manhattan Island 1498-1909.* New York: Robert H. Dodd, 1915. Six volumes. Reprinted 1998 by The Lawbook Exchange, Ltd. LCCN 97-30604. ISBN 1-886363-30-7. Cloth. $750.

Stone, Harlan F. *Law and its Administration.* New York: Columbia University Press, 1915. vii, 232 pp. Reprint available October 2001 by The Lawbook Exchange, Ltd. LCCN 00-021508. ISBN 1-58477-093-7. Cloth. $70.

Story, Joseph. [1779-1845]. *A Familiar Exposition of the Constitution of the United States:* Containing a Brief Commentary on Every Clause, Explaining the True Nature, reasons, and Objects Thereof; Designed for the Use of School, Libraries and General Readers. With an Appendix, Containing Important Public Documents, Illustrative of the Constitution. New York: Harper & Brothers: 1865. 372 pp. Reprinted 1999 by The Lawbook Exchange, Ltd. LCCN 98-50811. ISBN 1-886363-71-4. Cloth. $60.

[Story, Joseph]. [1779-1845]. Story, William. *Life and Letters of Joseph Story, Associate Justice of the Supreme Court of the United States and Dane Professor of Law at Harvard University, edited by his son, William W. Story.* Boston: Charles C. Little and James Brown, 1851. Two volumes. xii, 574; viii, 676 pp. Frontispiece. Reprint available January 2001 by The Lawbook Exchange, Ltd. LCCN 99-058777. ISBN 1-58477-071-6. Cloth. $195.

Story, Joseph. *Commentaries on the Conflict of Laws, Foreign and Domestic, in Regard to Contracts, Rights, and Remedies, and Especially in Regard to Marriages, Divorces, Wills, Successions, and Judgments. Second Edition. Revised, Corrected and Greatly Enlarged.* London: A. Maxwell, 1841. xxxiv, 927 pp. Reprint available May 2001 by The Lawbook Exchange, Ltd. ISBN 1-58477-146-1. Cloth. $125.

[Story, Joseph]. Story, William W., ed. *The Miscellaneous Writings of Joseph Story, Associate Justice of the Supreme Court of the United States and Dane Professor of Law at Harvard University, edited by his son, William W. Story.* Boston: C.C. Little and J. Brown, 1852. x, 828 pp. Reprint available February 2001 by The Lawbook Exchange, Ltd. LCCN 99-058559. ISBN 1-58477-072-4. Cloth. $125.

Tayler, Thomas. *The Law Glossary: Being a Selection of the Greek, Latin, Saxon, French, Norman and Italian Sentences, Phrases, and Maxims, Found in the Leading English and American Reports, and Elementary Works.* New York:

Lewis & Blood, 1856. 580 pp. Reprinted 1995 by The Lawbook Exchange, Ltd. ISBN 1-886363-12-9. Cloth. $65.

[Taylor, John]. [1753-1824]. *A Defence of the Measures of the Administration of Thomas Jefferson. By Curtius.* Washington: Samuel H. Smith, 1804. 136 pp. Reprinted 1999 by The Lawbook Exchange, Ltd. LCCN 99-24139. ISBN 1-886363-97-8. Cloth. $60.

Taylor, John. *Construction Construed and Constitutions Vindicated.* Richmond: printed by Shepherd & Pollard, 1820. iv, 344pp. Reprinted 1998 by The Lawbook Exchange, Ltd. LCCN 97-49411. ISBN 1-886363-43-9. Cloth. $65.

Taylor, John. *An Inquiry into the Principles and Policy of the Government of the United States.* Fredericksburg:Green and Cady, 1814. With an introduction by Roy Franklin Nichols, Yale University Press, 1950. 562pp. Reprinted 1998 by The Lawbook Exchange, Ltd. LCCN 98-11147. ISBN 1-886363-46-3. Cloth. $75.

Taylor, John, of Caroline. *New Views of the Constitution of the United States.* Washington City: Printed for the Author, 1823. [4], 316pp. Reprint available December 2001 by The Lawbook Exchange, Ltd. ISBN 1-58477-079-1. Cloth. $70.

Thomson, Richard. *An Historical Essay on the Magna Charta of King John: to which are added, the Great Charter in Latin and English, the charters of liberties and confirmations, granted by Henry III and Edward I, the original Charter of the forests, and various authentic instruments connected with them: Explanatory Notes on their Several Privileges; A Descriptive Account of the Principal Originals and Editions Extant, Both in Print and Manuscript; and Other Illustrations, Derived from the Most Interesting and Authentic Sources.* London: John Major and Robert Jennings, 1829. xxxii, 612 pp. Reprinted 2000 by The Lawbook Exchange, Ltd. LCCN 99-40987. ISBN 1-58477-030-9. Cloth. $95.

Tiedeman, Christopher G. *A Treatise on the Limitations of Police Power in the United States Considered from both a Civil and Criminal Standpoint.* St. Louis: The F.H. Thomas Law Book Co., 1886. lxv, 662 pp. Reprint available March 2001 by The Lawbook Exchange, Ltd. ISBN 1-58477-122-4. Cloth. $110.

Townley, James. *The Reasons of the Laws of Moses from the "More Nevochim" of Maimonides. With Notes, Dissertations, and a Life of the Author.* London: Longman, Rees, Orme, Brown, and Green, 1827. xi, 451 pp. Reprint available September 2001 by The Lawbook Exchange, Ltd. ISBN 1-58477-168-2. Cloth. $95.

Townsend, William H. *Lincoln the Litigant.* Boston: Houghton Mifflin Company, 1925. [ix], [117] pp. Frontis. Illus. Reprinted 2000 by The Lawbook Exchange, Ltd. LCCN 99-16499. ISBN 1-58477-021-X. Cloth. $60.

Trayner, John. [1834-1929]. *Latin Phrases and Maxims: Collected from the Institutional and other Writers on Scotch Law; with Translations and Illustrations.* Edinburgh: William Paterson, 1861. iv, [2], 356 pp. Reprint available July 2001 by The Lawbook Exchange, Ltd. LCCN 00-067012. ISBN 1-58477-174-7. Cloth. $75.

[Trials]. [Witchcraft Trials]. *Curious Cases and Amusing Actions at Law Including Some Trials of Witches in the Seventeenth Century.* Toronto: The Carswell Co., Limited, 1916. vii, 234 pp. Reprinted 2000 by The Lawbook Exchange, Ltd. LCCN 99-032361. ISBN 1-58477-012-0. Cloth. $65.

Tucker, Henry St. George. *Commentaries on the Laws of Virginia. Comprising the Substance of a Course of Lectures Delivered to the Winchester Law School. With an Introduction by David Cobin and Paul Finkelman.* Richmond: Shepherd and Colin, 1846. Two volumes. 34, 468; 24, 512 pp. Reprinted 1998 by The Lawbook Exchange, Ltd. LCCN 97-10313. ISBN 1-886363-26-9. Cloth. $175.

Tucker, Henry St. George. *Limitations on the Treaty-Making Power Under the Constitution of the United States.* Boston: Little, Brown, and Company, 1915. xxi, 444 pp. Reprinted 2000 by The Lawbook Exchange, Ltd. LCCN 99-31589. ISBN 1-58477-015-5. Cloth. $75.

Tucker, St. George. *Blackstone's Commentaries. With Notes of Reference to the Constitution and Laws, of the Federal Government of the United States, and of the Commonwealth of Virginia. In Five Volumes, with an Appendix to Each volume, Containing Short Tracts upon Such Subjects As Appeared Necessary to Form a Connected View of the Laws of Virginia As a Member of the Federal Union.* Philadelphia: William Young Birch and Abraham Small, 1803. Five volumes. Reprinted 1996 by The Lawbook Exchange, Ltd. LCCN 96-12566. ISBN 1-886363-15-3. Cloth. $450.

[Twiss, Sir Travers]. *The Black Book of the Admiralty, with an Appendix.* Monumenta Juridica. Edited by Sir Travers Twiss. Four volumes. 4, xciii,

491, [2]; 4, lxxxvii, 500, 31; 4, lxxxvi, 673, [1], 31; 4, clii, 559, 32 pp. LCCN 97-38809 ISBN 1-886363-39-0. 1871. Reprinted 1998 by The Lawbook Exchange, Ltd. Cloth. $495.

[Upshur, Abel Parker]. *A Brief Enquiry Into the True Nature and Character of Our Federal Government, being a review of Judge Story's Commentaries on the Constitution of the United States. By a Virginian.* Petersburg: Printed by Edmund and Julian C. Ruffin, 1840. 132pp. Reprinted 1998 by The Lawbook Exchange, Ltd. LCCN 97-11151. ISBN 1-886363-44-7. Cloth. $45.

Valmaer. [pseud]. [Ream, Michael]. *Lawyer's Code of Ethics. A Satire.* St. Louis: The F.H. Thomas Law Book Co., 1887. 143 pp. Reprint available Janaury 2001 by The Lawbook Exchange, Ltd. LCCN 00-021508. ISBN 1-58477-047-3. Cloth. $65.

Vinogradoff, Paul. *Custom and Right.* Oslo: H. Aschehoug, 1925. 110 pp. Reprinted 2000 by The Lawbook Exchange, Ltd. LCCN 99-0474851. ISBN 1-58477-048-1. Cloth. $45.

Vinogradoff, Paul. *Roman Law in Mediaeval Europe.* London: Harper & Brothers, 1909. 136 pp. Reprint available March 2001 by The Lawbook Exchange, Ltd. LCCN 00-039068. ISBN 1-58477-109-7. Cloth. $65.

Vinogradoff, Sir Paul. *Outlines of Historical Jurisprudence.* London: Oxford University Press, 1920. Two volumes. 428; x, 315 pp. Reprinted 1999 by The Lawbook Exchange, Ltd. LCCN 98-42298. ISBN 1-886363-64-1. Cloth. $150.

Walker, James. *The Theory of the Common Law.* Boston: Little, Brown and Co., 1852. xxiv, 130pp. Reprinted 1998 by The Lawbook Exchange, Ltd. LCCN 98-9522. ISBN 1-886363-45-5. Cloth. $65.

Warren, Charles. *History of the Harvard Law School and of Early Legal Conditions in America.* New York: Lewis Publishing Company, 1908. Three volumes. xiv, 543; iv, 560; 397 pp. Illustrated. Reprinted 1999 by The Lawbook Exchange, Ltd. LCCN 99-29193. ISBN 1-58477-006-6. Cloth. $275.

Wheaton, Henry. [1785-1848]. *Elements of International Law with a Sketch of the History of the Science.* Philadelphia: Carey, Lea & Blanchard, 1836. xiv, 375 pp. Reprint available May 2001 by The Lawbook Exchange, Ltd. LCCN 00-066335. ISBN 1-58477-170-4 . Cloth. $80.

White, Edw. J. *The Law in Scriptures. With Explanations of the Law Terms and Legal References in Both the Old and the New Testaments.* St. Louis: Thomas Law Book Company, 1935. xxiv, 422 pp. Reprinted 2000 by The Lawbook Exchange, Ltd. LCCN 99-059102. ISBN 1-58477-076-7. Cloth. $80.

Whiting, William. *War Powers under the Constitution of the United States. Military Arrests, Reconstruction & Military Government. Also, Now First Published, War Claims of Aliens with Notes on the Acts of the Executives & Legislative Departments During Our Civil War & a Collection of Cases Decided in the National Courts. 1864. Tenth edition.* Boston: Little, Brown, and Company, 1864. xvii, 342 pp. Reprint available April 2001 by The Lawbook Exchange, Ltd. LCCN 99-049360. ISBN 1-58477-055-4. Cloth. $80.

Whitney, Henry C. *Life on the Circuit with Lincoln. With Sketches of Generals Grant, Sherman and McClellan, Judge Davis, Leonard Swett, and Other Contemporaries.* Illustrated. Boston: Estes & Lauriat, 1892. viii, 601 pp. Reprint available March 2001 by The Lawbook Exchange, Ltd. ISBN 1-58477-115-1. Cloth. $110.

Wiener, Leo. [1862-1939]. *Commentary to the Germanic Laws and Mediaeval Documents.* Cambridge: Harvard University Press, 1915. lxi, 224 pp. Reprinted 2000 by The Lawbook Exchange, Ltd. LCCN 99-23969. ISBN 1-58477-005-8. Cloth. $60.

Willoughby, Westel W. *The Supreme Court of the United States. Its History and Influence in our Constitutional System.* Baltimore: The Johns Hopkins Press, 1890.124 pp. Reprint available August 2001 by The Lawbook Exchange, Ltd. LCCN 00-068896. ISBN 1-58477-147-X. Cloth. $60.

Woodbine, George E. *Four Thirteenth Century Law Tracts. A Thesis Presented to the Faculty of the Graduate School of Yale University in Candidacy for the Degree of Doctor of Philosophy.* New Haven: Yale University Press, 1910. vi, 183 pp. Reprinted 1999 by The Lawbook Exchange, Ltd. LCCN 99-29294. ISBN 1-58477-007-4. Cloth. $50.

Woolsey, Theodore D. *Divorce and Divorce Legislation, Especially in the United States. Second Edition Revised.* New York: Charles Scribner's Sons, 1882. x, [9]-328 pp. Reprint available February 2001 by The Lawbook Exchange, Ltd. ISBN 1-58477-118-6. Cloth. $75.

[Worrall, John and Edward Brooke]. *Bibliotheca Legum Angliae. Or, a Catalogue of the Common and Statute Law Books of This Realm, and Some Others*

Relating Thereto: Giving an Account of Their Several Editions, Ancient Printers, Dates, and Prices, and Wherein They Differ. [With a Supplement to 1800]. Part I Compiled by John Worrall, Part II and Supplement Compiled by Edward Brooke. Parts I, II and Supplement bound in one volume. London: Printed for Edward Brooke, 1788-1800. [15], 272, [26]; viii, 40, 49-255, [1]; [3], 45, [2] pp. 1788-1800. Reprinted 1997 by The Lawbook Exchange, Ltd. LCCN 97-12962. ISBN 1-886363-29-3. Cloth. $110.

Wright, John S. *Citizenship Sovereignty.* Chicago: Published for American Citizens, the True Maintainers of State Sovereignty, 1864. Reprinted 1998 by The Lawbook Exchange, Ltd. LCCN 98-15940 ISBN 1-886363-55-2. Cloth. $65.